Running Mainframe z on Distributed Platforms

How to Create Robust Cost-Efficient Multiplatform z Environments

Kenneth Barrett

Stephen Norris

ca
technologies

CA Press
Apress®

Running Mainframe z on Distributed Platforms: How to Create Robust Cost-Efficient Multiplatform z Environments

ISBN-13 (pbk): 978-1-4302-6430-9

ISBN-13 (electronic): 978-1-4302-6431-6

President and Publisher: Paul Manning
Acquisitions Editor: Robert Hutchinson
Editorial Board: Steve Anglin, Mark Beckner, Ewan Buckingham, Gary Cornell, Jonathan Gennick, Jonathan Hassell, Robert Hutchinson, Michelle Lowman, James Markham, Matthew Moodie, Jeff Olson, Jeffrey Pepper, Douglas Pundick, Ben Renow-Clarke, Dominic Shakeshaft, Gwenan Spearing, Matt Wade, Tom Welsh
Coordinating Editor: Rita Fernando
Copy Editor: Carole Berglie
Compositor: SPi Global
Indexer: SPi Global
Cover Designer: Anna Ishchenko

Distributed to the book trade worldwide by Springer Science+Business Media, LLC., 233 Spring Street, 6th Floor, New York, NY 10013. Phone 1-800-SPRINGER, fax (201) 348-4505, e-mail orders-ny@springer-sbm.com, or visit www.springeronline.com.

For information on translations, please e-mail rights@apress.com, or visit www.apress.com.

Apress and friends of ED books may be purchased in bulk for academic, corporate, or promotional use. eBook versions and licenses are also available for most titles. For more information, reference our Special Bulk Sales–eBook Licensing web page at www.apress.com/bulk-sales.

Contents at a Glance

About the Authors.. xv

Foreword xvii

Acknowledgments xix

Preface xxi

■Chapter 1: Understanding the Mainframe Environment, Technologies, and Methodologies 1

■Chapter 2: Creating a Mainframe Virtualized Environment: Requirements and Choices 13

■Chapter 3: Building the Hypervisor Host 31

■Chapter 4: Creating a Base Environment 53

■Chapter 5: Constructing the z/VM Environment 69

■Chapter 6: Establishing a DASD Repository for a Multi-Server Environment...................95

■Chapter 7: Staging for z/OS Optimization..109

■Chapter 8: Migrating to Mainframe zEnterprise DASD 127

■Chapter 9: Customizing the z/OS Environment with Symbols.........................161

■Chapter 10: Updating the Environment 189

■Chapter 11: Preparing for Recovery 201

■Chapter 12: Deploying Virtualized Mainframe Environments.........................213

■Appendix A: Software Licensing..231

Appendix B: Setting the Standards and Conventions 233

Appendix C: IEASYS Member Example 245

Appendix D: LOAD Member Example 249

Glossary.. 251

Index... 257

Contents

About the Authors... xv

Foreword xvii

Acknowledgments xix

Preface xxi

■Chapter 1: Understanding the Mainframe Environment, Technologies,
and Methodologies 1

The IBM Mainframe Virtualization Technology 1

Understanding the zPDT 1090 2

zPDT Capabilities...2

    Multi-User Capability 2

    Cryptographic Processor 3

    Mainframe Look and Feel 3

    Knowing the Mainframe Platform...3

    Input and Output Definitions...4

    Direct Access Storage Devices 5

    Data Sets 6

Catalogs 6

    Master Catalog 7

    User Catalog 7

    Shared Master Catalog 8

Learning How to Share z/OS Parameters and Symbols 9

Mainframe Practices in a Distributed Environment...9

    Network-Attached Storage for Backups...9

    Remote Network-Attached Storage...10

    Using Network File Systems as Repositories 11

Recognizing the Potential for Cloud Enablement 12

Summary...12

■**Chapter 2: Creating a Mainframe Virtualized Environment:**
Requirements and Choices **13**

Use Cases...13

Hardware Considerations and Options 15

    CPU Requirements...16

    Memory Usage...16

    Hard Drive Space and I/O Requirements...17

    Connectivity...18

Recovery for System Failures and Outages 19

    Hardware Fault Tolerance..19

    Disaster Recovery...20

Software Update Requirements 23

Sharing Data...23

Failsafe System..25

Case Studies 27

    Case 1: Single Laptop System for Mainframe Developer 27

    Case 2: Server Class Machine Hosting Multiple Mainframe Systems for Software QA Testing............28

■**Chapter 3: Building the Hypervisor Host** **31**

Networking Design Considerations 32

    Remote Access to the Physical Server 32

    Network Connectivity Planning..35

Hard Drive Configuration 40

    RAID Configuration Consideration...41

    Other Storage Technologies..42

Installing the Linux Operating System..43

    Network Time Protocol Server...43

    File System Creation...44

    Software Packages...45

    Software Updates..46

Configuring the Linux Host Network Settings 46

Case Studies 47

    Case 1: Single Laptop System for a Mainframe Developer..47

    Case 2: Server Class Machine Hosting Multiple Mainframe Systems for Software QA Testing...........49

■Chapter 4: Creating a Base Environment 53

Create a User...53

Install the z1090 Software (Emulator) 54

Copy the Supplied DASD Files...55

Create the Device Map 57

    Device Map Location 57

    Stanzas..58

Start the Base System..64

Case Studies 66

    Case 1: Single Laptop System for Mainframe Developer 66

    Case 2: Server Class Machine Hosting Multiple Mainframe Systems for Software QA Testing...........67

■Chapter 5: Constructing the z/VM Environment 69

Installing the Base z/VM System..70

    DASD Files..70

    z/VM Device Map..70

    Verify z/VM System...71

Optimizing the z/VM Environment..71

    Attaching New Volumes to the z/VM Virtual Machine...72

    Updating the Network for z/VM 75

    Defining New Users and Service Machines...81

    Configuring the z/VM Performance Monitor 88

Conclusion 88

Case Studies 88

    Case 1: Single Laptop System for Mainframe Developer 88

    Case 2: Server Class Machine Hosting Multiple Mainframe Systems for Software QA Testing 88

■Chapter 6: Establishing a DASD Repository for a Multi-Server Environment 95

A DASD Repository Built on a Network File System Server 95

Product Development Requirements 95

zEnterprise Availability on a Distributed Platform 96

Current Software Levels 96

Process for Using zEnterprise Mainframe Software 97

The Lab Environment May Grow 98

    Service and Support Challenges 99

    Service Methodology 99

Network File System Server 101

DASD Repository Efficiencies 103

    Server Storage Efficiency 103

    Transfer-on-Demand Efficiency 103

    Individual Product Transfer Efficiency 104

    Disruption Reduction Efficiency 104

Case Studies 104

    Case 1: Single Laptop System for Mainframe Developer 104

    Case 2: Server Class Machine Hosting Mainframe Systems for Software Quality Assurance Testing 105

Summary 107

■Chapter 7: Staging for z/OS Optimization 109

DASD Volume Updates to the Virtualized Mainframe Environment 110

    Creation and Organization of New DASD Files 110

    Updates to the Device Map 114

    Updates to the User Directory 115

    Initializing the New DASD Devices 116

System Volume..116

DASD Repository 117

    Accessing the Emulated DASD Volumes on the Repository...117

    Updating the Device Map..118

    Updating the User Directory 119

Progress and Prospectus 120

Case Studies 121

    Case 1: Single Laptop System for a Mainframe Developer...121

    Case 2: Server Class Machine Hosting Multiple Mainframe Systems for Software QA Testing........122

■**Chapter 8: Migrating to Mainframe zEnterprise DASD** 127

Backing Up the Base Environment 127

Starting the Vendor System...127

    Verify New DASD Volumes..128

    Shared DASD Volume...128

System Manipulations 128

    The Storage Management Subsystem..128

    Catalog Updates 128

Procedure Libraries..132

    Procedure Library Concatenations..132

    Procedure Library Members 133

Parameter Libraries..133

    Parameter Library Concatenations..134

    Parameter Library Members...135

System Migration Considerations 136

    Build the Page and Spool Data Sets 136

    Parameter Library Manipulations 136

    Dynamic Dump Data Sets...139

    Resource Access Control Facility 139

    Add Users 140

    System Data Sets 140

JES2 Migration Considerations 141

Virtual Telecommunications Access Method (VTAM) 141

Internet Protocol Activity 142

Interactive System Productivity Facility (ISPF) 142

Coupling Facility 144

Sharing Data Sets and Volumes 144

Starting the New System Environment 144

Verifying the New System 145

Summary 145

Case Studies 146

Case #1: Single Laptop System for Mainframe Developer 146

Case #2: Server Class Machine Hosting Mainframe Systems for Software Quality Assurance Testing.............160

Chapter 9: Customizing the z/OS Environment with Symbols.......................................161

Reserved Symbols...161

MVS Operating System Management..162

LOADxx 162

IEASYMxx...163

IEASYSxx...165

IODF 165

Establishing Shared Parameter Libraries 165

Parameter Overriding 166

LOADxx Members 168

IEASYS Members 170

Creating Shared Master Catalog 170

Manipulating with System Symbols..170

Operating System DASD Volume Serial 171

Page Data Set Naming Standard 172

Starting a z/OS Virtual Guest 173

Start to Finish with Symbols 174

    Symbol Substitutions...174

    Job Entry Subsystem..177

Summary 183

Case Studies 183

    Case 1: Single Laptop System for Mainframe Developer 183

Conclusion..185

    Case 2: Server Class Machine Hosting Multiple Mainframe Systems for Software QA Testing........................ 186

■Chapter 10: Updating the Environment 189

Maintain z/OS Operating Systems with IBM Recommended Service Updates...........................189

    Server Upgrade Process for the Operating Systems 189

    Operating System Upgrade Is Complete... 198

Maintain Subsystems with IBM Recommended Service Updates...198

Summary 199

Case Studies 199

    Case 1: Single Laptop System for Mainframe Developer 199

Conclusion..200

    Case 2: Server Class Machine Hosting Multiple Mainframe Systems for Software QA Testing........................ 200

Conclusion..200

■Chapter 11: Preparing for Recovery 201

Backup/Restore Process 201

    Full Backup of the Linux Host... 202

    Virtual System Backup/Recovery 202

    Location of Backup Files 204

    Conclusion... 204

Backup Volumes 205

Emergency Recovery System 206

    ER System for a First-Level Operating System...206

    ER System for a z/OS Guest Operating under z/VM 207

Conclusion...210

Case Studies 210

    Case 1: Single Laptop System for Mainframe Developer 210

    Case 2: Server Class Machine Hosting Multiple Mainframe Systems for Software QA Testing.........211

■Chapter 12: Deploying Virtualized Mainframe Environments...........................213

Creating and Hosting the Deployment Image..214

    Hosting the Deployment Image on a NAS Device 214

    Hosting the Deployment Image on a USB Flash Drive 217

    Hosting the Deployment Image in the Cloud 218

Pre-Deployment Requirements 219

    Hardware Configuration..219

    Linux Installation and Configuration 220

    z1090 Installation and Configuration 220

Deploy the Base Image...221

    NAS...221

    USB Flash Drive 223

    Cloud...224

Post-Deployment Activities 224

    Update DASD File Locations and the Device Map..225

    Virtual Systems Updates..225

Considerations to Simplify Deployment 226

    User Volume Naming Convention 226

    Networking Pre-Configurations 227

Conclusion 228

Case Studies 228

    Case 1: Single Laptop System for Mainframe Developer 228

    Case 2: Server Class Machine Hosting Multiple Mainframe Systems for Software QA Testing....................228

■Appendix A: Software Licensing..**231**

IBM Software Licensing, Approval, and Certification...231

Third-Party Software Licensing, Approval, and Certification 231

Summary..231

■Appendix B: Setting the Standards and Conventions **233**

z/OS System Naming Standard 233

DASD Volume Serial Naming Convention 234

    Operating System 234

    Time Sharing Option/Extensions 235

    Auxiliary Storage 235

    Job Entry Subsystem (JES)..236

Data Set Naming Standards 237

    Auxiliary Storage 237

    Job Entry Subsystem 238

Network Naming Standards 239

Application Naming Standards...240

Naming Standards Explained 240

    Step 1: System Names are Standardized 240

    Step 2: DASD Volume Serials Are Standardized..241

    Step 3: Data Set Names Are Standardized 241

    Step 4: Network Names Are Standardized..241

    Ease of Creating a Virtual System 241

Modifications for the Distributed Environment..242

    System Names..242

    DASD Naming Conventions..243

    Data Set Naming Standards 244

■**Appendix C: IEASYS Member Example** **245**

IEASYS Member 245

Summary 247

■**Appendix D: LOAD Member Example** **249**

LOAD Member 249

Summary 250

■**Glossary** **251**

Index **257**

About the Authors

Kenneth Barrett is Director of Information Technology and Infrastructure Engineering at CA Technologies, responsible for the development of pristine mainframe work environments on the zEnterprise and distributed platform. He is a CA technical and management leader for all new IBM mainframes and the architect of a zPDT lab which provides private mainframe environments on Intel-based servers. Previously he was a systems programmer and manager at CA technologies, responsible for a suite of virtual z/OS guests. He has over 30 years experience as a systems programmer and mainframe manager with particular expertise in DOS, VM, z/OS, datacenter management, mainframe security, and disaster recovery. Barrett has a BS in Mathematics and Computer Science from California State College in Pennsylvania.

Stephen Norris is Director of Software Engineering at CA Technologies, responsible for engineering teams that develop enterprise automation and performance solutions. Prior to this role, Norris was instrumental in deploying IBM zPDT technology to create virtualized mainframe environments through which mainframe operations on a z series server can be transitioned to a distributed platform. At CA Technologies and previously at Legent, his projects have included updating and expanding network management tools, assisting customers with solution deployment, creation of automation tool kits, and virtualization of lab environments. His experience has enabled him to drive the transition of several CA Technologies Research and Development mainframe environments to a distributed platform quickly and seamlessly. Norris holds a BS in Electrical Engineering from West Virginia University and an MBA from Indiana University of Pennsylvania.

Foreword

In my more than a quarter century of work on the mainframe platform, both with IBM and CA, I have had the misfortune ("opportunity," in management-speak) to have had to deal repeatedly with the conundrum: "How do I provide an easily obtainable, flexible, and inexpensive environment for prototyping, developing, and testing code for the z/OS (nee OS/390, fka MVS) platforms." Prior to the advent of effective hardware emulation, the answer was invariably some variation of the same theme: obtain a smallish 390 or System z server, put z/VM on it, and then virtualize my way to a brighter tomorrow. This, however, was only a limited solution, really available only to a serious player in the S/390 and System z software markets. Even with the deep discounting available to IBM PartnerWorld participants, the total cost of acquisition and ownership of such a system is beyond the mythical "two guys in a garage" software outfit.

Near the end of the last millennium, I was at Share and met a guy named Carl Ross, who was demonstrating his new "mainframe on a laptop" solution which he called FLEX-ES. Carl came to this idea one day when he decided to build enough of a simulator of the computing environment that his father had been brought up on: the System/360 and 370. I introduced myself as being the lead developer for some of the operating system, and Carl was more than happy to let me take a test drive. From what I could tell, the implementation was flawless and the system was at least as responsive as the z/VM guests that I was using back at the lab in Poughkeepsie.

Carl's timing and implementation were right on target for the needs of the day and provided a blueprint for the future. x86 clock speeds were routinely outpacing S/390 and early System z machines, so emulation could easily reach 15-25 MIPS on an IBM ThinkPad T20 and software emulation of mainframe oddities like ECKD was merely an exercise in tedium. The actual architecture was readily available on the internet. Linux was an easily extensible platform to code an architectural harness into and had good programming support for multi-programming and multiple processors, so a user could buy a multi-CPU machine (this is before multi-core and SMT) and get fairly good performance for a two- or three-man show. IBM could see the value in this kind of architecture emulation (especially as the cost/value proposition on their own P390 machines was waning), so they partnered with Ross to allow him to supply his machines, along with the IBM software stack on easily installable CDs to provide development-grade machines to small- and medium-sized ISVs.

Fast forward to today: IBM has brought the emulation forward into the 21st century with nearly complete emulation of all of the zEC12 architecture at a price point that rivals development environments for other platforms (check out what a full Microsoft Visual Studio license costs). However, it is still z/OS, with a 40+ year legacy of systems-management needs, processes and procedures. What good is a really cheap development environment if you still have to have a full systems programming staff to keep it up and running? While it is reassuring that all one has to do to recover the system is reload it from scratch, it would still be very helpful to have easily-implemented solutions to back up your work and maintain configuration integrity based on industrial-strength best practices.

At CA Technologies, we have the luxury of having our own zEC12 and related "real kit" on a real raised floor with a real z/OS systems programming team. At the same time we could see the value in having a bunch of these zPDTs around for everything from destructive system testing to being able to demo product at a customer site where internet connections are less than stellar or nonexistent. We could also see that just letting these loose in our environment was probably an invitation to machines going from very useful to becoming fancy doorstops after an amateur foray into systems programming went bad.

The authors of this book, Kenneth Barrett and Stephen Norris set out on a task to figure out what the best practices were to build and maintain a cadre of these very useful machines without creating a full systems programming support staff around them. What you have in your hands is the culmination of years of research, experimentation and experience around the use of these machines. Should you choose to implement zPDT (or RDz-UT or RD&T) in your team's arsenal, you will find their insights, genius, and hard work illuminating as to how to rationally and economically manage the environment.

Scott Fagen
Chief Architect, System z Business
CA Technologies

Acknowledgments

The authors would like to thank the following people for their unwavering support of this work:

Mahendra Durai for his enthusiastic support of this book. His encouragement and enthusiasm helped get this project off the ground and running.

Diane Norris for her early review of each chapter. Her experience as a software engineer provided insightful analysis of information presented from a product developer vantage point. Her observations and recommendations were invaluable as each chapter proceeded from rough to final copy.

Debbie (Barrett) Myers for her review of early drafts from a non-technical point of view. Her notes and suggestions for outline and structure assisted in creating a smoother layout and transitions for the final project.

Richie Boyle for his CA Technologies review of this book.

Joyce Barrett for her unshakeable support and enthusiasm for this project. She was instrumental in supporting and encouraging this project.

Pam (Barrett) Shirley, Anna Barrett, Mike Norris and Jon Norris for their support and enthusiasm.

Preface

This book reveals alternative techniques not covered by IBM for creatively adapting and enhancing multi-user IBM zPDT environments so that they are more friendly, stable, and reusable than those envisaged by IBM. The enhancement processes and methodologies taught in this book yield multiple layers for system recovery, 24x7 availability, and superior ease of updating and upgrading operating systems and subsystems without having to rebuild environments from scratch.

Most of the techniques and processes covered in this book are not new to either the mainframe or distributed platforms. What is new in this book are innovative methods for taking distributed environments running mainframe virtual machine (VM) and multiple virtual storage (MVS) and making them look and feel like mainframe MVS systems.

CHAPTER 1

■ ■ ■

Understanding the Mainframe Environment, Technologies, and Methodologies

This chapter provides a cursory review of the aspects of mainframe technology that are commonly practiced and implemented on the zPDT environment. It serves to orient readers toward the in-depth information on mainframe and distributed technologies we present in the subsequent chapters. Although we assume that most of our readers have prior knowledge of mainframe technologies, we couch our descriptions of it so that non-mainframers and even novices can follow along.

The IBM Mainframe Virtualization Technology

zPDT is an IBM technology whose full name is the *IBM System z Personal Development Tool*. IBM offers this product to qualified and IBM-approved *Independent Software Vendors* (ISVs) as a development tool. For non-ISVs, IBM offers the *IBM Rational Development and Test Environment for System z*, which is based on zPDT.[1]

The solutions developed in this book are premised on the ability of the zPDT technology to run one or more emulated System z processors and provide emulation for many input/output device types. The zPDT has a machine type designation of 1090 and can run on x86 processor-compatible platforms.

■ **Note**   Servers installed with the zPDT technology will be referred to in various ways throughout this book, including *server*, *PC-based server*, *distributed server*, and *distributed platform server*. Whenever you encounter such a reference, you may make the tacit assumption that zPDT technology is installed on the server unless specified otherwise.

---

[1] Details of both programs are available on various IBM websites. Please refer to IBM websites or contact IBM directly to get the latest updates and options that may fit the requirements of your company. IBM licensing and approval are required.

Understanding the zPDT 1090

The zPDT 1090 consists of the two following components:

- *The software*: Provides the processor function and emulation. It also has built-in utilities.

- *The USB key* (*dongle*): Determines the number of System z processors to be emulated on the server and authenticates the environment. A process is performed with IBM or its partners to certify the USB key. The USB key will provide the authentication for running the 1090 software.

Once the 1090 software is installed, a virtual System z environment is possible. Figure 1-1 is an illustration of steps toward creating a System z environment once the server and Linux host have been configured.

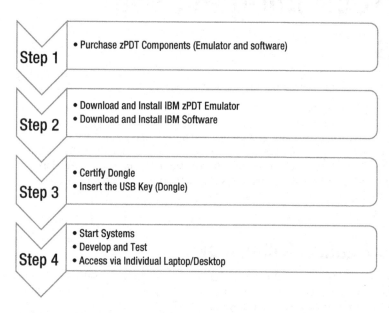

Figure 1-1. *Steps to implement zPDT software and base systems*

zPDT Capabilities

This section discusses the capabilities of the zPDT. The purpose is to convey some of the technology capabilities of this environment that make the distributed server configuration appear more closely linked to the mainframe than just running emulated software and hardware.

Multi-User Capability

The implicit premise of a Personal Development Tool (PDT) is that it is for a single person. When the systems are set up in an environment with network connectivity, multiple users may sign onto the systems concurrently. While this may seem a simple concept when dealing with mainframe environments, the concept can be lost when dealing with a distributed environment running mainframe operating systems.

Cryptographic Processor

Depending on the nature of the development or usage of the mainframe environment, security may be needed to protect data or may be required for testing of security products. A feature that is provided (but which must be set up) is the ability to utilize a virtualized cryptographic processor.

Mainframe Look and Feel

To a developer or tester who has signed onto a system installed with zPDT technology, the server environment has the look and feel of any mainframe system, including the following properties:

- The system is multi-system capable.

- The system is multi-user capable.

- The environment looks the same as the mainframe.

- The software service levels are the same as the mainframe.

Although a mainframe environment has far greater capabilities than a distributed server running mainframe software, the end user performing normal functions notices no differences between the two.

Knowing the Mainframe Platform

The *IBM zEnterprise System* is an integrated system of mainframe and distributed technologies. The zEnterprise has three essential components:

- *System z Server*: Examples include the zEC12 or z196 enterprise class server or mainframe.

- *BladeCenter Extension* (zBX): This infrastructure includes blade extensions for Power Blades, Data Power Blades, and x86 Blades.

- *Unified Resource Manager* (zManager): All systems and hardware resources are managed from a unified console.

▨ **Note**   References in this book to the zEnterprise will be based on the System z enterprise class server only.

A System z server comprises many parts, including the following:

- General purpose processors

- Specialty processors

- Logical partitions (LPARs)

LPARs can be created to run native operating systems such as z/OS, z/VM, z/VSE, and z/Linux. Figure 1-2 is a depiction of a mainframe with many LPARs:

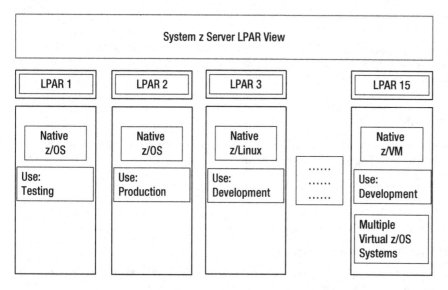

Figure 1-2. *LPAR view of a System z server*

In Figure 1-2, LPARs 1, 2, and 3 are running native operating systems. Each of them serves a singular purpose. LPAR 15, which is running z/VM, is hosting multiple virtual z/OS guests for development purposes. This allows many different individual z/OS instances to execute differently from and independently of each other. There are other LPARs not listed that perform various functions.

A zPDT server can create an environment similar to LPAR 15—for example, a z/VM environment with multiple virtual z/OS guests running underneath. Several configurations can be established:

- *The z/OS systems are fully independent of each other.* There is no need for data sharing, but there is a need for independence.

- *The z/OS systems are connected to each other via a coupling facility.* This configuration allows the systems to share data in a Parallel Sysplex. This environment permits data sharing among multiple systems with data integrity.

- *A combination of systems sharing data and systems that are independent of each other.*

Input and Output Definitions

A System z server has a configuration of devices. All of these devices must be defined to the operating system in order to utilize them. A precise hardware configuration must be defined using IBM utilities and processes.

To support product development and testing, it is necessary to manipulate the input/output definitions. There are many requirements for the diverse products and product-development teams. Understanding how to manipulate and update the input/output configuration is essential. A few items that may require adding or updating include:

- Devices such as *direct access storage devices* (DASDs) and terminals

- Channel paths

- Processors

- Switches

Direct Access Storage Devices

DASD *volumes* are used for storage. They come in different architectures and can be allocated in different sizes. Each volume has a *volume table of contents* (VTOC) that contains information about each data set, including its location on the volume.

■ **Note**   The following discussion of DASDs is based on IBM 3390.

A volume may contain many different types of data, including the following:

- Operating system
- Subsystem
- Products
- Temporary data
- Program executables

Figure 1-3 depicts examples of DASD volumes and their associated content. The figure shows that DASD volumes can be configured in different sizes, depending on DASD usage requirements.

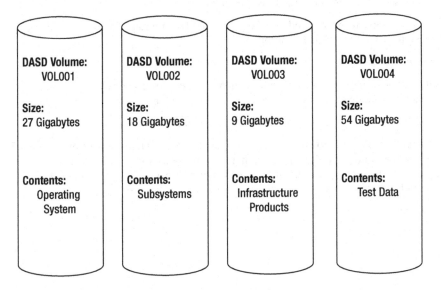

Figure 1-3. *DASD volumes of various sizes and usages*

As the requirements for larger data grow each year, enhancements are continually made to DASDs. For example, the 3390 DASD's limitation to 65,520 cylinders was lifted as IBM created larger 3390 volumes known as *extended address volumes* (EAVs). The extra space conferred by the EAVs is called *extended addressing space* (EAS). Before implementing EAVs, it is necessary to certify that the products have the capability to access the EAS for reading, writing, and updating.

For product development and testing purposes, there are a number of considerations that require more DASD than provided in the base configuration. Examples include the following:

- Large work spaces

- Large databases

- Many volumes and sizes for certification

- Large amounts of testing data

Data Sets

Data that reside on DASD are stored in a data set. Each data set on a DASD volume must have a unique name. A data set typically contains one or more records.

There are many types of data sets and access methods. Two commonly distinguished types of data sets are *sequential* and *partitioned*:

- *Sequential data sets*: The data-set records are stored one after the other.

- *Partitioned data sets*: These data sets have individual members and a directory that has the location of each member, allowing it to be accessed directly.

Data sets can be *permanent* or *temporary*:

- *Permanent data sets*: The resident data are permanent, such as payroll.

- *Temporary data sets*: Such data sets are exemplified by a data set created in one step of a job that is passed to another step for manipulation and output.

Data sets can be *cataloged* or *uncataloged*:

- *Cataloged data sets*: Such data sets may be referred to only by name, without specifying where the data set is stored, because a catalog contains the data-set attributes and the location.

- *Uncataloged data sets*: Such data sets must be specified by both name and location.

Virtual storage access method (VSAM) applies both to data sets and to an access method for accessing and maintaining various types of data. VSAM maintains records in a format that is not recognizable by other access methods, such as those used for data sets in the preceding bulleted list. VSAM can define data sets in the following ways, which differ in respect of the ways in which the respective data sets store and access records:

- Keyed sequential data set (KSDS)

- Entry sequence data set (ESDS)

- Relative record data set (RRDS)

- Linear data set (LDS)

Catalogs

A *catalog* keeps track of where a data set resides and its attributes. Most installations utilize both a *master catalog* and one or more *user catalogs*. Each catalog regardless of its type can be shared and provides a seamless means for accessing data sets across multiple systems without needing to keep track of each data set's location.

Master Catalog

Every system has at least one catalog. If a system is utilizing only one catalog, then it is using the master catalog. Using only the master catalog would be inefficient, however, as it would be maintaining information about all data sets on the system. Figures 1-4 depicts a system with a single catalog. In this case, all data sets on the system are fully cataloged and maintained by a single catalog.

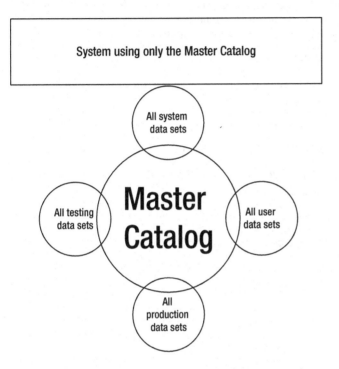

Figure 1-4. Master catalog configuration with no user catalogs

To provide a better separation of data, user catalogs are used, as discussed in the next section.

User Catalog

In large environments, data sets are generally separated by the first part of the data-set name, known as a *high-level qualifier* (HLQ). By way of a simple example, the HLQs are just the first levels of the following data-set names:

- *USER1*.TEST.DATA
- *USER2*.TEST.DATA
- *USER3*.JOB.CONTROL
- *USER4*.DATABASE.BACKUP

The HLQs USER1, USER2, USER3, and USER4 have an *alias* defined in the master catalog with a reference to the user catalog. The user catalog in turn tracks the data set.

The user catalogs and associated HLQs are normally further separated on a system, as in the following examples:

- User Catalog 1: All user data sets

- User Catalog 2: Production data sets for Payroll

- User Catalog 3: Production data sets for Finance

The separation of data sets by functionality creates efficiency in the sense that each user catalog defines specific data sets for specific functions. This provides ease of management and greater flexibility.

The process of linking a user catalog to a master catalog consists of the following steps:

1. The master catalog is defined as part of the system.

2. A user catalog is defined.

3. The user catalog is connected to the master catalog.

4. An alias (HLQ) is defined to the master catalog relating it to a user catalog.

5. The user catalog now tracks the data sets with the HLQ defined in step 4.

A simple view of a master catalog linked with four user catalogs is depicted in Figure 1-5.

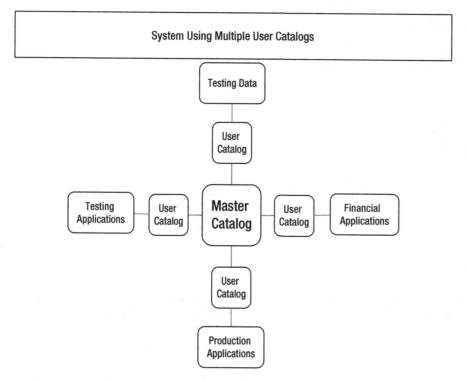

Figure 1-5. *Master catalog and user catalog relationships*

Shared Master Catalog

In a multisystem environment where systems are connected and sharing data, you should consider sharing a master catalog. In a large shop with many systems and master catalogs, just keeping the alias pointers and user catalogs in sync at all times can be cumbersome. A shared master catalog eliminates duplication of effort across systems and concerns that a catalog is not in sync. Moreover, when a new application, product, or user is introduced into a shared environment with a shared master catalog, the efforts to add the new facility or function are simpler and more flexible. The process of linking each user catalog and each alias can be performed just once.

Learning How to Share z/OS Parameters and Symbols

To create a pristine, easy-to-update multiple system z/OS environment, first create a shared parameter library (PARMLIB) data set to maintain all system- and subsystem-related parameters. This allows all systems to share the same commands to start each system independently without the need to maintain multiple PARMLIB data sets and parameters.

Part of sharing system startup parameters involves the use of symbols that are used within PARMLIB members to differentiate the systems and other components when starting a virtual system, as discussed in Chapter 9 in connection with techniques and methodology to facilitate an environment that is easily updated with new operating systems versions and other software.

Mainframe Practices in a Distributed Environment

This section discusses methods for translating common mainframe practices and services into the distributed environments.

Network-Attached Storage for Backups

To provide backup and recovery, a backup plan needs to be put into place that is easily maintained and serviceable for providing proper support for the systems. A *network-attached storage* (NAS) solution suffices for this requirement. To ensure that your backup plan provides multiple levels of recovery depending on the need, you need to perform regular backups and incremental backups at critical points of development and system setup.

Figure 1-6 illustrates the possible backups for a single server.

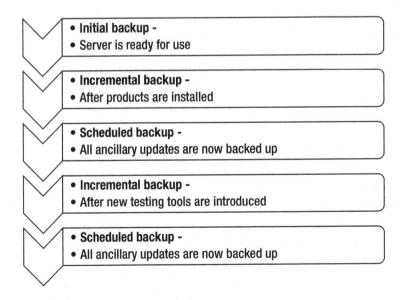

Figure 1-6. Backup scenarios for a server

Backups serve the following purposes:

- Recovery in the event of a hardware failure

- Recovery in the event of software or product-related system corruption

- Ability to restore the systems to a known environment

Backups on local NAS devices provide peace of mind and a methodology for restoring a server to a point in time. Depending on the use of the systems, you may need to regularly restore a system to a point in time, as illustrated by the following example.

■ **Example**   A group of developers is learning the proper installation and setup of a product. They require a base system setup and two infrastructure products before beginning the training. This part of the setup is not considered part of the training, but will be the starting point for each developer. As each person completes his or her training, a restore is performed so that the next person begins at the same point without a need to rebuild the system environment.

Figure 1-7 shows some of the many advantages of using the NAS devices for backups.

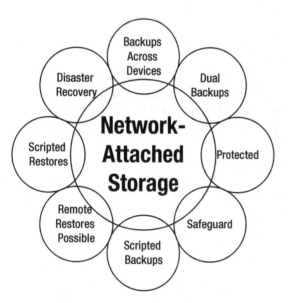

Figure 1-7. *Network-attached storage server*

Remote Network-Attached Storage

Another step to providing peace of mind and better recovery is placing NAS devices in a remote location, allowing another layer of backup and better recoverability in the event of a localized incident, such as damage to the lab. Figure 1-8 represents the different layers of backups:

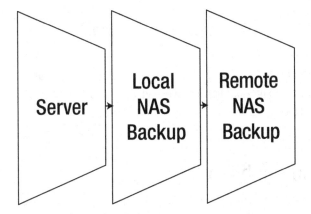

Figure 1-8. *Server backups to multiple locations*

Using Network File Systems as Repositories

You can gain the benefits of a network file system server for storing frequently used software—such as operating systems, subsystems, and integration/infrastructure products—by using NAS devices. The use of the network file system servers located in the same lab as the other servers creates a means for warehousing a lot of software in a common place. Having the warehoused data in the same location reduces the transfer times between the repository and the servers, in contrast to the much longer transfer time to a distant mainframe. This solution also eliminates the need to copy all the software to the individual development servers and frees up storage on the server that can be better utilized for product development and testing. Figure 1-9 is a conceptual representation of a repository.

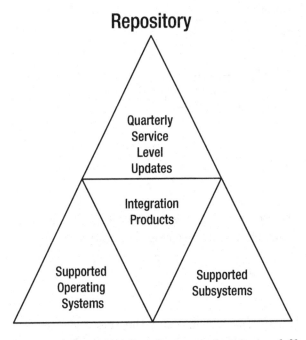

Figure 1-9. *Repository for software stored on a network file system*

Maintaining multiple service levels for each generally available operating system and subsystem provides flexibility for various development teams as special circumstance or needs arise, as illustrated by the following example.

■ **Example** A product developer has been working at the most current operating system service level when a customer reports a problem at the previous level. The developer can request the previous service level and attempt to recreate the customer's problem. The transfer can be performed quickly and easily.

Recognizing the Potential for Cloud Enablement

The potential for cloud enablement is tremendous, especially with respect to remote servers and mobile laptop devices. Cloud enablement of the sharing of the repositories and NAS backups with remote distributed platform servers and laptops allows the latter to download any software or recover their systems to a known instance (Figure 1-10).

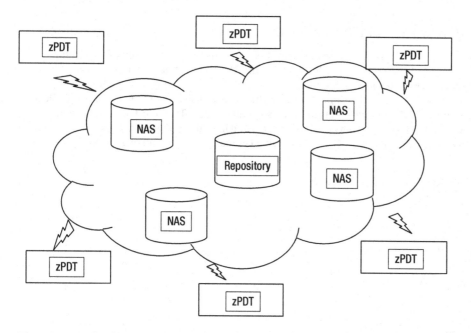

Figure 1-10. *Cloud Enablement*

■ **Note** Readers should assume throughout the remainder of this book that all the servers utilizing the zPDT technology are in a single lab setting, such that cloud enablement does not come into consideration unless specifically mentioned

---

Summary

This chapter provided insight into some common concepts of a mainframe environment and brief descriptions of how they are implemented in a distributed platform. Chapter 2 describes the many concerns and considerations you face in implementing a small one-system personal computer or a larger environment of servers.

CHAPTER 2

■ ■ ■

Creating a Mainframe Virtualized Environment: Requirements and Choices

Several factors that drive the configuration of the mainframe virtualized environment need to be taken into account when you define the requirements for virtualized systems. The most salient requirement is the *use case*—the objective that is to be achieved by utilizing the virtual systems. Once you define the use case, you can finalize the other requirements. These include access to the systems, the number of systems, hardware specifications, and data sharing.

After the environment has been built, another important consideration is how software updates and upgrades will be deployed. After you have made those decisions and created those processes, you need to resolve one last set of issues concerning downtime for the environment. You must investigate and prepare for potential problems, such as hardware errors, a prolonged environment outage, or complications that might prevent a virtual system from starting. Configuring and deploying a virtualized environment entails a significant investment, and it is incumbent on you to undertake a detailed recovery discussion and plan.

A thorough analysis of all these topics is essential to constructing a comprehensive and successful design.

Use Cases

The most important step in creating a virtualized mainframe environment is defining the use case. With the flexibility and scalability that are available, numerous configurations can be implemented. It is imperative to scope *how* the environment will be utilized in order to identify the most appropriate options. The project objective must be accurately identified to ensure that the mainframe environment is correctly generated. Figure 2-1 identifies several use cases based upon commonly defined goals.

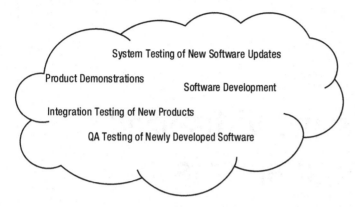

Figure 2-1. *Possible use cases for emulated mainframe environment system access*

Determining the type of access required to the emulated mainframe environment is another critical step in the creation of the lab. How many users will require access? What level of access will be needed? With the tools that are provided by both Linux and the emulator, there are several possible methods to access the virtualized systems. One possibility is to create a solution that is accessible by a single user using a local keyboard. This would allow for the protection of the physical hardware in a secure location and the control of access through physical security.

Another possibility is to create network connectivity so that the hardware can be protected in a secure location, but the users have the ability to log in remotely and physical access to the hardware is not required. Using the network and the software tools provided, the environment can be configured for multiple users accessing the system. User requirements and security policies must be reviewed to provide the optimal solution for both users and corporate security. The possibilities available are shown in Figure 2-2.

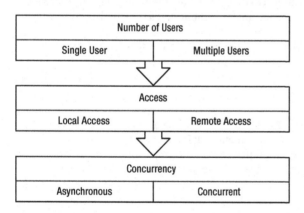

Figure 2-2. *Variables in configuring virtual system access*

Once the purpose and usage of the virtualized mainframe environment have been established, the number of systems necessary to satisfy the requirements needs to be decided.

- Can a single system accomplish the specified goals?

- Will two or more systems be necessary?

- Is a host/guest configuration essential?

- What mainframe operating systems are required?

- How many systems will be active at the same time?

If only a single system is needed, then a basic configuration of a single first-level OS would suffice. However, even if only a single system is required, there are several advantages to creating a zVM host and running the required virtual systems as guests. If multiple mainframe systems are critical, then a VM host is highly recommended. Depending on the performance requirements for the virtual environment specified in the use case, it is possible to start multiple first-level systems on the Linux host, but it introduces additional complexities. Your choice of configuration will depend on the system requirements for the specific virtual environment that you are creating (as suggested by the examples in Figure 2-3).

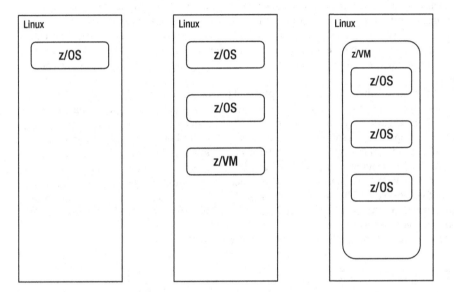

Figure 2-3. *Possible emulated mainframe configurations. (Left) A first-level z/OS system. (Middle) Three first-level systems, each independent of each other. (Right) A z/VM host with three z/OS guest systems*

Hardware Considerations and Options

The hardware requirements of a virtualized mainframe environment must be generated based upon the use case, access needs, and total number of systems previously defined. The main configuration options to consider are CPU specifications, memory usage, storage demands, and network connectivity. Before creating the hardware specifications for the physical machine, you must answer several questions:

- How many CPUs are required to support the host operating system and the emulated mainframe systems?

- What are the memory demands of the Linux host and the virtual systems?

- What are the hard drive space requirements of the virtualized systems?

- What are the hard drive I/O demands of the required virtual environment?

- • If network connectivity is required:

  - • What network transfer rates are desired?

  - • Are dedicated networks required?

These specifications need to be identified and quantified to construct a complete configuration of the hardware.

CPU Requirements

The CPU provides the power to perform calculations, drives I/O through the memory and hard drives, and is a determining factor in the capacity of the virtual environment that is being created. The driving factor behind performance of the virtualized environment is the number of CPUs available for use by the virtualized systems. Although the speed of the CPU is important, the cost of the processor is a contributing factor in the specific model that is selected. The requirements of the virtualized environment need to be considered when determining the model of the CPU purchased. The number of cores may be more of a factor than the actual speed of the CPU. When you purchase your licenses from a vendor, you will select an option for the number of CPUs that can be licensed for your emulated mainframe environment.

The recommendation for a minimum number of CPUs for the physical hardware is the number of CPUs licensed for the virtual systems +1 for the host operating system. Practical experience has shown that better performance can be obtained by providing a minimum configuration of the number of the CPUs licensed for the virtual systems +2. This provides extra capacity for the host operating system to perform work for the emulator and background tasks, without using the CPUs for the emulator and taking cycles away from the virtual systems. For example, if three CPUs are licensed, the minimum recommended configuration would be five CPUs. This is not a valid configuration with the current offerings from hardware vendors. With current manufacturing processes, the number of CPUs is restricted to a multiple of two. For example, a configuration could be ordered with six processors, or eight processors, but not seven. Given this constraint, our recommendation is to round up to six or eight CPUs. This will ensure the best performance from the CPUs that are allocated to the virtual systems.

An example how the CPUs of an eight CPU host might be utilized is shown in Figure 2-4.

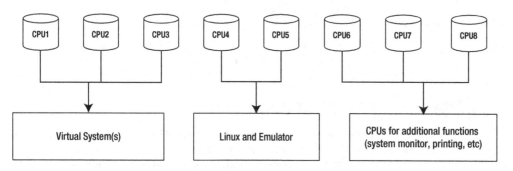

Figure 2-4. Sample CPU distribution workload for 3 CP dongle and 8 processor PC

Memory Usage

In production IT systems, use of a swap or a paging file needs to be minimized. In a virtualized mainframe environment, swapping/paging needs to be nonexistent for the virtualized systems. Any time data is swapped or paged out, I/O is required to a nonmemory data storage device. On a production system in which performance is critical, this can lead to degradation in responsiveness. In the virtualized environment that is being designed, a substantial amount of paging would lead to an unresponsive system that would quickly become unusable.

In the virtualized environment, this I/O is normally fulfilled by the hard drives that have been installed in the physical host. Because access times to physical hard drives are significantly longer than to memory, the former introduce delays in the work that is being performed. For that reason, it is important to identify the memory requirements of both the Linux host OS and the virtualized mainframe systems. The memory installed on the physical host machine needs to provide enough storage so that none of the operating systems needs to swap or page. Figure 2-5 shows an example of a physical server with 64 GB of memory installed, and how the memory could be allocated to the host Linux operating system and the emulated mainframe operating systems.

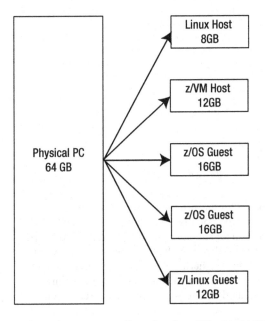

Figure 2-5. *Memory allocation for a PC with 64 GB of Memory*

Hard Drive Space and I/O Requirements

Possibly no other aspect of the physical environment will have as much of an impact on performance as the hard drives that are chosen for the physical server. For this reason, it is imperative that the storage I/O and space requirements be properly defined. Depending on the vendor chosen to supply the hardware, your choices might include *solid-state drives* (SSDs), *Serial ATA* (SATA) drives, *Serial Attached SCSI* (SAS) drives, or a fibre-attached *storage area network* (SAN). Each technology has its advantages and disadvantages, as summarized in Figure 2-6.

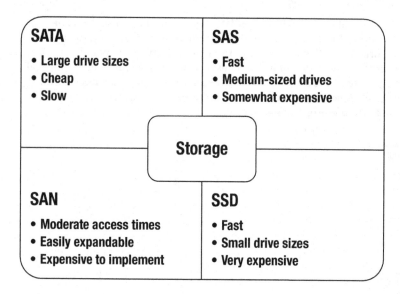

Figure 2-6. *Comparison of advantages and disadvantages of hard drive and storage technologies*

The first question to answer is how much actual space will be needed for the virtual systems. The answer may be the deciding factor in choosing a storage technology. There are a finite number of drives that can be mounted in the server chassis. If the storage requirements are large, the technology chosen for storage may be restricted to large SATA drives or a SAN. In addition to the space requirements, how responsive must the drives be to I/O requests? How many I/Os per second will be issued by the users of the systems? If it is critical that the hardware be responsive to a high rate of I/O, then this will also impact the decision. As with all other options for the hardware, there are advantages and disadvantages to all existing technologies. Each option needs to be evaluated to determine the optimal solution for creating the virtualized mainframe environment.

Connectivity

In the world today, all systems are interconnected. From small handheld devices, to large mainframe computers, to satellites orbiting the earth, everything is connected in some way. The emulated mainframe environment that you are designing is no different. Understanding the connectivity needs of the users is important when considering the hardware specifications of the physical machine. Although the basic configuration can be created and operated with only one network interface, that is not necessarily the best configuration. Network performance requires an analysis of how the environment will be utilized to determine the correct number of *network interface cards* (NICs).

- Will the emulated environment need connectivity to the local network? If so, how many physical connections are needed?

- Does the emulated environment need to be isolated from the network?

    - Are there security concerns such that the environment has to be isolated?

    - Does a NIC need to be included in the configuration?

- If network connectivity is required, how much bandwidth is needed?

- How many mainframe images will be created?

- Can they share the same physical connection?

- Does the Linux hypervisor layer need a dedicated network connection?

Depending on the objectives of the virtual mainframe environment, the optimal hardware configuration may contain one or several NICs. Figure 2-7 demonstrates the various types of connections that might be required, based upon the network specifications for both the physical and virtual environments. Understanding the connectivity requirements for the virtual environment as well as the hypervisor layer will ensure that a complete networking configuration can be constructed.

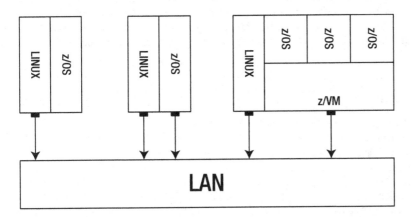

Figure 2-7. *Network connectivity possibilities for three possible environment configurations*

Recovery for System Failures and Outages

As with any other hardware or software environment, there is potential for some type of failure. The failure could be due to a problem with the hardware, or it could be the impact of an external failure, such as a building power outage or a fire. How will any failure or system outage affect the project? What are the tolerance levels for the environment being unavailable for any length of time? Depending on the answers to these questions, there are both hardware and software solutions that can be used to remediate these issues. Redundancies can be configured within the hardware to tolerate some forms of device problems, and backup solutions can be utilized to remediate full system failures. If a disaster occurs at the location of the physical host machine, a disaster recovery plan can be used to reduce the length of time that the virtual environment is unavailable to the user. However, before creating processes to resolve a disruption in the availability of the virtual systems, it is critical to define the consequences of the outage, because any remediation will add cost and overhead to the construction and maintenance of the physical and virtual environments.

Hardware Fault Tolerance

One of the most critical considerations is the issue of fault tolerance. The creation of a virtualized mainframe environment is a significant investment in a project. Such an investment is an indicator of the critical nature of accomplishing the objectives quickly. The hardware architecture that is to be utilized to create the virtualized environment has to reflect the relative importance of stability.

- How tolerant of failure does the hardware need to be?

- If there is a failure, what is the impact to the project?

- How long can an outage last before there is in impact to commitments?

Once this information has been gathered, then the technology can be analyzed and the best options can be identified. Depending on the tolerance for hardware failure there are several available options. The choices range from a *redundant array of independent disks* (RAID) configuration for the hard drives, to a backup solution, to nothing at all.

The advantage that RAID provides is the ability to recover from a single hard drive failure. Two common RAID configurations for fault tolerance are RAID 1 and RAID 5. RAID 1 is commonly known as *disk mirroring*. This method simply copies data to two locations, Disk 1 and Disk 2. If one of the drives fails, then all the data is available on the secondary drive. This allows the physical machine to remain viable while the failed drive is either repaired or replaced. RAID 5 uses *parity data striping* to allow for drive failures. Simply put, parity data is stored on the device array to allow for continuity of operation if a drive fails. This enables the hardware to operate until the failed drive is repaired or replaced. As with all technologies, there are advantages and disadvantages to both. RAID 1 tends to be a little slower and is more expensive, but if a failure occurs, there is no degradation in performance. RAID 5 tends to be faster and is cheaper for large storage requirements. These factors, outlined in Figure 2-8, need to be considered in choosing either option.

RAID 1	RAID 5
• Disk mirroring • Requires a secondary disk for every primary disk • Minimum disk configuration is 2 • Expensive • No performance loss if disk failure	• Redundancy through parity striping • Requires a minimum of N+1 disks • Minimum disk configuration is 3 • Less expensive solution for large storage requirements • One drive failure is tolerated, but performance is affected

Figure 2-8. Comparison of RAID 1 and RAID 5

Backups are another import consideration when determining how long outages can be endured. If the outage is due to an event more serious than a hard drive failure and requires a system rebuild or completely new hardware, how quickly does the environment have to be restored? Backups can considerably shorten outages of this nature. There are several methodologies that can be implemented depending on the available resources and the time that can be invested in crafting the solution. Options for backup/restore processes will be discussed later, but if a backup solution is desired, it will impact the hardware required for the environment being created.

The cost of acquiring and maintaining a virtualized mainframe environment underscores the low threshold for system outages. As a result of both the financial and time investment in creating and maintaining these environments, there is a high value placed on their availability. Therefore most implementations will require a combination of hardware redundancies and software recovery solutions.

Disaster Recovery

If the physical host is lost at its original location for a long period of time, how will that impact the business? *Disaster recovery* (DR) is another factor to consider. Hardware configurations can alleviate failures at the PC level, but what about environmental failures, natural disasters, or emergencies? How important is this environment to the project? If the physical host is unable to be utilized at its original location for a long period of time, how will that affect the business? The full impact of any disruption needs to be understood in order to plan the DR process. If the outage can last for several days without having an effect, then DR planning may not be necessary; the users can wait until the situation has been resolved and the environment is restored. However, in many cases, a disruption of services for longer than a few days will have a significant impact on the users and cannot be tolerated. If this is the case, then the next step is to determine what options are available for disaster recovery, and which of these alternatives is optimal for the business.

For instance, is there another location that can host this environment? If so, does it have hardware that meets the minimal viable hardware required for adequate performance? (Read "minimal not in the sense of the minimal requirements as stated in the installation guides for the software that is used, but rather the minimal requirements to provide a useful environment for the users.) Normally this is closer to the equipment used in the original lab than the specified hardware in the installation guides. If suitable hardware is not readily available in a secondary location, a process to quickly acquire a satisfactory machine needs to be established.

Having replacement hardware in a viable location to host the environment is only one piece of the DR solution. The hardware is meaningless without the software to run on it. A process to restore the software environment is required to facilitate a rapid redeployment of the environment. To craft the DR solution, the following questions must be addressed:

- What is the starting point for the environment creation?

- Will the environment be restored from a backup?

    - Are there full system backups to restore?

    - Are the backups only of the virtualized environment?

    - Where are the backup files located?

- Where is the location of any necessary software?

- Is there a licensing dongle available for the physical machine?

■ **Tip** Disaster recovery plans are continually evaluated and modified, but every design begins with simple constructs.

Although these questions should have answers before the plan is created, most DR plans are reverse-engineered and the questions are used to help frame the processes to achieve the desired result. If the desired result is to have a fully restored environment that includes all changes made after the initial configuration, the answers will be different than if the DR plan is to simply put together a new environment and reengineer all the changes.

If the preferred solution is to create a fresh environment at a secondary site, major considerations in the process include the following:

- A suitable secondary site

- Satisfactory hardware at this site

- Availability of required network connectivity

- All of the required software:

    - Linux install media

    - Emulator install package

    - Virtualized system media or backup

- Obtainability of an appropriate licensing dongle

■ **Caution** Depending on the conditions attached to the licensing dongle, IBM may need to be notified of any location changes of the environment.

If the desired outcome is to fully replace the existing environment quickly, then the basic considerations are similar:

- A suitable secondary site

- Satisfactory hardware at this site

- Availability of required network connectivity

- Accessibility to the latest backup files

- Obtainability of an appropriate licensing dongle

Once the DR plan has been created, the hardware to support the plan needs to be factored into the creation of the virtualized environment. This may include hardware ranging from additional host machines, to *network-attached storage* (NAS) devices, to cloud storage. Figure 2-9 illustrates a DR plan that has a backup set of physical machines in Phoenix that can be used if there is a serious problem in the New York datacenter. The machines are similar to the original hosts and are available when needed. All backups of the initial environments are hosted on storage provided by a cloud archive provider and are accessible from both locations. A process has been created to overnight the licensing dongles from the New York datacenter to Phoenix. This is an over simplification of a complicated process, but it demonstrates the core components of a successful strategy.

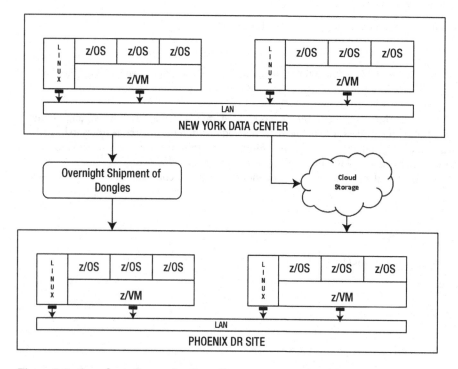

Figure 2-9. *Sample configuaration for a disaster recovery scenario*

Software Update Requirements

With the effort required for the initial implementation of the virtualized mainframe systems, the longer each environment can be sustained without a rebuild, the higher the return on the initial investment. The problem with maintaining operating systems and software environments for long periods of time is that they become dated very quickly. Each software vendor with operating systems or programs utilized in the environment has a team of engineers continually providing functional updates and patches for problems. To maintain the viability of the virtualized system, a method will need to be created to apply software updates. Considerations in developing an approach that will satisfy the needs of the user include the following:

- How many virtualized operating systems are required?

- What virtualized operating systems are required? z/OS? z/VM? z/Linux? z/ VSE?

- How many virtualized operating systems will be run concurrently?

- How often are updates provided that will need to be installed?

- How often will software patches need to be applied?

- What non-operating system software is critical to the success of the project?

- What are the patching/updating procedures for each software package?

Once the maintenance requirements for each operating system and independent piece of software have been identified, then procedures can be created to complete the updates. For software packages installed after the operating system has been configured, this should be a straightforward task performed according to the vendor supplied procedures. However, operating system updating and patching can be much more complex and will require a more sophisticated approach. Operating system installation and maintenance procedures will be covered later, and will be focused specifically on z/OS as it is the most common operating system utilized in these environments. However, similar procedures could be created for other mainframe operating systems.

Sharing Data

In a multiple system environment, does the data need to be shared? In most mainframe environments, when multiple systems are created, data is shared on some level. The following questions need to be answered:

- In the virtualized environment that is being created, is data sharing a requirement?

- Will there be multiple shared volumes and a shared master catalog, PARMLIB, and Unix file systems?

- Will there be multiple independent systems whereby each system will have its own virtualized data stores?

If data does not need to be shared, then the implementation of the virtualized mainframe environment is much easier, although it requires a significantly larger data footprint. The advantage to this approach is that each system is truly independent, and changes or problems on one system will not affect the other systems installed in the same environment. The main disadvantage is that any system modifications or updates that are required may need to be replicated across every virtual system in the environment. A sample configuration of three systems with independent DASD volumes is presented in Figure 2-10.

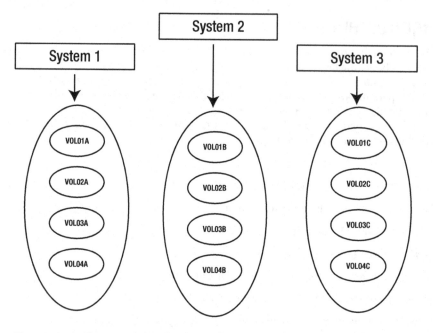

Figure 2-10. *Three systems with unique DASD volumes*

If data is to be shared across systems in the virtualized environment, sharing a master catalog has several advantages. It allows the sharing of emulated DASD units between the virtualized systems. This can help to dramatically reduce the footprint of the virtualized systems on the Linux host hardware. Sharing DASD also reduces management overhead in that operating system configuration datasets can be shared. This allows changes made on one system to be utilized by all systems sharing the dataset. It also allows the option to share installed software. Any software solution installed on one system could be used by any image sharing the same volume. In addition to lowering management overhead and reducing the data footprint on the storage devices, it also allows for interoperability testing. If testing or development needs to be done across systems, or with multiple systems with diverse operating system versions, this can be accomplished easily. The one drawback to this configuration is that a resource sharing tool needs to be installed, configured and maintained to ensure data integrity. Figure 2-11 schematizes three systems sharing six volumes labeled VOL001- VOL006.

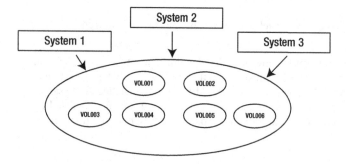

Figure 2-11. *Three systems sharing six DASD volumes (VOL001–VOL006)*

The decision on sharing data is obviously dependent on the requirements for the environment, but it is a decision that impacts the complexity of the configuration. It will affect the creation of the environment and impact the choice of the hardware that is necessary for the implementation. If data is to be shared, it will also impact the procedures created to update the operating system and other software packages, because the updates could impact all systems within the complex.

Failsafe System

A major concern with maintaining the virtual systems is overcoming configuration errors made after the full environment has been supplied to the users. As with any operating system, even a simple change to a parameter, executable, or library might cause a virtualized system startup to fail. Without thorough planning, the only options would be to restore the latest backup and start over again. Once a configuration change has been made and the system fails to restart, it is extremely difficult to make a correction since there is no way to use the normal mechanism to effect changes.

The emulator software provides a method that will allow updating existing datasets, but it is somewhat cumbersome and requires the technician to know what mistake has been made and how to correct it. A better option would be to have an emergency system on standby that has access to the virtualized volumes that need to be modified. With the flexibility provided in the virtualization tool, and some careful configuration changes, a simple recovery environment can be built to help correct simple configuration errors. This can easily be done by using the software volumes that are provided to create base virtualized environments. The volumes that have configuration datasets can be attached to the emergency system. If there is a problem and the real system will not start, the emergency system can be started, and the problem can be addressed in a normal operational environment. A sample configuration is represented in Figure 2-12.

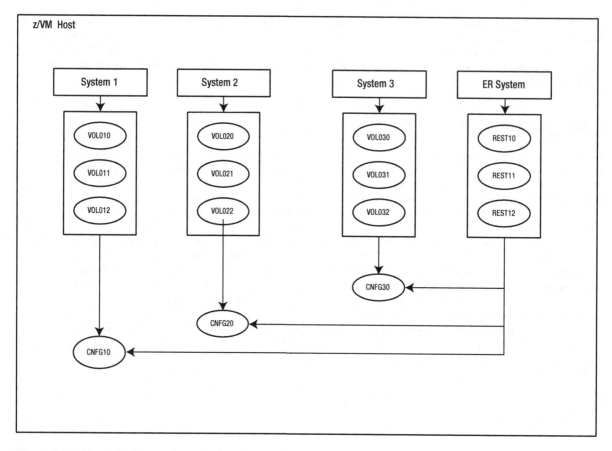

Figure 2-12. *Example of connections allowing an emergency repair system to access DASD volumes from a production system*

In Figure 2-12, the following volume assignments have been created:

- VOL010, VOL011, VOL012 are attached only to System 1
- VOL020, VOL021, VOL022 are attached only to System 2
- VOL030, VOL031, VOL032 are attached only to System 3
- REST10, REST11, REST12 are attached only to ER System
- CNFG10 is attached to both System 1 and ER System
- CNFG20 is attached to both System 2 and ER System
- CNFG30 is attached to both System 3 and ER System

■ **Caution** Sharing data without a resource protection tool is dangerous and not recommended. The ER system should be started only after systems 1, 2, and 3 have been stopped.

In the design in Figure 2-12, the configuration datasets needed to properly start systems 1, 2, and 3 are stored on each system's respective CNFGxx volumes. Sharing these volumes with the emergency restore system allows easy access to the information contained on them should one of the three production systems fail to start due to a configuration error. For example, if a parameter is specified incorrectly on System 1 and the system will not start, ER System can be started, the dataset with the error accessed from the ER System and the problem resolved. Then the emergency restore system can be stopped and System 1 restarted.

Case Studies

After careful analysis of the use case, the hardware considerations, and the recovery requirements, a high-level design of the virtualized mainframe environment can be completed. The two following case studies each describe a specific use case for a virtualized mainframe environment and detail the thought process used to construct the architecture. Once the environment has been designed, the PC and the Linux host need to be constructed. This requires a more detailed analysis of the use case, and deeper considerations of the hardware technologies available.

Case 1: Single Laptop System for Mainframe Developer

A developer working in a small mainframe shop is tasked with creating a process to move billing information from the database on a Unix cluster to a more powerful database on the production mainframe system to allow for faster reporting. Because of the sensitivity of the data and the perceived risk to the production systems, a single virtual mainframe system on an isolated environment is determined to be the best solution for the development work. It will isolate the development environment from the critical systems, but allow the software engineer access to the same technology that is current running on the production mainframe. The developer works with teams around the world and often works at night or weekends to collaborate with colleagues. Since he is working with databases, hard drive access is critical as slow response times will dramatically impact development. Incremental backups of changes are not essential, but a quick recovery if the system has a critical error is important as there are financial penalties if the project is not completed by the specified deadline. To balance the need for a quick recovery with the expense of a full backup/recovery plan, a mechanism to quickly fix system parameter library configuration errors is desired so that simple problems can be alleviated without the need for a full system restore.

Based on the specifications, a four-CPU laptop has been ordered to provide environment mobility as the user needs access to the environment at both the office and at home. Only one z/OS system has been requested so a single first level z/OS image will be created. A three-CPU dongle has been allocated to the environment to allow for both maximum processing power and the ability to test multi-threading. The Laptop has 32 GB of RAM and two 512GB SSD's to reduce paging and also provide fast access to data. A full environment backup will be performed after the environment is initially built to provide the ability to have the base configuration operational quickly in case of a problem. To resolve simple errors preventing the system from starting, a failsafe system will be provided to enable access to specific volumes from a secondary system. A summary of the decisions and the reasoning is shown in Figure 2-13.

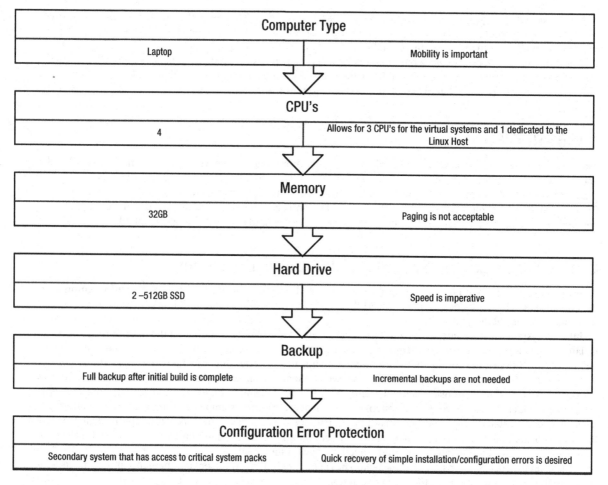

Figure 2-13. *System configuration for Case 1*

Case 2: Server Class Machine Hosting Multiple Mainframe Systems for Software QA Testing

A team of QA engineers in a software development company is tasked with testing a new mainframe solution. The new software package is designed to run on multiple z/OS systems and shares data between the images. The solution gathers data and stores it in a database on a periodic basis. While performance is important, the ability to warehouse large volumes of data is vital. Several large DASD volumes are essential to maintain database performance. Remote access to the environment is mandatory as there are several engineers allocated to the project that will need simultaneous access. Because of the critical nature of the project long systems outages cannot be tolerated.

Based on the specifications, an eight-CPU Server has been ordered. This will provided the extra performance demanded by the database applications. With the specification of a three z/OS complex, a z/VM host with three z/OS guest systems will be configured. To provide processing power for this many systems a three-CPU dongle has been ordered. This will enable three CPUs to be allocated to the emulated systems and allow five CPUs to service tasks for the Linux operating system and the emulator. The server has been constructed with 64GB of RAM to allow for sufficient memory to satisfy the demands of the virtual systems. Twelve 600GB, 15K RPM SAS hard drives have been allocated to provide ample space, while maintaining acceptable performance. This will provide a balance between hard-drive performance and the availability of space for large quantities of data. Hardware redundancies and regularly scheduled backups will be used to help remediate system failures. The critical nature of this project will require a fully functional DR plan to quickly restore the virtual environment if there is a disaster at the original host site. A failsafe system will also be created to alleviate any configuration issues that prevent a system from being able to start. The basic configuration and the reasons for the choices are shown in Figure 2-14.

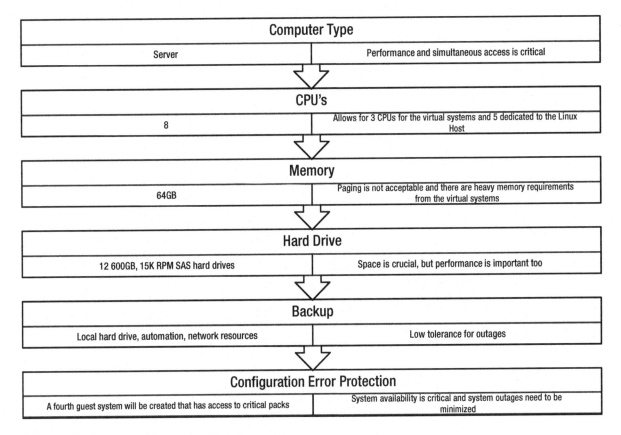

Figure 2-14. *System configuration for Case 2*

CHAPTER 3

■ ■ ■

Building the Hypervisor Host

Once the use case and requirements for your virtualized system environment have been specified (Chapter 2), you have to design the networking scheme, implement the storage configuration, and install and configure the Linux operating system.

■ **Step 1**   Design the networking scheme.

To complete the creation and implementation of the networking scheme, the specifications are analyzed in order to calculate the number of physical ports and determine the IP configuration needed. It is vital to identify the number of physical network connections required so that the IT department can verify that there are enough available connections to satisfy the requests. Early identification of the IP configuration is also important. Depending on the number of static and DHCP addresses required, a reconfiguration of the local IP network may be necessary. The requirements for maintaining and operating the full environment define the factors vital to a successful networking design.

■ **Step 2**   Implement the storage solution.

The implementation of a storage configuration that meets the stated objectives for the environment is another important aspect of building the hypervisor host. The following factors constrain the storage solution:

- What are the I/O demands?
- How much space is needed?
- What is the level of redundancy needed for fault tolerance?

■ **Step 3**   Install and configure the Linux operating system.

Once the network design and the storage solution have been created, the next step is to install the Linux operating system. During installation, the environment requirements and hardware specifications must be examined and the correct Linux installation parameters selected. Some of the factors that influence the installation may include the following:

- Storage configuration
  - Number of hard drives
  - RAID configuration

- Software packages required by the emulator

- Network Time Protocol Server configuration

- Development environments required for automation or utility creation

- Configuration of the primary NIC if networking is required

After the base operating system has been installed, any optional packages are evaluated and required/recommended software updates are applied. Installing the updates will protect the environment from outages due to known issues with the software.

Configuration of any additional network interfaces is the final stage in setting up the base Linux host. If there are additional NICs required by the virtualized environment design, they need to be configured and attached to the network. Once all of these steps are finished, the creation of the Linux host is complete.

Networking Design Considerations

Networking design considerations fall broadly into two areas: remote access to the physical server, and network connectivity planning.

Remote Access to the Physical Server

A key issue when configuring the hardware for the virtualized mainframe environment is remote access. Is there a requirement to remotely control the hardware? Is there a need to remotely restart or shutdown? If this is a specification, then the appropriate hardware must be installed and configured. Two common methods utilized to provide remote access are network *keyboard/video/mouse* (KVM) devices and *remote access cards* (RAC).

Network KVM

A network KVM solution provides access as if the user is actually using the keyboard and mouse attached to the machine. The hardware itself is a combination of a KVM and a remote viewer. The KVM is attached to the keyboard, mouse, and video ports of the machine and then attached to the network. The remote user is given either the hostname or the IP address assigned to the network port of the KVM. When users log on with the hostname/IP address, they are provided with a remote view of the physical machine's desktop. With this interface, users can interact with the physical hardware as if they were using the actual keyboard and mouse attached to the machine. For example, a server can be provisioned in New York and connected to a networked KVM. The hostname/IP address of the KVM is then given to a user in Denver who can log into the KVM and control the server as if he were physically at the New York location.

Remote users can modify the BIOS and restart/power off the machine. However, if the machine is powered off, the KVM does not provide the ability to remotely power on the machine, which may eliminate this choice as a viable option. One major advantage of a network KVM solution is its ability to manage multiple physical machines from one management console. This solution requires only one physical network connection and one IP address. By decreasing the number of physical devices used to remotely control PCs, the overhead of applying patches and updates is greatly reduced. Depending on the requirements of the environment and the facility that is hosting the hardware, a networked KVM solution may provide a practical remote access solution.

Figure 3-1 illustrates a typical network KVM solution. A keyboard, mouse, and monitor are physically connected to the KVM. This provides direct access to the three physical machines as needed. Cables are attached to the USB or PS2 ports on the PCs to provide the input from the keyboard and mouse. As another connection on this cable or as a separate cable, the video-outs of the PCs are also connected to the KVM to relay the video data. The KVM is also connected to the LAN so remote users can utilize the KVM to control the PCs just as if they were at the physical keyboard. As shown in Figure 3-1, the PCs do not need to be connected to the network to be controlled through the networked KVM.

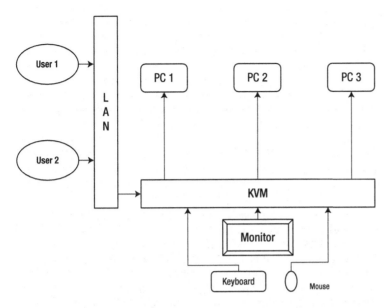

Figure 3-1. *Network KVM solution*

RAC

A common option to remotely control the environment is a *remote access card* (RAC). A RAC is a feature that is available with most new server configurations. If older hardware or nonserver machines are part of the hardware design, a RAC may still be available from a hardware vendor. The machine model and age determine if a RAC solution is viable.

Similar to network KVMs, RACs provide the ability to interact as if the user were operating the input devices physically attached to the machine. However, a RAC also provides the capability to control the power state of the hardware. This feature allows users to remotely power on the hardware if there is an outage. In addition, they can power down the hardware if there is a need to do so.

Figure 3-2 shows two servers configured with RACs. Each RAC has a unique port on the PC with a dedicated connection to the network. User 1 and User 2 are in remote locations and can use the LAN to connect to the RAC and control the PC. As shown in Figure 3-2, the NICs that would be used by an operating system installed on the PC do not need to be connected to the network for the machine to be remotely controlled through the RAC.

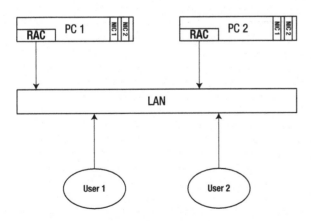

Figure 3-2. *RAC configuration*

A significant advantage of some RAC solutions is the ability to remotely mount an ISO image. To control a machine remotely through a RAC, each user is provided with a client that is installed on his local machine. In most cases, this software is simply used to take control of the desktop of the remote machine or its power state. However, some manufacturers have provided the additional functionality of allowing the local user to configure the RAC on the remote machine to access a local ISO image as if it were mounted on the remote machine. This allows the machine that is being controlled through a RAC to access the ISO image as if it were physical media mounted in the machine's optical drive. This functionality provides the ability to perform a remote build of the host system or a recovery of a failed host system.

■ **Tip**   RAC software may provide additional functionality.

The ability of some RACs to use a client to remotely mount ISO images is illustrated in Figure 3-3. In this configuration, Server Z is connected to the network and controlled with a RAC. A user logs into PC 1 and initiates a connection to Server Z via client software provided by the RAC manufacturer. The client software allows the user on PC 1 to access the RAC on Server Z and virtually mount a Linux ISO that is physically located on PC 1. The Linux ISO image is virtually mounted on Server Z. Once the configuration is completed, the BIOS on Server Z accesses the ISO image on PC 1 as if it were physically mounted on an optical drive on Server Z (Figure 3-4). This allows the user to install or update the Linux operating system on Server Z though the network connection provided by the RAC.

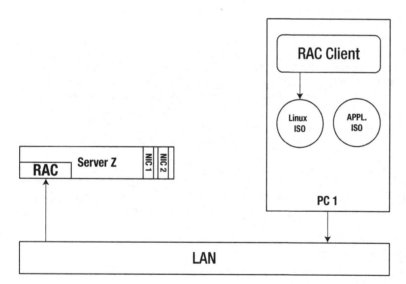

Figure 3-3. *Remotely mounted ISO to install Linux OS*

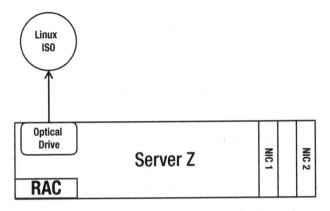

Figure 3-4. *Linux ISO virtually attached through a RAC*

Network Connectivity Planning

In the current technological environment, almost every electronic device is simply a component of a larger structure. This creates tremendous opportunity for change and advancement, but it also introduces additional complexities into IT architectures. The networking requirements of the virtualized mainframe systems running on Linux hosts vary according to the use and configuration of each environment. It is critical therefore that the connectivity needs of this environment be clearly communicated to the local IT organization to ensure that necessary changes are in place by the time that the virtual systems are built and ready to be utilized.

The first issue to be addressed is connectivity requirements for the environment. It is crucial that the needs of the physical hardware, Linux host, and virtual system are acknowledged to ensure that the plan to implement the specifications is complete. Information should be gathered to answer the following questions:

- How many virtual systems are to be created?

- Do all the virtual systems require network access?

- If a z/VM host is used, will the VMSWITCH machine be sufficient for the guest images?

- Are any of the network connections wireless?

- Is there a separate remote access port on the physical server?

- What connection speed is necessary?

- Does the Linux host need a static IP address?

Incomplete information regarding the network will create a situation where only partial connectivity may be achieved and the virtual system usage will be compromised.

Physical Network Connections

The number of physical connections to the network is important to the local IT staff. The number of available network ports will need to be researched to determine if there is enough capacity to satisfy the request. An early analysis of the needs is essential to ensure that the IT staff has sufficient time to procure any additional hardware that may be required.

The first consideration in establishing the total number of ports is remote access to the physical machine. Is the hardware equipped with a mechanism to remotely control configuration and status? If so, does it need a distinct network connection for communication, or can it share a port with the operating system? If a unique connection is mandatory for remote access, this will need to be factored into the network connection requirements.

A second consideration is the connectivity of the host system. If network connectivity is crucial to the virtual systems, then a physical port must be available to the host Linux system. If a network connection is not required for the emulated mainframe systems, then the demand for a connection is based simply on the needs of the Linux host. To determine the necessity of a host network connection, the following questions must be answered:

- Will the software running on the physical host require access to the network?

    - How are the operating system patches applied?

    - How is the emulator updated? How are changes to the virtual system software deployed?

- Will the users of the virtual environment need remote access?

- Should the full environment be isolated from the network for security concerns?

Depending on the answers to these questions, the Linux host may require a network connection to satisfy essential needs outside the connectivity requirements of the virtual systems. If the analysis of these questions determines that a Linux network connection is mandatory, then this data will have to be added to the information given to the IT staff.

In addition to resolving the issue of providing a network connection for the Linux host, the specifications for the virtual systems must be analyzed to determine how many connections are required. To determine the number of connections, the following information must be evaluated:

- How many virtual systems comprise the environment?

- Is there a z/VM host with guest systems?

    - Can the guest systems share a single physical connection?

    - Is a secondary, failover, connection required?

    - How many unique connections are necessary?

    - Can the z/VM host share a physical connection with Linux host?

- Does each system require a physical connection?

Careful analysis of these specifications and the technologies that are available within the emulated environment is needed to create an optimal network configuration. For example, within z/VM a virtual switch can be configured so that all guest machines will share a single physical network port. Or, if needed, physical ports can be dedicated to individual guest systems. A mix of the two, dedicated and shared, is also available as a valid networking solution for a z/VM and guest environment. Some possible configurations are shown in Figures 3-5, 3-6, and 3-7.

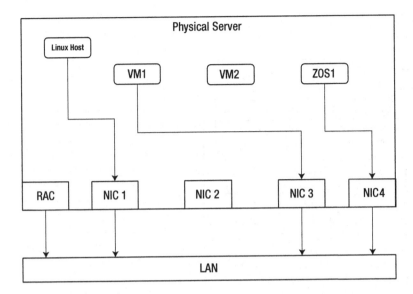

Figure 3-5. *Mix of virtual machines with and without network connections*

Figure 3-5 depicts an environment that has a RAC with a dedicated connection. The Linux host machine has a dedicated port to communicate over the LAN. There are three first-level virtualized systems. Two systems, *VM1* and *ZOS1*, have dedicated NICs to communicate through the LAN. The third virtual system, *VM2*, is isolated and has no connection to the local network.

With this configuration, one physical connection is required for the RAC and three more are needed for the Linux host and virtual machines. So even though the hardware itself will support up to five physical network connections, only four are really required. In order to reduce the physical network connections and IP address requirements, NIC 2 is not physically attached to the local network.

A more complicated environment is depicted in Figure 3-6. In this scenario, the RAC has a dedicated connection to the network. The Linux host also has a direct connection. The virtualized configuration is more complex. There is a z/VM host with three z/OS guest systems (*ZOS1*, *ZOS2*, and *ZOS3*). The z/VM host, *VM1*, has a dedicated connection to the LAN. Configured within the z/VM environment are two virtual switches, *vSwitch 1* and *vSwitch 2*. Both switches have connections to the local network. Each of the z/OS guest systems has a connection to both virtual switches, providing network connectivity for the guest systems and also redundancy. If one of the virtual switches fails, the other provides failover. This configuration requires five physical network connections. One is for the RAC and the remaining four are allocated for each of the NICs that are used by the Linux host and the virtualized systems.

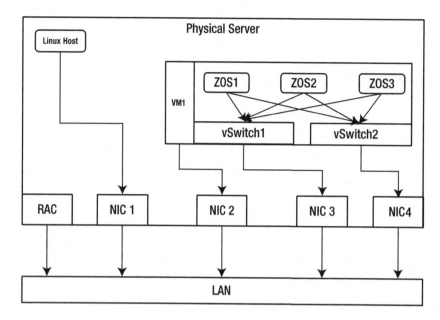

Figure 3-6. *Configuration of multiple z/OS guest using the vmswitch machine to share network ports*

Figure 3-7 demonstrates a possible configuration for a laptop that is used to create a virtualized mainframe environment. In this scenario, there are two network interfaces. The Linux host utilizes the wireless interface to communicate on the network, while the virtualized z/OS system uses the hardwired connection to the LAN. The laptop requires only one physical connection and wireless access to the network.

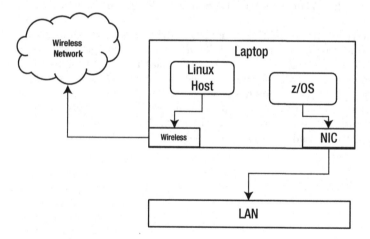

Figure 3-7. *Laptop computer with wireless NIC*

IP Configuration

The issues discussed in the preceding section in respect of establishing the number of physical network ports required to satisfy the connectivity requirements are also critical to determining the IP configuration for the environment, as follow:

- Is there a unique physical port for remote management of the hardware?
  - Does it require a static IP address?
- Does the Linux host require an IP address?
  - If so, does it need a DHCP or static address?
- How many first-level systems are in the environment?
  - Do they each need access?
- Is there a z/VM host system?
  - Does it require network access?
  - How many guest systems exist?
  - How many require network access?
  - Do the guest systems require connectivity to each other but not the outside network?

The answers to these questions determine what IP configuration is needed for the environment. The total number of IP addresses required is the sum of the physical connections and the virtual machines that need network connectivity. For example, if the environment has three physical connections, at least three IP addresses will be required. If there are four virtual machines that need network connectivity, then there will be four additional IP addresses, for a total of seven.

Another phase in the network configuration is the determination of how many of the IP addresses are dynamic and how many are static. The corporate IT requirements for IP addressability dictate part of the configuration. If the virtualized systems are considered part of a production environment, then static IP addresses may be required for all connections. If this is not a requirement, then DHCP addresses are permissible for all of the physical network connections to the hardware environment. However, static IP addresses are required for any virtualized z/VM, z/OS or z/VSE systems. In the previous example with three physical connections and four virtual machines, the IP requirement consists of three DHCP addresses and four static IP addresses. The final design includes the number of IP connections required and their classification as either static or dynamic.

In Figure 3-8, there are three physical network ports on the server. If the requirements state that these ports can have DHCP addresses, then three DHCP addresses are required. The Linux host system is attached to NIC 1 and uses that IP address for network communication. The z/VM host, *VM1*, is also using NIC 1 for communication, but to communicate over the network it requires a unique IP address. The IP addressability restrictions placed on it by the z/VM operating system VM 1 require one static IP address. The z/OS guest systems (*ZOS1, ZOS2,* and *ZOS3*) are connected to virtual switches running under z/VM. Although the switches pass the information through and do not require IP addresses, each z/OS guest system requires one static address. The total IP requirements for this environment are three DHCP addresses and four static IP addresses.

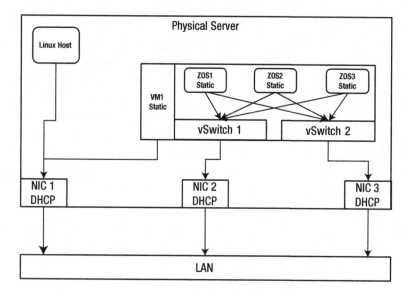

Figure 3-8. *Static and DHCP address configuration*

Hard Drive Configuration

Before the Linux host operating system can be installed, the hard drive configuration must be constructed. The specifications for the virtualized environment must be analyzed to answer the following questions bearing on the choice of technologies and configuration design:

- Is redundancy required to provide hardware fault tolerance?

- Is performance or capacity critical to the success of the virtual environment?

    - Is solid-state performance required?

    - Will high-speed spindle drive performance be sufficient?

    - Are large spindle drives necessary to meet capacity requirements?

- How many physical hard drives will be included in the hardware implementation?

- Is RAID part of the solution?

    - What RAID level is employed?

    - How many hard drives compose each array?

- Is there a mix of storage technologies?

    - Are there SSDs?

    - Is a SAN part of the storage solution?

These questions are important in determining the configuration of the storage environment that will host the Linux operating system and the virtual mainframe environment.

■ **Tip**   The advantages and disadvantages of the different technologies available must be weighed when creating the optimal solution.

RAID Configuration Consideration

RAID technology provides variations that deliver a large degree of flexibility when designing storage solutions. Each RAID level has a precise purpose and, when aligned correctly with specific requirements, provides powerful solutions. Of the several levels of RAID technology, the most common RAID solutions are RAID 0, RAID 1, and RAID 5.

- RAID 0
    - Commonly known as *disk striping*
    - Data spans multiple disks
    - Essentially converts two or more smaller drives to a larger drive (array)
    - No fault tolerance
        - If one drive fails, all data is lost
    - Tends to be used to meet high capacity demands
- RAID 1
    - Commonly known as *disk mirroring*
    - Data is duplicated across multiple disks
    - Provides a 1-1 backup for each disk in the array
    - Provides fault tolerance for hard drive failure
        - If one drive fails, the array continues to function
        - When the failed drive is repaired or replaced, the data is copied from the existing drive to the new drive to complete the array
    - Tends to be used where capacity is secondary to reliability
- RAID 5
    - Parity data is distributed across all disks in the array
    - Provides fault tolerance for hard drive failure
    - If one disk fails, the array continues to function
        - When the failed drive is repaired or replaced, parity data is used to rebuild the array
        - Tends to be used where capacity, speed and fault tolerance are all important
    - Probably the most common RAID configuration in server environments

If the mainframe environment is created in a server environment that is using RAID, it will most likely employ a combination of the technologies. RAID 1 may be used for important data that is not easily replaced and is critical, while a RAID 5 configuration may be used to create a larger array that contains data that needs fault tolerance, but is not as critical. One drive may be configured as a RAID 0 to host temporary data that is easily replaced.

Figure 3-9 shows one possible configuration, in which the machine has a total of eight hard drives. The first two drives are allocated to a RAID 1 array to provide maximum performance in case of a hard drive failure. Because all the data is duplicated on both drives in the array, if one of the drives fails, there is no impact to performance. If one disk fails, the PC simply extracts the requested data from the remaining disk. The next two drives are configured in a RAID 1 array for the same reason: data are still important, but performance is not a factor. In case of a failure, the next three drives are allocated to a RAID 5 array. In RAID 5 configuration, the data is striped across all the disks in the array. If one disk fails, the data is still available, but the array is running in a degraded state, which is often slower, and if another failure occurs, all data in the array will be lost. Disk 8 will contain transient information or data that is easily recovered from a failure, and so this is configured as RAID 0 to maximize speed and capacity.

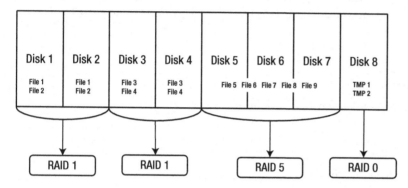

Figure 3-9. *RAID configuration combining multiple RAID levels*

Other Storage Technologies

In addition to RAID, other storage technologies merit consideration. *Solid state* is one of the newest and most promising technologies that can be used as part of the storage solution. It provides considerable improvements over older technologies. Another technology to consider is *storage area network* (SAN). Though not usually a full solution owing to a desire to have the operating system located on a local disk, it can provide an important component to a full storage strategy.

Solid-state technology is a relatively new entrant into the storage market, but it has several compelling advantages urging its consideration as part of the designed solution. The read/write speeds on *solid-state drives* (SSDs) far outperform those on the fastest spindle drives. This technology also has no moving parts, reducing power consumption and heat generation. Depending on all the requirements for the environment, these may be very persuasive arguments for using solid state as the storage solution. However, there are a few downsides to this technology. The capacity of SSDs is much smaller than the capacity of older technologies. Also, because this is a newer technology, SSDs are much more expensive than older storage components. For this reason, the requirements of the environment need to be thoroughly analyzed to determine if solid state is a viable option.

A storage design that includes SAN provides several options that are not available in a normal hard drive storage environment. The architecture of a SAN provides the ability to quickly expand storage capacity. It also offers the capability of upgrading the storage hardware of the environment without modifying the configuration of the physical PC or server. For example, if a new hard drive technology is discovered, a new SAN built on these enhancements can be created and the data stored on the older SAN can easily be migrated and made available. Another advantage of using SAN technology is in the area of disaster recovery. A SAN can be designed to span multiple locations. If a storage replication solution is employed, then the information that is stored on the local drives can be replicated to a secondary location, providing an essential element of a DR solution. However, the cost of implementing a SAN can be significant. And most current implementations still require at least one local hard drive to host the operating system. These issues must be considered when evaluating a SAN solution.

Figure 3-10 demonstrates the capabilities of a SAN solution. The physical machine has two hard drives configured in a RAID 1 array that will hold the operating system and other required programs, such as the emulator. The storage provided by a SAN is attached via a fiber channel. The SAN storage will hold all of the virtualized DASD files. In this scenario, the Linux host will not be affected if more capacity is needed by the virtual systems. The SAN will simply be reconfigured to provide the space and no upgrades will be required for the Linux host machine, thus providing a more stable hardware platform.

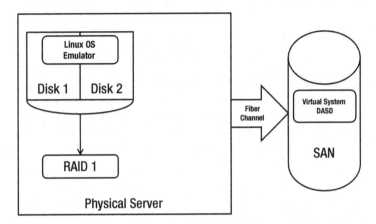

Figure 3-10. *Storage solution utilizing SAN technology*

Installing the Linux Operating System

Once the hardware has been configured, the next step is to install the Linux operating system. The installation documentation for the z1090 software provides information on the compatible releases of Linux. However, the list provided is simply the list of versions that have been tested with the emulator and are confirmed to work. There are several other Linux platforms that perform just as well. The only caveat is that complications that are seen on a non-supported release may not be addressed as a problem. For this reason, if you choose a non-supported Linux platform, you must allocate time to perform testing to confirm compatibility.

The installation of Linux is a simple process. The basic installation procedure for most Linux versions include many of the packages required by the emulator software. There are five steps in the installation process that need to be evaluated and customized to the needs of the environment that is being created. The first step is the decision whether to use a *Network Time Protocol* (NTP) server (discussed in the next section). The second step is the creation of the file systems on the storage solution. The selection of software to install is the third step in the installation process. This step of the process requires careful planning to ensure that all the required packages are installed and available to both the emulator and the users. After the operating system installation has been completed and any additional packages selected, outstanding software updates should be applied to all components on the system. The last step of the installation process is to update the networking configuration in Linux and validate the network connections. The completion of these steps establishes a solid foundation for the virtual environment that is being constructed.

Network Time Protocol Server

If the Linux host system is connected to the network, an NTP server can be utilized to keep the operating system in sync with other devices connected to the network. The primary purpose of an NTP server is to allow all computers connected to a network to synchronize time. For example, many applications rely on consistent timing or time accounting for transactions. To maintain data integrity, an NTP server may be utilized to ensure that all time clocks on the machines used in these processes are synchronized. NTP servers are powerful tools for providing data integrity, and most major corporations have internal NTP servers to provide this service.

File System Creation

The configuration of the file systems on the Linux host machine is one of the most complicated processes of the Linux installation. The design of the storage solution will impact the number and size of the file systems. The IT department may have specific guidelines for the file systems required by the Linux operating system. For example, they may have basic requirements for the location and size of the /swap file system or a specific size /boot file system. At a minimum, each Linux installation needs a swap and root file system. Other file systems—such as the /boot, /tmp, or /usr—can be specified and created individually, but this is not required.

Swap File System

The *swap file system* is a location that the operating system uses to temporarily store data that is not currently needed for operation. When software is executing, the program and the data it uses has to be located in the memory of the machine. If, however, there is data that is not required for the program to function at a particular point in time, it can be moved out of memory into a temporary location until it is required again. In Linux, this temporary location is the swap file system, /swap. The operating system determines when data can be swapped out and when it needs to be moved back to real memory.

Root File System

The *root file system* is the primary mount point for the Linux operating system. Every other file system is mounted off the root file system. The root file system is accessed as /. As other file systems are created, they are mounted, or attached, to either the root file system, or some other file system that is already mounted under root. For example, if there are three hard drives or RAID arrays on a system, the first drive might be initialized as root and all of the Linux operating system file systems default to mounting directly under root. The other drives may be allocated to specific projects. A mount point might be created under root as /projects, and these other drives might be mounted as */Project/ProjectA* and */Project/ProjectB*. This scenario is depicted in Figure 3-11. Mounting file systems under Linux is a powerful organizational tool, as it allows the users to create logical organization out of complex hardware configurations.

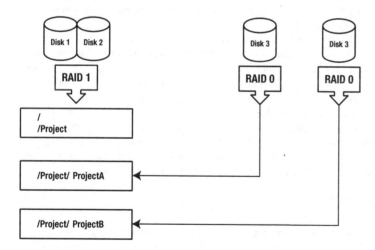

Figure 3-11. Drives mounted in a project file system

Virtual System Data

Although it is not a requirement to have the Linux host create a separate file system to house the data files for the virtual systems, it is desirable to create a distinct file system for organizational purposes. Creating a separate location to host all the data files for the virtual systems makes any required housekeeping duties straightforward. The file system does not necessarily need to be a separate physical device, although in many cases this provides performance benefits. The main objective is to simply create an organizational structure that makes finding and accessing the data files uncomplicated.

Figure 3-12 represents a possible file system layout for a system with multiple raid configurations. The volumes used by the virtual systems are stored on a RAID 1 array with a mount point of /Volumes. Temporary storage is stored on a RAID 0 volume with a mount point of /tmp. The RAID 5 array contains the operating system and the swap files, mounted at / and /swap, respectively.

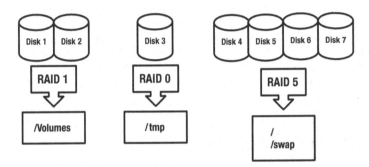

Figure 3-12. *File system layout for a Linux host*

Software Packages

Most of the software needed by the mainframe emulator is installed as part of the default Linux list of software packages. To ensure that everything required is installed, refer to the current installation guides for the emulator software. In addition to the required packages, a few other types of software may warrant consideration.

3270 Application

To use the virtual system locally, a 3270 application needs to be available on the Linux host. This application provides the ability to connect to the virtual mainframe image without a network connection. Most versions of Linux provide a 3270 application as part of the packages supplied by the install, but if one is not available, many internet sites offer downloadable versions.

Graphical FTP utility

The first additional software package to consider is a graphical FTP program. If it is necessary to move large volumes of data with nested directories, then a graphical FTP software package that can easily navigate through file systems and directories will make this task much easier. In addition to clearly picturing how the data is moved, graphical FTP utilities simplify training others on the team how to perform the task by providing them intuitive visual methods rather than complex command line instructions.

Automation/Programming Tools

Automation of routine functions can provide a tremendous increase in the usability of the virtualized environment. Depending on the requirements for the environment, several tasks may be performed on a regular basis. Using one of the programming environments available on Linux to automate these tasks not only reduces the manual efforts to maintain the environment but also, if a scheduler is added to the solution, ensures that the activities are performed on time and completed successfully. Linux has several programming environments that can be employed to create these utilities. They range from full-scale compilers for languages such as C and Java to scripting environments for languages such as Tcl and Python. The skills of the programmer and the requirements will determine which solution is optimal.

Software Updates

The last phase in the installation of the Linux host software is to download and apply the outstanding updates to the operating system and all additional software packages. Most Linux distributions come with a utility that analyzes the software installed and presents a list of outstanding defects and recommended updates. The application of the updates is as simple as checking the desired updates and then clicking OK/Apply. If the Linux distribution that is being utilized does not have a tool similar to this, the task is a little more difficult and may require research to determine what updates are needed. As always, refer to the installation guide for the emulator software to identify the critical updates and kernel levels required for proper operation.

Configuring the Linux Host Network Settings

Once the operating system has been installed and the software has been updated, the networking configuration of the Linux host needs to be customized to match the requirements. Most Linux distributions provide a graphical interface to modify the network configurations for the NICs. There are three important steps in this process.

■ **Step 1**   Validate that NICs are recognized by the Linux host.

The first step is to confirm that all the required NICs are recognized by the operating system. Each physical NIC that is installed should be recognized by Linux.

■ **Step 2**   Configure the NIC for network connectivity.

After the NICs have been defined and recognized by the operating system, the next step is to configure them for IP access. At this point, the decision to configure them with either static or DHCP addresses becomes important. If the network interfaces are to use DHCP, they need to be configured to utilize the DHCP server. The advantage of using a DHCP server is that the network settings such as the IP address, Subnet mask, IP gateway, and DNS servers are provided automatically. If the decision has been made to use static IP addresses for the network interfaces, values for the following settings must be specified:

- IP address
- Subnet mask
- IP gateway
- DNS servers

This information must be provided by the IT department prior to making the adjustments. Care must be used when making these modifications, as any errors will prevent the NIC from connecting to the IP network. If a graphical interface is available to define the network information, then making these modifications for both static and DHCP configurations is a straightforward task.

■ **Step 3**   Confirm the correct operation of all required NICs.

Once all the changes have been made and the network cards have been enabled, the final step is to test each interface to confirm that they are operational. In most cases a simple ping from an external system will confirm that they are functioning correctly. Figure 3-13 illustrates a successful ping request.

```
-> Ping Linux-host
Pinging linux-host.company.com [192.168.2.18]   with 32 bytes of data:
Reply from  192.168.2.18:  bytes=32 time<1ms TTL=128
Reply from 192.168.2.18:  bytes=32 time<1ms TTL=128
Reply from  192.168.2.18:  bytes=32 time<1ms TTL=128
Reply from 192.168.2.18:  bytes=32 time<1ms TTL=128
```

Figure 3-13. *Successful ping request*

If a ping fails, ensure that there are no errors in the configuration. If there are no obvious problems, contact the local IT team to verify that the network ports are active and functioning properly.

Case Studies
Case 1: Single Laptop System for a Mainframe Developer

The laptop that was designed and ordered in Chapter 2 has arrived and needs to be configured and the Linux operating system installed. Because this mobile system will be used only by the developer, no remote access is needed. Although the virtualized system will not have access to the network, the Linux host is to be configured to enable the ability for quick updates to the system. Performance of the virtual system is critical. The developer will potentially need to move large volumes of data, so any utilities to enable this are important. Verification of the installation of an x3270 application is also critical, as there is no network access to the virtual systems. All connections to the virtualized systems will have to be initiated locally from the laptop.

Based on the specifications, the Linux operating system will be configured to use both the wireless and the hardwired LAN connection. Since there is no network connectivity requirement for the virtual system, DHCP servers will be utilized to provide the networking information to Linux. Because only two DHCP addresses and no RAC or networked KVM support are needed, the local IT staff does not need to be called on to add more ports to the switch or to configure static IP addresses. To provide maximum performance for the virtual environment, the swap and root directories are created on one of the solid state devices and the emulated DASD volumes are located on the second device. To facilitate the transfer of data, a graphical FTP tool is provided after the Linux install. A Python development environment is also be provided for automation or creation of utilities. As part of the post installation validation process, verify that an x3270 application is available on the system and, if one has not been provided as part of the base Linux configuration, locate and install a suitable application.

Figure 3-14 illustrates the network and file system configuration for the laptop. The Linux operating system is configured to utilize both the wireless and physical LAN port, while the z/OS host is isolated from the network. One of the solid state devices has been formatted and the root and swap files systems are mounted on it. The second drive has been mounted as /zDATA and contains the emulated DASD volumes. Figure 3-15 represents the hardware configuration and Linux installation created for the developer using the laptop.

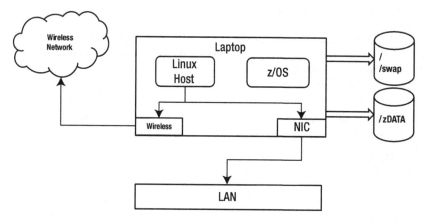

Figure 3-14. *Case 1 network and file system configuration*

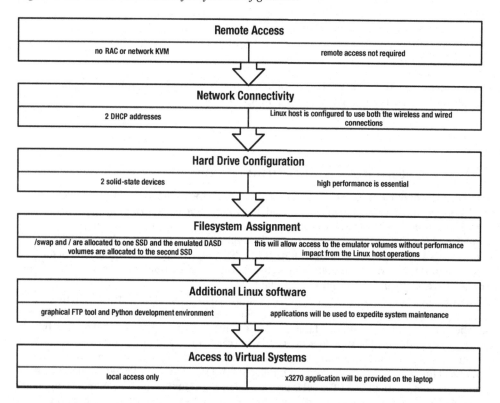

Figure 3-15. *Base hardware and Linux configuration for Case 1*

Case 2: Server Class Machine Hosting Multiple Mainframe Systems for Software QA Testing

The server for the QA team designed in Chapter 2 has arrived and is ready to be configured. Based on the specifications provided, the machine was ordered with a RAC and four network ports. Each virtual system will need connectivity to the network to provide the team members the access that they require. The server has been configured with twelve hard drives that need to strike a balance between performance and capacity. Since the virtual systems will occasionally connect to other mainframe systems on the network, it is imperative that the system clock be kept synchronized with the real systems. On account of the critical nature of the project, any automation that can be written to perform routine tasks is vital and any tools or utilities to enable automation are essential.

To provide the networking configuration according to the specifications, the local IT team has been contacted. With the RAC and the three NICs, a total of four physical connections need to be available when the environment is brought online. In addition, three DHCP addresses (one for each NIC attached to the system) and five static IP addresses (one for the RAC and one for each of the virtual systems) are required. Because of the large number of network ports and IP addresses required, it is important to involve the IT team quickly.

Figure 3-16 shows the network configuration for this server—in particular, the four physical network connections that are needed for accessing the network: one for the RAC and three for the Linux host and mainframe virtual systems. The figure also labels each connection with the type of IP address that is required. Note that the Linux host shares the DHCP address with NIC 1.

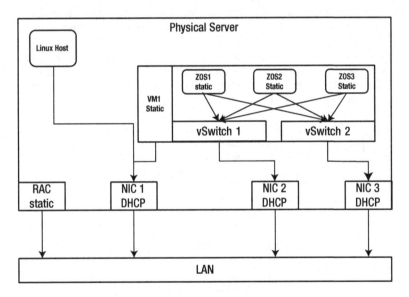

Figure 3-16. *Case 2 network configuration*

To provide the capacity, performance, and reliability required by the environment specifications, the following hard-drive configuration with the following attributes is created:

1. Two 600GB drives in a RAID 1 array

    -   Provides high availability in case of failure

    -   Provides approximately 550GB of storage capacity

    -   File system mounted as /zDATA/cr

2.   One 600GB drive in a RAID 0 array

   • Provides fast access for temporary, noncritical data

   • Provides approximately 550GB of storage capacity

   • File system mounted as /tmp

3.   Nine 600GB drives in a RAID 5 array

   • Provides fault tolerance in case of drive failure

   • Provides approximately 4.5TB of storage capacity

   • File systems mounted as

      • /

      • /swap

      • /zDATA

The Linux installation places the root and swap files on the RAID 5 array. After the installation of the operating system, a file system (/zDATA) is created on this array to hold most of the emulated DASD volumes for the virtual systems. The two-disk RAID 1 array holds a file system that stores the emulated DASD volumes that contain critical data and are needed to maintain performance in case one of the drives fails. The critical volumes are accessed at the location /zData/cr. This file system is mounted under the /zDATA file system so that all the emulated volumes are organized in one logical area.

Figure 3-17 shows the hard-drive configuration, as well as the file systems created during the install. The first two hard drives are configured in RAID 1, and the file system created is mounted at a location called /zDATA/cr. The third hard drive is configured as a RAID 0 drive and is mounted in the /tmp location. Disks 4 through 12 are configured as RAID 5 and the root, swap, and /zDATA file systems are created at this location.

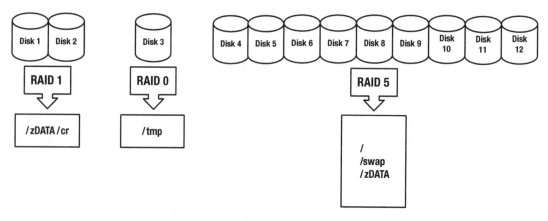

Figure 3-17. *Case 2 hard drive and file system configuration*

As part of the Linux installation, a graphical ftp utility is installed to help the users migrate data from the Linux host to other systems. To help create automation or other utilities JAVA, Tcl, Python, and Perl development environments are installed. To enable local diagnostics of virtual system issues, an x3270 environment is installed and configured.

Figure 3-18 demonstrates the hardware configuration and Linux installation created for virtual environment to be utilized by the QA team.

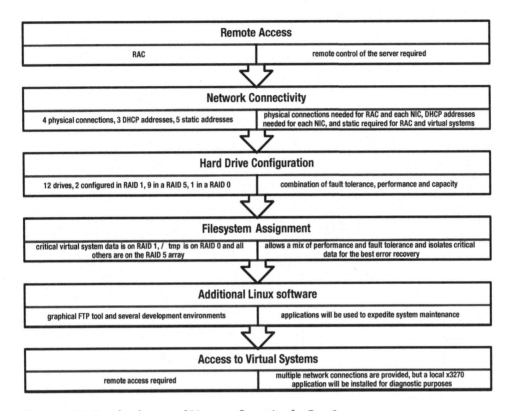

Figure 3-18. *Base hardware and Linux configuration for Case 2*

CHAPTER 4

■ ■ ■

Creating a Base Environment

Creating a basic virtualized mainframe environment is dependent on the mainframe architecture required. There are several schemes that can be employed. The first is a simple, single system configuration. This configuration can be expanded to include two or more systems running independently. Another, more complex virtual environment consists of a first level z/VM host and one or more guest systems. Any combination of these configurations can be utilized depending on the use case for the virtual environment. Regardless of which architecture is desired, the procedure for creating the environment is the same:

- Create a user.
- Download and install the z1090 software (emulator).
- Copy the supplied DASD files (simulated volumes) to the appropriate file system.
- Create the device map which defines the
    - terminals
    - DASD volumes
    - networking devices
    - channel-to-channel (CTC) devices
- Start the virtual systems to confirm that the environment is configured correctly.

■ **Note** The material covered in this chapter provides background information on the creation of a basic virtual system. It covers several key concepts and provides insight into decision processes utilized to optimize a simple configuration. For more detailed information on the topics covered, refer to the documentation provided by the vendor.

Create a User

In all distributed environments, a base install of an operating system creates what is commonly called a super user. In a Windows operating system, this userid is most often referred to as the Administrator ID. In a Linux environment the userid is root. These IDs are reserved for operations that require high levels of security. For daily operations, more limited userids are created and used for system access.

As a precursor to installing the z1090 software, one or more userids need to be created on the Linux host machine. Each first level virtual system will require an instance of the emulator. Each emulator instance requires a unique Linux userid. With this stipulation, the number of userids required will depend on the number of first level virtual systems that will be created. For example, if the virtual environment that is to be created on a Linux host is composed of two z/OS systems running as first level systems, then two userids would need to be created. In Figure 4-1, two userids have been created, zuser1 and zuser2. The userid zuser1 will be used to build and run the virtual system zsys1. Userid zuser2 will be used to build and run system zsys2.

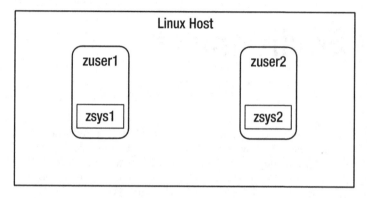

Figure 4-1. *Linux host with two userid and two first-level systems*

■ **Note**   It is a requirement that each instance of the emulator be associated with a unique Linux userid.

Install the z1090 Software (Emulator)

Before installing the z1090 software that was delivered as part of the original contract, the vendor should be contacted to obtain the latest version and any software patches that may be available. Along with the z1090 software, the vendor should provide installation and configuration instructions. These instructions will detail a step-by-step procedure for both installing the emulator software and making system modifications to the Linux host to allow the software to function properly.

The z1090 software package includes an installer and by following the instructions provided by the vendor, the installation of the emulator should be completed quickly. After the software is installed, there are several manual configuration changes that need to be made to the Linux host. These steps are also specifically detailed in the supplied installation instructions.

While performing the manual updates, care must be taken to ensure that the right files are updated. Several of the adjustments are modifications to the Linux kernel and require the authority of the root superuser ID. As such, each change must be evaluated to ensure that the modifications do not harm the host operating system.

■ **Note**   The kernel modifications recommended by the vendor documentation may need to be adjusted based upon the hardware specifications of the machine hosting the virtualized mainframe environment.

In addition to the kernel changes, there are modifications that need to be performed that are specific to the userid that will be running the emulator. These modifications will need to be performed for each userid defined on the Linux host that will be responsible for an emulator instance. For example, in Figure 4-2, the Linux host has five userids defined to the system: root, zuser1, zuser2, maint and guest. On this system zuser1 and zuser2 each control an instance of the z1090 software. Therefore, all the modifications for each userid specified in the vendor documentation have to be performed on zuser1 and zuser2.

```
                              Linux Host

     root      - super user
     zuser1    - user ID associated with first z1090 instance
     zuser2    - user ID associated with second z1090 instance
     maint     - user ID that will be used to perform maintenance
     guest     - guest user ID provided for other non-critical functions
```

Figure 4-2. *Example of userids defined to a Linux host*

■ **Note**   If several virtualized environments are to be built and maintained, it may be expedient to create scripts, applications, or automation to perform updates.

Copy the Supplied DASD Files

Once the emulator has been installed and the system and userid updates completed, the vender supplied DASD files need to be copied to the Linux host. The vendor may supply these files via physical media, or by an ftp download. The files will need to be uncompressed and placed on a file system on the Linux host. These files are the initial volumes delivered by the vendor to create and implement a basic virtualized mainframe environment. They contain the operating system DASD file and any subsystem DASD files that are provided as part of the contract.

The files that are supplied are images of DASD volumes that the emulator reads and translates for the end user of the virtual system. A simulated DASD volume is one large file that contains the information that would be stored on a physical DASD device. The emulator has a device manager that opens this file and translates the information for the operating system running under the emulator so that the virtual system perceives it as a real DASD device.

In Figure 4-3, there are two simulated DASD volumes, VOL001 and VOL002, which have been copied to the Linux host system, LinuxH1. The two simulated DASD volumes are large binary files that have been copied to the file system /zDATA that is attached to the physical hardware. LinuxH1 sees these simulated volumes as large files, but the virtual system ZS01 cannot recognize this format. When ZS01 needs data from these volumes, it expects the data on them to be presented in a format it understands. The emulator has functionality that translates the information in the large file on LinuxH1 to a format that ZS01 understands. When ZS01 needs dataset ZSYS1.PROD.DS01, the emulator translates this to a request for data from the file VOL001 hosted on the LinuxH1 /zDATA file system and gets the appropriate data.

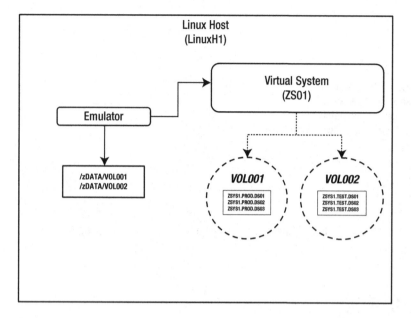

Figure 4-3. *Conversion of VOL001 and VOL002 by the emulator for the virtual system*

An important consideration when copying the files to the Linux host is the location of the files from an organizational point of view, determined by answering the following questions:

- Is there a need to isolate vendor supplied DASD files from any new DASD files that may be created to support the use case for the environment?

- Should the operating system volumes be isolated from subsystem volumes?

- Is there a desire to separate the volumes based upon function?

Figure 4-4 shows a possible organization of volumes based upon function. All of the volumes required by the virtual operating system are stored in /zDATA/System. The volumes that contain the applications that are run on the virtual systems are located in /zDATA/Application, and the volumes that hold data, such as databases or logs, are placed in /zDATA/Data.

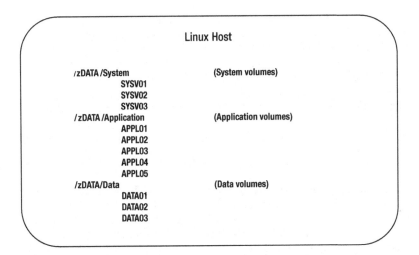

Figure 4-4. *Organization of the DASD files based on function*

While the location of the DASD files is not critical to the functioning of the emulator, a logical, well designed configuration will reduce the overhead of maintaining the files. The vendor periodically distributes updates to the DASD files to provide access to updated versions of their mainframe software. Also, as the virtual environment is used, it may become necessary to create additional simulated volumes. A small environment with only one or two users may not require many modifications to the DASD files, but a larger environment with whole teams utilizing the virtual systems may require more modifications.

■ **Note** The userid that will be associated with the emulator instance must have read/write permissions to the file system where the DASD files are located.

Create the Device Map

After the simulated DASD volumes have been uncompressed and copied to the desired location, a device map must be created. The device map is a mechanism used by the emulator to translate information from the Linux host to the virtualized operating system.

Device Map Location

Each instance of the emulator requires a unique device map. While the emulator does not require a specific location for the device map, for maintenance purposes, it is recommended that the placement be considered when determining the location of the files needed for the virtual systems.

One logical location is in the home directory of the userid that will be using the device map when starting the emulator. An advantage of placing the device map in the user's home directory is that it is obvious the map is to be associated with that specific userid. For example, if device map zSystem1 is located in the home directory of Linux userid zUser1, then it is obvious that when zUser1 is starting the emulator, it should use the device map zSystem1.

Another possible placement for the device map is with the DASD files that will be used by that specific instance of the emulator. While this does not present the intuitive connection between the userid and a device map, it does provide a closer link between the device map and the DASD files that will be utilized by the emulator instance using the device map. This can be illustrated by Figure 4-4. In this figure, the DASD files used by the device map are all located in /zDATA, or a file system attached to /zDATA. To organize the device map with the DASD files that will be accessed using the map, the device map would also be placed in /zDATA.

Once the location of the device map has been determined, the device map needs to be generated. The map itself is a simple text file, so any available Linux text editor can be used to create it. To create the map file, simply start the editor and open a new file. To ensure that the file is saved in the correct location, the recommendation is to save the file with the correct device map name in the desired location. Once the text file has been initially saved, then the next step is to start adding the required stanzas.

Stanzas

The stanza is the basic building block for the device map. There are three types of stanzas. The first is called a *system stanza*. This defines configuration information that is specific to the emulator instance. Parameter specifications include items such as memory allocations and processor definitions. The second stanza type is the *adjunct-processor stanza* and it is used to define a connection for a cryptographic adapter. The *device manager stanza* is the third type. The device managers handle the translation of distributed technologies to a format that is understood by the virtualized mainframe systems.

System Stanza

The first keyword in the system stanza shown in Figure 4-5 is *[system]*, denoting that the stanza will specify parameters specific to the emulator. The three most common parameters in the system stanza control the amount memory that will be allocated by the emulator, the port number that will be used for 3270 communication, and the processors defined to this instance of the emulator.

```
[system]
memory 48000m
3270port 3270
processors 3 cp cpziip
```

Figure 4-5. *System stanza*

In the example in Figure 4-5, the first parameter specified is the amount of memory to be allocated by the emulator. In this example, 48 GB of memory is to be allocated by the emulator. This will be used by the device managers started by this instance of the emulator and the virtual systems that are controlled by this instance.

The next parameter is the port number on the system that will be used for 3270 communication with the system. The default port is normally 3270. This parameter is important if there are multiple emulator instances running on the system. Each instance will need a unique port number for 3270 communication. For example, if a second instance is required for the environment, then a value of 3271 might be used for the 3270 port parameter.

The processors parameter controls both the number and type of processors that will be available to the emulated system. The number of processors cannot exceed the quantity authorized by the dongle attached to the Linux host machine. If the dongle is configured to authorize only two processors, then the maximum number of processors in this statement is two.

The next keyword in this example is the parameter that specifies the processor information. By default, all authorized processors will be CPs. However, if there is a need, other mainframe processors such as zIIP, zAAP, and IFL can be specified. In Figure 4-5, the processors statement defines three processors: two are CP processors and the third is a zIIP.

Adjunct-Processor Stanza

The adjunct-processor stanza is used to define a cryptographic adapter to the emulator. An example of an adjunct-processor is shown in Figure 4-6. In this figure, the first keyword, *[adjunct-processors]*, specifies that this stanza is for a cryptographic adapter. The next line contains the parameter *crypto 1*, which defines an adapter at index 1.

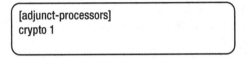

```
[adjunct-processors]
crypto 1
```

Figure 4-6. *Adjunct-processor stanza*

Device Manager Stanza

The emulator has several device managers that handle the translation of distributed technologies to a format that is understood by the virtualized mainframe systems. All device managers are defined in the device map by creating stanzas. Each device manager stanza is created using a specific structure. While each device manager stanza has parameters that are unique to the device manager being defined, each stanza is initiated with a common structure. There are limits to how many virtual devices can be controlled by one manager. Depending on the number of devices that need to be defined and controlled, multiple stanzas of the same manager type may need to be created.

The vendor has supplied device managers to define and control most device types that are typically available in a traditional mainframe environment. The device managers available and the device types that can be defined to them are detailed in the vendor documentation. However, most implementations require only a subset of the device managers to be active. There are four common device managers used by most configurations are the following:

- *aws3274*   Terminal devices

- *awsckd*   DASD volumes

- *awsosa*   Network adapters

- *awsctc*   CTC devices

Figure 4-7 illustrates the common format of the initial statements in a device manager stanza. Every device manager stanza begins with *[manager]*. The next line in the stanza begins with the keyword *name* and this is followed by the device manager being defined, *awsckd* in Figure 4-7. The last common parameter on the second line of the stanza is a four character hexadecimal index. This is an internal control number for the emulator to track the device manager definitions and must be unique for every device manager. In Figure 4-7, the control index is *1000*.

```
[manager]
name awsckd 1000
```

Figure 4-7. *Common keywords for a device manager stanza*

A complete device manager stanza provides the information that the emulator requires to translate information flowing between the distributed environment and the virtual mainframe systems. The four common device managers are considered in turn in the following sections.

AWS3274

The *aws3274* manager simulates channel-attached communication to the virtual guest system. It allows the user of the virtualized system access to system consoles and sessions through a simulated VTAM connection. There are two limitations to the *aws3274* device manager. The first is that the maximum number of sessions that can be open at one time is 32. The second is that SNA is not supported. Through the use of the *aws3274* manager, the system users can access the systems locally through an x3270 application, or remotely by using a tn3270 application.

To connect to the virtual machine through a locally attached channel, the *aws3274* device manager can be configured with one or more devices. Figure 4-8 illustrates a sample *aws3274* stanza that defines sixteen devices. The first two lines in the stanza define the stanza type, *[manager]*; the device manager that is being created, *aws3274*; and a control index number, *0001*. The remaining statements in the stanza all begin with the keyword *device*. This keyword indicates that the following parameters will define a device that will be simulated by the emulator. The first parameter for the device statement is the address that will be used for the simulated connection. In Figure 4-8, the address for the first device defined is *0700*. The next parameter is the device type, followed by the control unit type—*3279* and *3274*, respectively. The last parameter of the device statement is the Logical Unit name (LUname). For the first device defined, the LUname is *L700*. This parameter is optional and not required for full functionality.

For Figure 4-8, a summary of the definition for the first device is:

- **Device address**   *0700*
- **Model**   *3279*
- **Controller**   *3274*
- **LUname**   *L700*

```
[manager]
name aws3274 0001
device 0700 3279 3274 L700
. . . .
device 070F 3279 3274 L70F
```

Figure 4-8. *Example of an aws3274 device manager stanza*

AWSCKD

The *awsckd* manager controls the information flow between the virtual systems and the simulated DASD volumes. The function of this manager is to ensure that the information stored in the large DASD files on the Linux host are translated properly so that the virtual systems believe that they are reading and storing data on true 3380 or 3390 devices.

An example of the *awsckd* device manager stanza is shown in Figure 4-9. As with the *aws3274* device manager stanza the first two lines of the stanza define this as a device manager stanza. The type is *awsckd* and the control index is *0002*. The remaining statements in the stanza define the DASD volumes that will be available to the virtual system. The first keyword in each statement is *device*. This indicates that the following parameters will define a physical device that is to be simulated by the emulator. This keyword is followed by the device address *(0101)*, DASD model number *(3390)*, and control unit type *(3990)* parameters. The last parameter on the device statement is the location of the DASD file on the Linux host file system that will be simulated as a DASD volume by the emulator. For the device that is being created at address *0101*, this location is */zDATA/VOL001*.

In Figure 4-9, these parameters are as follows for the first DASD unit defined:

- **Device address**   *0101*
- **Model**   *3390*
- **Controller**   *3990*
- **Linux file location**   */zDATA/VOL001*

```
[manager]
name awsckd0002
device 0101 3390 3990 / zDATA /VOL001
device 0102 3390 3990 / zDATA /VOL002
. . . .
device 010F 3390 3990 /zDATA/VOL00F
```

Figure 4-9. *Example of an awsckd device manager stanza*

___

■ **Note**   The *awsckd* manager is not restricted to model 1, 2, 3 3380 and model 1, 2, 3 and 9 3390 devices. The manager is also capable of handling Extended Address Volumes (EAV).

___

AWSOSA

The *awsosa* manager is critical if remote access is required for the virtual system. It allows the emulator to create networking connections for the virtual system it is controlling. This manager operates the bridge between the virtual network interfaces it creates on the virtual systems, and the real network interfaces that are located on the physical hardware and controlled by the Linux host.

For example, in Figure 4-10, the *awsosa* manager would control the flow of data so that the virtual z/OS system could use the NIC to access the LAN. This allows information to flow into and out of the virtual system through the physical network interface on the laptop. The *awsosa* manager controls the data so that the z/OS system can access the network as if it were physically connected and does not realize it is using a simulated connection.

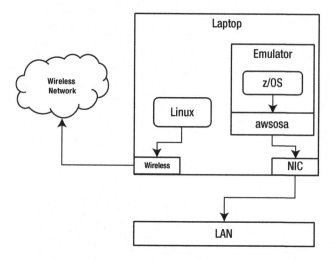

Figure 4-10. *The awsosa manager controls the network configuration so the z/OS system can access the network via the NIC*

Figure 4-11 shows an example of an *awsosa* stanza. Like the other device managers, the stanza starts with the keywords *[manager]*, *name*, device manager name *(awsosa)*, and the control index *(0003)*. However, for this device manager, there is another set of parameters on the second line of the stanza. The first parameter is *-path*. This parameter is the path to the NIC that will be used for network communication. In this case, the path is *F0*. The last parameter for this line is *-pathtype*. In Figure 4-11, the value for this parameter is *OSD*, which signifies that the interface will be simulating QDIO communication.

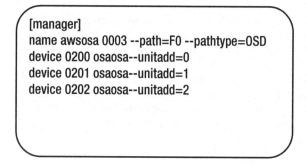

Figure 4-11. *Example of an awsosa device manager stanza*

The device line consists of the *device* keyword, the address *(0200)* and the keyword *osa* listed twice. The last parameter *-unitadd* designates the internal OSA interface number. In the case of the first device statement, the number is *0*.

Depending on the number of network interfaces that will be used by the virtual system, there may be several *awsosa* device managers, one for each interface. If multiple instances of the emulator are to be active simultaneously, care must be taken so that the same interface is not defined to more than one instance. This is accomplished by diligent accounting of the NIC assignments to the *-path* statement.

AWSCTC

While not required for a base system, CTCs are a common vehicle for communication between applications on systems. Couple this with the flexible implementation created by the vendor, and it is a very powerful option. The *awsctc* manager translates data movement for the virtual systems so it appears as if the virtual system is using actual CTC devices. Most configurations that need to utilize CTCs will simply define multiple addresses in the local environment to handle communication between systems within the same virtualized environment. However, the vendor has provided the ability to expand beyond this type of communication. The *awsctc* manager allows users to define remote IP addresses as part of the stanza. By doing so, the users have the ability to define CTC paths between systems in different virtualized environments.

Figure 4-12 shows a simple example of this type of configuration. In this instance, CTC addresses 301 and 302 have been defined on virtual system MVS1 that is hosted by Linux H1. CTCs at addresses 401 and 402 have been created on virtual system MVS2 that is hosted on LinuxH2. The CTC definitions were created so that they would use the network to communicate. In this configuration, CTC 301 sends data to CTC 401 and CTC 402 sends data to CTC 302. Using this design, MVS1 and MVS2 can communicate via CTC despite existing on separate physical servers.

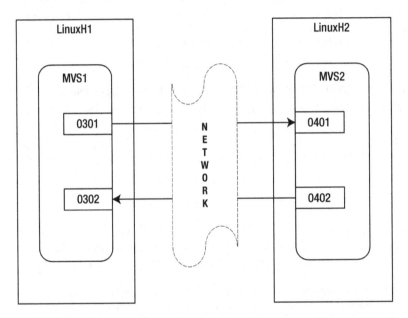

Figure 4-12. *CTC communication using the network to pair two virtual machines on different physical servers*

Figure 4-13 shows an example of an *awsctc* stanza. As with the other device managers, the stanza begins with *[manager]*, *name*, device manager name *(awsctc)*, and control index *(0004)*. The third line of the stanza begins with the keyword *device*, signifying that this will be a definition for a simulated device. The first parameter is the device address *(0301)*, followed by *3088 3088*, which signifies that this is a standard channel-to-channel device. The last parameter is actually a composite of several important pieces of information.

```
[manager]
name awsctc0004
device 0301 3088 3088 ctc://192.168.2.100:8000/0401
device 0302 3088 3088 ctc://192.168.2.100:8001/0402
device 0401 3088 3088 ctc://192.168.2.101:8000/0301
device 0402 3088 3088 ctc://192.168.2.101:8001/0302
```

Figure 4-13. *Example of a CTC stanza*

The first part of the parameter, *ctc://*, is required. The next piece of the parameter is the destination IP address for the CTC communication. In Figure 4-13, the IP address is *192.168.2.100* for the first two entries and *192.168.2.101* for the second pair. The next piece of the parameter is the port number. The parameter specifies the IP port on the destination address that will be used for communication. It is important to choose port numbers that will not be used by any other device or service. In this example, the port number that is used by the first CTC definition is *8000*. The last component of the parameter is the destination device number—in this case *0401*.

───

■ **Note**   In the I/O definition table provided by the vendor are specific addresses assigned for each supported device type. Please refer to the vendor documentation to determine the appropriate address ranges for each device type when creating device manager stanzas.

───

Start the Base System

Prior to starting the virtualized mainframe environment, the USB authorization key (aka dongle) must be activated. The steps required to authenticate the dongle are specified in the vendor documentation. The activated dongle needs be connected to the system before starting any instance of the emulator and must remain attached while any emulator instances are active.

Once the DASD files have been copied to the Linux host, the device map has been created, and the dongle activated, the emulator and virtual system are ready to be started. Starting the full virtual environment on a local machine is a three step process; the emulator is started, an x3270 session is created and attached to the emulator to monitor the virtual system, and the virtual system is started (*IPLed*).

To start an emulator instance, log into the Linux host with the userid associated with the virtual environment. Once the user has been logged into the Linux host, follow vendor documentation for starting an instance of the emulator. The critical information needed before starting the emulator is the name and location of the device map. When the emulator is started, it requires that the device map be used as an input parameter.

Once the emulator has been started, a framework has been created to support the virtual system. An example of how the emulator uses device managers is depicted in Figure 4-14. In this example, the emulator uses the *awsckd* device manager to connect to the DASD files and the *aws3274* device manager to connect to a 3270 session. The *awsctc* and *awsosa* device managers are connected to the NIC and use the network to provide information to the network and CTC connections on a configured virtual machine.

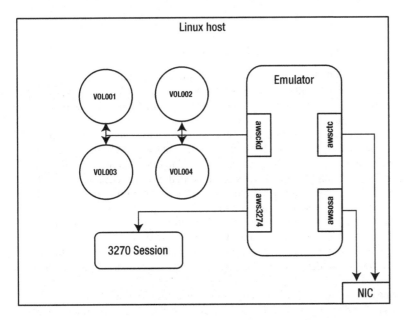

Figure 4-14. *How the emulator uses device managers to connect to the distributed environment in order to provide information for the virtual system*

To view the operator console of the system being started, start a local x3270 session and connect to the local system using the port specified for the first console specified in the aws3724 stanza. If the 3270 port specified in the system stanza is 3270 (as shown in Figure 4-5) and the default x3270 that ships with most Linux versions is used, the following command can be used to start a local x3270 session:

x3270 -port 3270 -model 3279-4 localhost &

This command will open up a 3270 terminal connection to the emulator on port 3270. This terminal connection is used to monitor the operation of the virtual system.

After the emulator and x3270 session have been started, the virtual system can be started. The vendor documentation provides instructions for how to IPL the virtual system. To start a z/OS image, you need several essential pieces of information. The first is the device address of the DASD volume that has the operating system files needed to IPL a z/OS system. The second is the device address of the DASD volume that holds the IODF and SYS1.IPLPARM data set. The SYS1.IPLPARM data set contains the load instructions for the operating system. The two-character suffix of the *LOAD* member to be used is added to the second device address to create the loadparm. (Chapter 8 will provide more information about these parameters.) As the system is starting, messages will appear in the x3270 session that was previously started. The messages should be monitored for errors. Any errors should be researched and resolved.

At this point, a base virtualized mainframe environment has been created that will function as designed by the vendor. While this environment is robust and useful in its current form, it may not provide enough functionality to meet all the user requirements, as in the following situations:

- The user(s) of the environment may require periodic updates to the virtual operating system.

- There may be a need to have multiple systems.

Chapter 5 sets out the rudiments of the process for creating an environment to handle more complex requirements. In particular, it will focus on creating a first-level z/VM system that allows multiple virtual systems to run in the same emulator instance. While the focus is on creating a z/OS environment, the concepts can be applied equally to z/VSE and z/Linux guests.

Case Studies

Case 1: Single Laptop System for Mainframe Developer

The developer laptop has the Linux host software installed and now needs to have the base virtual environment created. The z1090 software needs to be installed, the DASD files transferred, the dongle authenticated, and the device map created. While there will be modifications made to customize the environment, the immediate need is to validate that performance of the environment will be adequate.

To run the z1090 environment, user zuser is created on the laptop. As specified in the Linux configuration in Chapter 3, the DASD files will be located in /zDATA, therefore zuser is given ownership of the /zDATA file system.

The zuser ID is then used to open a browser and connect to the vendor website. The most recent copy of the emulator software is downloaded to the Linux host. When the download is completed, the software is installed and the post installation steps specified in the vendor documentation are used to configure the environment. The Linux kernel modifications are performed as root and zuser for specific user-related changes.

After the emulator is installed and configured, all of the vendor-supplied DASD files are uncompressed and copied to the /zDATA file system. These include all the files needed to start the virtual system. In addition to noting all the files that have been moved to the /zDATA file system, the vendor documentation is used to determine the path that will be used for the network interface for the *awsosa* device manager. The dongle is then authorized to license three processors to be run by the emulator.

Once these steps are completed, a device map, zuser-map, is created in the /zDATA file system. The device map is shown in Figure 4-15. The device map was defined with sixteen 3274 connections and eight DASD volumes. There is also a definition for one network connection using the *awsosa* device manager.

```
[system]
memory  24000m                              #Storage allocated to the emulator
3270port  3270                              #3270 Port Number
processors 3  cp cp cp                       #Number and type of processors

[manager]
name aws3274  0001                          #aws3274 device mgr  Control  Idx 0001
device 0700 3279 3274   Master              #First console defined, normally master
. . . .
device 070F 3279 3274

[manager]
name awsckd 0002                            #awsckd device mgr  Control  Idx 0002
device 0AB0 3390  3990 / zDATA/ xxxres      #Operating System Volume
device 0AB1 3390  3990 /zDATA/  xxxsys      #IODF and IPLPARM Volume
. . . .
device 0AB7 3390 3990 / zDATA/ xxxprd       #product volume

[manager]
name awsosa 0003 --path=F0 --pathtype =OSD  #awsosa device mgr  Control  Idx 0003
device 0400  osa osa --unitadd =0           #Device definitions for Network
device 0401  osa osa --unitadd =1                        Connections
device 0402  osa osa --unitadd =2
```

Figure 4-15. *Device map definition for Case 1*

Once the device map has been created, the base virtual environment can be started. After the virtual environment has been started, testing is completed to verify the network connections and DASD volumes. Any problems will need to be corrected. Figure 4-16 shows a summary of the decisions made for this case.

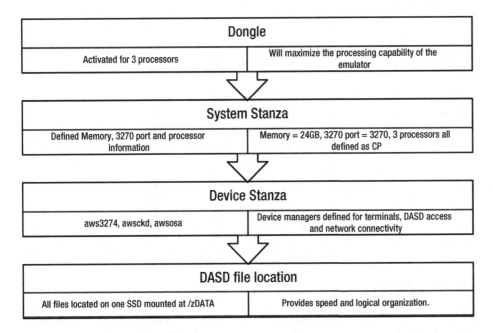

Figure 4-16. *Summary of decisions for Case 1*

Case 2: Server Class Machine Hosting Multiple Mainframe Systems for Software QA Testing

The QA server has the Linux host software installed and now needs to have the base virtual environment created. The z1090 software needs to be installed, the DASD files transferred, the dongle authenticated, and the device map created. While the final environment will consist of a z/VM host with three z/OS guest systems, the critical objective at this point is to evaluate the hardware and Linux host environment to ensure that it has been built correctly and to validate the dongle.

To run the z1090 environment, user zuser is created on the server. As specified in the Linux configuration in Chapter 3, critical DASD files will be located in /zDATA/cr while most of the DASD files will be located in /zDATA. Although all of the DASD files will be placed in /zDATA for the initial testing, zuser is given ownership of the /zDATA and /zDATA/cr file systems at this time.

The zuser ID is then used to open a browser and connect to the vendor website. The most recent copy of the emulator software is downloaded to the Linux host. When the download is completed, the software is installed and the post-installation steps specified in the vendor documentation are used to configure the environment. The Linux kernel modifications are performed as root and zuser for specific user-related changes.

After the emulator is installed and configured, all of the vendor-supplied DASD files are uncompressed and copied to the /zDATA file system. These include all the files needed to start the virtual system. In addition to noting all the files that have been moved to the /zDATA file system, the vendor documentation is used to determine the path that will be used for the network interface for the *awsosa* device manager. The dongle is then authorized to license three processors to be run by the emulator.

Once these steps are completed, a device map, zuser-map, is created in the /zDATA file system. The device map is shown in Figure 4-17. The device map was defined with sixteen 3274 connections and 12 DASD volumes. There is a definition for one network connection using the *awsosa* device manager for the initial testing, although more will be added later. Six CTC definitions have been created with the *awsctc* device manager for internal communication if needed when the full z/VM configuration is created.

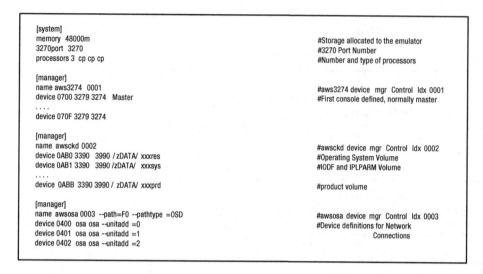

```
[system]
memory  48000m                                          #Storage allocated to the emulator
3270port  3270                                          #3270 Port Number
processors 3  cp cp cp                                  #Number and type of processors

[manager]
name aws3274  0001                                      #aws3274 device  mgr  Control  Idx 0001
device 0700 3279 3274    Master                         #First console defined, normally master
. . . .
device 070F 3279 3274

[manager]
name awsckd 0002                                        #awsckd device mgr  Control  Idx 0002
device 0AB0 3390   3990 /zDATA/ xxxres                  #Operating System Volume
device 0AB1 3390   3990 /zDATA/  xxxsys                 #IODF and IPLPARM Volume
. . . .
device 0ABB 3390 3990 / zDATA/ xxxprd                   #product volume

[manager]
name awsosa 0003 --path=F0 --pathtype =OSD              #awsosa device mgr  Control  Idx 0003
device 0400  osa osa --unitadd =0                       #Device definitions for Network
device 0401  osa osa --unitadd =1                                             Connections
device 0402  osa osa --unitadd =2
```

Figure 4-17. *Device map definition for the Case 2*

Once the device map has been created, the base virtual environment can be IPLed. After the virtual environment has been started, testing is completed to verify the network connections and DASD volumes. Any problems will need to be corrected before starting the customization of the environment to migrate it to a z/VM host/guest configuration. Figure 4-18 summarizes the decisions made for this case.

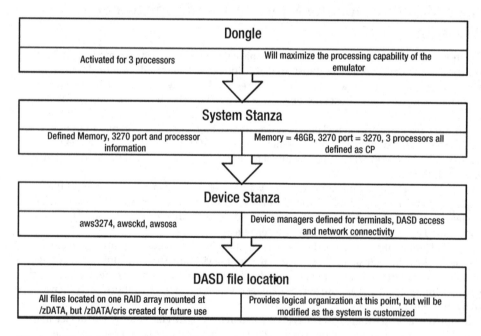

Dongle	
Activated for 3 processors	Will maximize the processing capability of the emulator

System Stanza	
Defined Memory, 3270 port and processor information	Memory = 48GB, 3270 port = 3270, 3 processors all defined as CP

Device Stanza	
aws3274, awsckd, awsosa	Device managers defined for terminals, DASD access and network connectivity

DASD file location	
All files located on one RAID array mounted at /zDATA, but /zDATA/cris created for future use	Provides logical organization at this point, but will be modified as the system is customized

Figure 4-18. *Summary of decisions for Case 2*

CHAPTER 5

■ ■ ■

Constructing the z/VM Environment

While simple use cases can be satisfied with a single virtual system, more complicated use cases will require an environment consisting of multiple virtual systems. Here are several methods for providing multiple virtual systems, with their pros and cons:

- Multiple Linux servers, each hosting a single virtual machine

    - An expensive solution

    - Sharing data between systems introduces complexity and has many points of failure

- Multiple first-level virtual machines on the same Linux host

    - Limits the number of machines to the maximum number of processors authorized by the dongle

    - Less expensive than supporting several distinct environments

    - Sharing data between virtual systems is complex

- A first-level z/VM virtual machine hosting several guest systems

    - Allows sharing of processors between guest systems, increasing the maximum number of systems that can run concurrently

    - Simplifies sharing of data between the guest systems

    - Less expensive than supporting several distinct environments

- Some combination of the above

    - Any combination, while adding flexibility, will increase complexity and create more points of failure

    - Could dramatically increase cost

Depending on the requirements, any of the above solutions may be viable, but the most versatile and economical solution is to create a z/VM host machine that will support several guest images.

A base z/VM environment is available from the vendor and comes preconfigured to run multiple z/OS images in a SYSPLEX environment. This standard design is detailed in the vendor documentation, with instructions for implementation.

While the standard configuration provided by the vendor is functional and provides many advantages over a single stand-alone virtual system, it may not be flexible enough to meet the environment requirements. However, with some modification and optimization, the supplied z/VM host running guest systems should provide a practical solution for most use cases requiring multiple virtual systems.

To optimize the vendor-provided z/VM configuration, there are several changes that need to be made to enhance the entire virtualized mainframe environment:

- Additional DASD volumes need to be created

- The network configuration has to be modified

- New z/VM service machines and users need to be defined

- The z/VM performance monitor should be configured and activated

---

■ **Note** Properly defining users is a critical process in creating a z/VM environment with guest machines. The users that are defined are often referred to as *service machines*. Throughout this and subsequent chapters, the term *z/VM users* will refer to the userids that are defined to run as the guest systems. The term *z/VM service machines* will refer to other userids that are defined to run specialized z/VM services.[1]

Installing the Base z/VM System

The first step in creating a z/VM environment that can run multiple guest systems is installing the base z/VM system. This process is very similar to creating a base z/OS environment:

1. Obtain the DASD files from the vendor and place them on the Linux host.

2. Create a device map for the z/VM system.

3. IPL the z/VM system to verify the configuration.

DASD Files

Just as the vendor has a set of DASD files for z/OS, there is also a set of DASD files to start a z/VM virtual system. Once these files have been obtained from the vendor, they need to be uncompressed and copied to the Linux host system.

The same Linux userid created in Chapter 4 for the z/OS test system can be used for the new z/VM system. The important part of this process is to ensure that the userid associated with the emulator instance to be started has read/write permissions to the file system where the DASD files are located.

z/VM Device Map

Once the files have been placed on the Linux host system, the next step is to create a device map that the emulator will use for the z/VM virtual machine. Like the z/OS device map created in Chapter 4, this device map will consist of both system and device stanzas. The system stanza will contain basic information for the memory, 3270 port, and processors. The device manager stanzas will be for the aws3274, awsckd, and awsosa device managers. Figure 5-1 illustrates a possible device map for the base z/VM system.

---

[1]For more information about z/VM, the use of service machines, and the user directory, see the IBM z/VM documentation.

```
[system]
memory 48000m                                    #Storage allocated to the emulator
3270port 3270                                    #3270 Port Number
processors 3 cp cp cp                             #Number and type of processors

[manager]
name aws3274  0001                               #aws3274 device  mgr  Control  Idx 0001
device 0700 3279 3274 Master                     #First console defined, normally master
. . . .
device 070F 3279 3274

[manager]
name awsckd 0002                                 #awsckd device mgr  Control  Idx 0002
device 0AB0 3390  3990 /zDATA/ xxxres            #Operating System Volume
device 0AB1 3390  3990 /zDATA/ xxxpag            #Paging volume
. . . .
device 0ABB 3390 3990 / zDATA/ xxxprd            #product volume

 [manager]
name awsosa 0003 --path=F0 --pathtype =OSD       #awsosa device mgr  Control  Idx 0003
device 0400  osa osa --unitadd =0                #Device definitions for Network
device 0401  osa osa --unitadd =1                                    Connections
device 0402  osa osa --unitadd =2
```

Figure 5-1. *Sample device map for z/VM system*

Verify z/VM System

After the z/VM device map has been created, the next step is to verify the virtual system. While the process to start the z/VM virtual environment is very similar to z/OS, there is a specific process that should be followed for a proper initialization. The vendor documentation should be used to create the process for starting the z/VM virtual environment. It is important that the console be monitored for errors and any that any problems found during the system startup be corrected before customizing the environment.

Optimizing the z/VM Environment

After the base z/VM virtual system has been installed and verified, there are several modifications that need to be performed to create a more flexible and robust environment.

- Create and add new volumes
  - Paging
  - Spool
- Update Networking
  - Update the z/VM network configuration
  - Add VMSWITCH service machines
  - Configure guest systems to use the VMSWITCH service machines

- Create new users

  - Add coupling facility (CF) machines

  - Update guest system user definitions

- Configure Performance Monitor

These changes will create a virtual environment that allows more flexibility in utilizing the physical hardware used to create the virtualized mainframe environment.

Attaching New Volumes to the z/VM Virtual Machine

While the base system supplied by the vendor provides a fully functional environment, depending upon the requirements of the use case, it may not deliver the performance or the flexibility desired. One constraint of the environment involves the capacity of the paging and spool volumes. While the volumes delivered with the base DASD files will provide adequate space and performance for light usage, if the guest systems are very active and configured with large memory pools, the paging and spool volumes supplied by the vendor will not deliver satisfactory performance. To resolve this problem, new volumes will need to be created.

Creating the DASD Files for New System Volumes

The *alcckd* utility is provided by the z1090 vendor to allow the user to create new DASD files as needed. These files can be added to the device map, attached to the virtual system as new volumes, and initialized to perform any function required. In a traditional mainframe environment there are standard sizes for DASD volumes. For 3380 devices, there are models 1, 2 and 3. For 3390 devices, there are models 1, 2, 3, 9, and A. The model numbers 1, 2, 3, and 9 give the approximate size of the DASD volume in gigabytes, and *model A devices* is a generic term for various nonstandard sizes.

The *alcckd* utility can be used to create any of the standard models available to a mainframe system. It can also be used to generate non-standard sized volumes. With new storage technologies, it is possible to purchase a large storage device, attach it to a mainframe and customize DASD volume sizes. This enables the creation of DASD volumes smaller than one gigabyte, or larger than nine gigabytes, to be created and attached to a mainframe. For this reason, the *alcckd* utility allows the specification of a specific number of cylinders through the use of a cylinder parameter (-s).

A cylinder is a disk size unit on the mainframe based upon old hardware architectures. As storage technology has evolved, the physical construction of a DASD device that relies on physical cylinder boundaries is no longer applicable. However, mainframe operating systems are dependent upon the older hardware configuration definitions. The *alcckd* utility used to create new DASD files takes input based upon the cylinder size of the DASD volume desired, translates it to gigabytes and creates a DASD file with the appropriate size. The following three examples of the `alcckd` command demonstrate the flexibility that this utility provides:

- `alcckd /zDATA/VOL001 -d3390-9`

  - Creates a 3390 model 9 device

  - File /zDATA/VOL001 is 8,539,292,672 bytes

- `alcckd /zDATA/VOL002 -d3390 -s100`

  - Creates a 3390 device with 100 cylinders

  - File /zDATA/VOL002 is 85,248,512 bytes

- `alcckd /zDATA/VOL003 -d3390 -s81249`

  - Creates a 3390 device with 81249 cylinders

  - File /zDATA/VOL003 is 69,263,148,032 bytes

The *alcckd* utility is used to generate the DASD file on the Linux host. However, before this file can be used by a virtualized mainframe system, it needs to be added to the device map. After it has been added to the device map, the emulator needs to be restarted so that the virtual systems can initialize the new device for use. Each mainframe operating system has unique steps to initialize the new volume for use. Refer to the IBM documentation to determine the proper procedure for the types of volumes that are being added to the system.

Adding a Paging Volume

Paging volumes are used by z/VM to move information that is not currently in use by the system out of memory and into a paging data set created on a DASD volume as a location to store program information when it is not currently required for execution. This allows the operating system to perform more efficiently with fewer hardware resources.

In a z/VM environment, page volumes are not only used to free memory for z/VM operation activities, they are also used to optimize memory operations for guest systems and service machines that are running. For this reason, the more service machines and guest systems that are running, the greater the need for paging space.

The paging volume delivered with the base system is sufficient for a simple configuration with a limited number of service machines and a few guest systems with minimal activity. However, as the z/VM environment grows and becomes more complex, the supplied paging space becomes inadequate. This can lead to a slow or unresponsive environment.

To determine if the paging volume is being expended, z/VM has the following command that can be used to display current usage: Q ALLOC PAGE. The output from this command is shown in Figure 5-2, and it displays the current usage of the paging volume, *610PAG*. This command is very useful in tracking the utilization of paging space on z/VM.

VOLID	RDEV	EXTENT START	EXTENT END	TOTAL PAGES	PAGES IN USE	HIGH PAGE	% USED
610PAG	0203	1	599	107820	103889	107820	100%

Figure 5-2. *Output of* Q ALLOC PAGE *command*

The pertinent information in this display that helps determine the current paging file usage and predict future needs is the following:

- TOTAL PAGES— Total number of pages allocated to the volume

- PAGES IN USE— Total number of pages currently in use

- HIGH PAGE— Peak number of pages in use since system start

- %USED— Percentage of the file currently in use

Figure 5-2 shows that although the usage is under 100 percent, there is only one small paging volume available. If system activity is expected to grow, a second paging volume should be allocated to provide room for more activity.

If additional paging capacity is desired, the first step is to determine the size of the desired paging volume. In Figure 5-2, *610PAG* is the paging volume supplied as part of the base z/VM configuration. This volume is very small and will fill quickly if the z/VM environment becomes active. To address this concern, *PAG002* will be created as a 3390 model 9 device to provide addition paging capacity. The command used to create the DASD file for the new paging volume and place it in /zDATA is:

```
alcckd /zDATA/PAG002 -d3390-9
```

After the DASD file is created, the next step is to add the volume to the device map. To add the PAG002 volume at device address 020C, the following statement would be added to the existing awsckd device manager stanza:

```
device 020C 3390 3990 /zDATA/PAG002
```

While it is not a requirement that the devices in the device map stanzas be ordered according to the address, it is recommended as it helps to ensure duplicate addresses are not used.

Once the device has been added to the device map, the z/VM system needs to be IPL'd. Once the z/VM system has been started, follow the IBM documentation for the processes on how to format the new volume to be used as a paging device and add it to the system so that it will be recognized and used by the z/VM system for paging activities. Figure 5-3 shows the output from a Q ALLOC PAGE command after PAG002 has been successfully added to the z/VM host system.

VOLID	RDEV	EXTENT START	EXTENT END	TOTAL PAGES	PAGES IN USE	HIGH PAGE	% USED
610PAG	0203	1	599	107820	107820	107820	100%
PAG002	020C	0	10016	1761K	0	0	0%

Figure 5-3. Output of Q ALLOC PAGE command after adding an additional paging volume

IBM recommends that all paging volumes attached to a system be the same size. For this reason, 610PAG should be removed from the system so that PAG002 is the only volume in use. To remove the volume from use by z/VM, follow the IBM documentation. Once it has been removed from the z/VM operating system, simply delete the line defining the volume in the device map and restart the z/VM operating system.

Adding a Spool Volume

Spool volumes are used by the z/VM operating system to hold output from jobs, service machines, and users on the system. The output can take the form of logs, data streams, and other output. The spool volume can retain data between system restarts so it must be properly managed to ensure that the volumes are not filled with outdated information. However, even with good management, on an active system the spool volumes can fill quickly.

The spool volume delivered with the base system may be sufficient for a simple configuration with few service machines and a limited number of guest systems with nominal activity. There are methods and procedures for managing the data on these spool volumes; with a small environment, the procedures may be sufficient to allow these spool volumes to satisfy the needs of the z/VM environment. But if the z/VM environment grows and becomes more complex, the supplied spool volumes may be inadequate. This can lead to serious performance problems.

To determine if there is enough spool space to support your current activity on the system, issue the following command to get the current statistics:

```
Q ALLOC SPOOL
```

The output from this display is shown in Figure 5-4. It shows the current usage of the spool volume, 610SPL. With the % USED at 100, the current spool volume is full and the situation needs to be rectified quickly. Without a second spool volume, the z/VM system and/or its guest systems could suffer performance problems or, worse, system instability could result.

VOLID	RDEV	EXTENT START	EXTENT END	TOTAL PAGES	PAGES IN USE	HIGH PAGE	% USED
610SPL	0204	1	599	107820	107820	107820	100%

Figure 5-4. *Output of Q ALLOC SPOOL command*

To add a second spool volume, the first step is to determine the size of the desired spool volume. In Figure 5-4, *610SPL* is the spool volume supplied as part of the base z/VM configuration. This volume is currently 100% utilized. This indicates that there may be a lot of spool activity on the system. A second spool file, *SPOOL2*, can be created as a 3390 model 9 device and the entire volume configured as a spool volume. The command used to create the DASD file for the new spool volume and place it in /zDATA is:

```
alcckd /zDATA/SPOOL2 -d3390-9
```

After the DASD file for the spool volume is created, the next step is to add the volume to the device map. To add the file at device address 020A, the following statement can added to the existing awsckd device manager stanza:

```
device 020A 3390 3990 /zDATA/SPOOL2
```

While it is not a requirement that the devices in the device map stanzas be ordered according to the address, it is recommended as it helps to ensure that duplicate addresses are not used.

Once the device has been added to the device map, the z/VM system needs to be IPL'd. Once the z/VM system has been started, follow the IBM documentation for the processes on how to format the new volume to be used as a spool device and add it to the system so that it will be recognized and used by the z/VM system for spool data. Figure 5-5 shows the output from a Q ALLOC SPOOL command after SPOOL2 has been successfully added to the z/VM host system.

VOLID	RDEV	EXTENT START	EXTENT END	TOTAL PAGES	PAGES IN USE	HIGH PAGE	% USED
610SPL	0204	1	599	107820	107820	107820	100%
SPL002	020A	0	10016	1761K	144106	144106	7%

Figure 5-5. *Output of Q ALLOC SPOOL command after adding an additional spool volume*

Updating the Network for z/VM

One of the most critical modifications to z/VM involves updates to provide network access for both the z/VM host system and the guest systems. The z/VM host system requires IP configuration updates to allow it to access the local network. After configuring the z/VM host to access the network, the next step is to review the networking requirements of the guest systems. In many instances, there will be more guest systems active than there are network connections available to use. In this case, the easiest solution is to configure a virtual switch. This allows all of the guest systems to share the same network connection. If multiple network ports are available for use, then more than one virtual switch can be configured to provide redundancy.

Updating the z/VM Network Configuration

IBM provides the *IPWIZARD* utility to expedite the network configuration for z/VM. This utility is a step-by-step process to set up the network definitions for the z/VM host, documented by IBM. To complete the configuration, the following information is required:

- Userid of the TCP/IP service machine; the default service machine name is *TCPIP*

- Hostname

- Domain name

- Gateway IP address

- Domain name server address—up to three addresses

- z/VM interface name—default is ETH0

- Device number, obtained from the device map

- IP address of the z/VM host system

- Subnet mask

- Interface type; default is QDIO, but verify it is the same as defined in the device map

Once the IPWIZARD utility has completed and this information has been entered, either the z/VM operating system or the TCP/IP service machine can be restarted to activate the new network configuration.

Although not part of the network configuration for the z/VM host system, one last task to keep the naming convention in synch is to update the system name for the z/VM host. This information is contained in the *system config* file. To set the correct system name, open this file for edit, search for the keyword *SYSTEM_IDENTIFIER_DEFAULT* and change the system identifier to the correct system name. An example of this statement specifying a system name of *VM01* is shown in Figure 5-6.

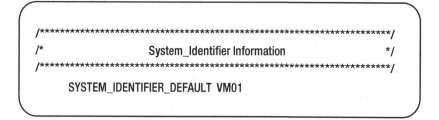

```
/*******************************************************************/
/*                    System_Identifier Information              */
/*******************************************************************/
        SYSTEM_IDENTIFIER_DEFAULT VM01
```

Figure 5-6. System name parameter in the system config file

Creating a Virtual Switch in z/VM

■ **Note**   The virtual networking provided by IBM as part of the z/VM operating system is extremely powerful and flexible. Most of the features that are available are not needed to allow multiple z/VM guest systems network access via a limited number of physical connections. However, if a more complex networking environment is desired, refer to the IBM z/VM networking documentation.

When there are a limited number of physical network connections for z/VM guest systems to use, a common solution is to define a virtual switch. Using a virtual switch allows the z/VM environment to provide network connectivity to numerous guest systems utilizing only a few physical network connections. By using a virtual switch, constant network reconfiguration on the z/VM host and/or the Linux environment is not required to meet the networking needs of the virtualized mainframe environment.

As part of the base z/VM configuration supplied by the vendor on their DASD volumes, there are definitions in the user directory for two virtual switch service machines, *DTCVSW1* and *DTCVSW2*. Although these machines are defined in the user directory provided by the vendor, they may be inactive. To verify that these service machines are defined and active, open the user directory and search for them. If they are defined and active, then the user directory can be closed. If they are defined but inactive (the first character of each statement is an *), remove the * character, save the user directory and then activate the new configuration. If the service machines are not defined at all, refer to IBM documentation on how to install and activate them.

After validating the z/VM virtual switch service machines, the virtual switch that is being created must be defined. The switch is defined in the same *system config* file that was updated earlier to designate the system name. Open the *system config* file for editing and search for the *vswitch* keyword. If one is found, simply update the existing definition with the information for the switch that is being created. If an existing definition is not found, a new statement must be added to create the virtual switch.

An example of the statement to create the virtual switch is shown in Figure 5-7. The *DEFINE* keyword specifies that this statement defines a new device. The second keyword, *VSWITCH*, specifies that this is a definition for a virtual switch. The third word in the statement is the name of the virtual switch, *VMSWITCH*. The next keyword, *RDEV*, specifies that the following parameters will contain the addresses of the real OSA devices to be used by the switch for communication through the local network. The device addresses specified in this statement must match device definitions specified in the device map for OSA devices. If the addresses specified do not correspond to network adapters in the device map for the emulator, then the vswitch that is being created will not be able to connect any users to the local network.

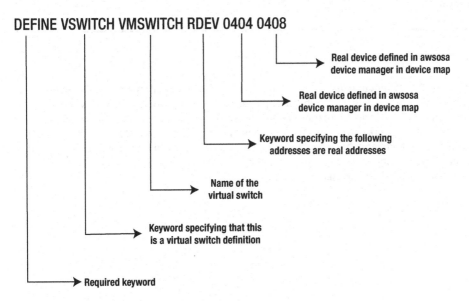

DEFINE VSWITCH VMSWITCH RDEV 0404 0408

Real device defined in awsosa device manager in device map

Real device defined in awsosa device manager in device map

Keyword specifying the following addresses are real addresses

Name of the virtual switch

Keyword specifying that this is a virtual switch definition

Required keyword

Figure 5-7. VSWITCH definition

Figure 5-8 shows an example of device map definitions for the emulator adapters that will be used. In this example, there are three network adapter definitions for the emulator. The first adapter will be used for another connection, but the adapters at path *F1* and *F2* are built to use addresses *404* and *408* respectively. The addresses must match with the device addresses used in the define statement for the VMSWITCH definition in the *system config* file.

```
[system]
memory 48000m                              #Storage allocated to the emulator
3270port 3270                              #3270 Port Number
processors 3 cp cp cp                      #Number and type of processors


......
 [manager]
name awsosa 0012 --path=F0 --pathtype =OSD     #awsosa device mgr  Control  Idx 0012
device 0400  osa osa --unitadd =0              #Device definitions for Network
device 0401  osa osa --unitadd =1                          Connections
device 0402  osa osa --unitadd =2

[manager]
name awsosa 00013 --path=F1 --pathtype =OSD    #awsosa device mgr  Control  Idx 0013
device 0404  osa osa --unitadd =0              #Device definitions for Network
device 0405  osa osa --unitadd =1                          Connections
device 0406  osa osa --unitadd =2

[manager]
name awsosa 00014 --path=F2 --pathtype =OSD    #awsosa device mgr  Control  Idx 0014
device 0408  osa osa --unitadd =0              #Device definitions for Network
device 0409  osa osa --unitadd =1                          Connections
device 040A  osa osa --unitadd =2
```

Figure 5-8. *Device map definition for VMSWITCH adapters*

In addition to adding the *DEFINE* statement in the *system config* file for the new virtual switch, a MAC prefix needs to be created for the new device. Because there may be multiple virtual switches running on a network, IBM created a mechanism to ensure that the MAC address of these virtual devices can be unique. This is important as duplicate MAC addresses on the same network can cause data routing problems. To address this issue, IBM provided the ability to create MAC addresses by modifying the first six digits of the MAC address with the macprefix statement. This statement should be added directly after the *DEFINE* statement for the VMSWITCH definition in the *system config* file. An example of this command is shown in Figure 5-9.

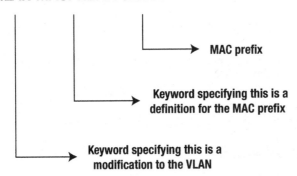

Figure 5-9. *MACPREFIX definition*

In this example, *VMLAN* signifies that this statement will modify the vmlan definition. Keyword *MACPREFIX* specifies that this statement will create a MAC prefix for all the MAC addresses created by the virtual LAN for users that are connected to the virtual switch. The last parameter is the MAC prefix itself. The first two digits, *02*, are required for every VMLAN definition. The next four characters can be any hexadecimal value, but must be unique in the networking environment. If there are multiple virtual environments using z/VM virtual switching, this value must be unique for each virtual switch. For example if z/VM system VM01 has a *MACPREFIX* of 020001, then no other *MACPREFIX* on the network can be 020001.

■ **Note**   If there are no current virtual switch definitions in the file, it is recommended that the statements defining a new virtual switch be added to the end of the *system config* file to reduce the efforts required to make future changes.

After activating the two switch service machines and adding the virtual switch definition statements to the *system config* file, the service machines should be configured to auto start. This is accomplished by updating the *profile exec* logon script for the autolog userid (AUTOLOG1 by default). To make the required changes, log onto the z/VM system as the autolog user and add the following lines to the *profile exec* file:

```
'CP XAUTOLOG DTCVSW1'
'CP XAUTOLOG DTCVSW2'
```

The last step needed to configure the virtual networking environment is authorizing the guest machines that will require access to the network. These changes should also be made in the autolog user's *profile exec*. These commands must be placed after the updates previously entered to start the switch service machines. The command required to grant a virtual machine access to the switch is illustrated in Figure 5-10. In this example, guest userid *MV11* is granted access to the virtual switch *VMSWITCH*.

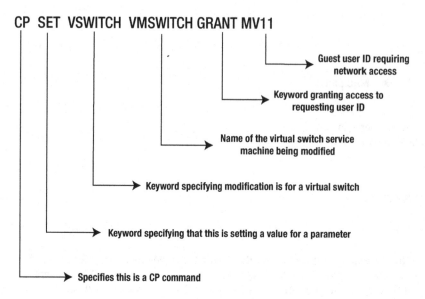

CP SET VSWITCH VMSWITCH GRANT MV11

Guest user ID requiring
network access

Keyword granting access to
requesting user ID

Name of the virtual switch service
machine being modified

Keyword specifying modification is for a virtual switch

Keyword specifying that this is setting a value for a parameter

Specifies this is a CP command

Figure 5-10. *Guest system authorization statement*

The commands required for starting the switch virtual machines and granting guest machines access to the virtual switch are system commands that can be issued at any time. However, placing them in the *profile exec* of the autolog userid allows the system to automatically start the service machines and grant access at system start time. Figure 5-11 displays a sample entry from the profile exec of an autolog machine. The entry includes the commands required to start the switch service machines. Following the start commands for the switch service machines are the commands granting access for three guest systems to the virtual switch *VMSWITCH*.

```
'CP XAUTOLOG DTCVSW1'
'CP XAUTOLOG DTCVSW2'
'CP SET VSWITCH VMSWITCH GRANT MV11'
'CP SET VSWITCH VMSWITCH GRANT MV21'
'CP SET VSWITCH VMSWITCH GRANT MV31'
```

Figure 5-11. *Sample profile exec to autostart a virtual switch configuration*

Once the configuration has been completed, the virtual switch will be activated after the next restart of the z/VM system and will be available for use by any of the z/VM guest systems. New guest systems requiring access to the network through the virtual switch will need to be granted access through the command listed in Figure 5-10.

A diagram of a z1090 environment using a z/VM host and virtual switching for guest systems is illustrated in Figure 5-12. In this example, the Linux host and z/VM system are sharing the same NIC, which is at path F0. There is a virtual switch configured on the z/VM system at device address 0404. This switch is created with the name *VMSWITCH*. This switch is defined to use address 0404 to communicate through path F1 (NIC 2) over the network. All three guest systems are configured to use virtual switch *VMSWITCH* when they need to communicate over a network connection. For example, if *MV11* sends information to another system on the network, it will direct the data to the network connection defined in the network configuration for system *MV11*. However, the z/VM system, *VM01*, will intercept the request and send the data through the virtual switch defined on the system at address 0404. At that point, the emulator directs the data to path F1, which corresponds to NIC2. Any responses are then directed in the reverse order to ensure that the returned data is delivered to system *MV11*.

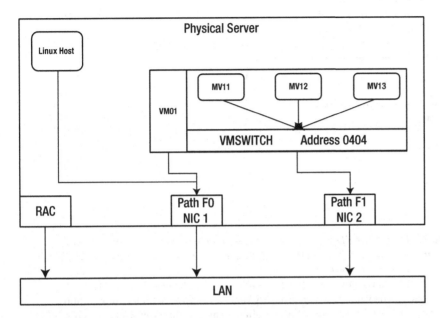

Figure 5-12. *Example of virtual switching configuration for a z1090 implementation*

Defining New Users and Service Machines

In a z/VM environment, all users are defined in a location called the user directory. The user directory contains the userid and password of the system being defined, as well as other resources that will be provided to the user by the z/VM host. In the z/VM environment that is being created, there are two categories that will be employed to refer to users being defined.

The first category is service machines. These provide a service to other defined users of the system. The *DTCVSW1* and *DTCVSW2* users that were defined to create the virtual switch environment are examples of service machines. The next service machines that need to be created or updated define a virtual *coupling facility* (CF).

The second category is users of the z/VM environment. This category consists of the proxy user and the z/OS guest systems for the z/VM configuration being constructed.

Coupling Facility

When initially introduced by IBM, the CF was a hardware-based solution that provided a mechanism for software running on different logical systems to quickly share data across memory. With the success of the hardware solution, IBM ported this technology to z/VM so that virtual CFs could be created to be used by guest systems running under the z/VM system. This allows z/VM guest systems to use the virtual CF's facilities as if they were real hardware solutions.

In order to provide a scalable and redundant virtual CF under z/VM, the recommendation is to create at least three service machines. This configuration consists of two CF machines and a manager, called the *CF console*.

The vendor documentation provides excellent instructions on the procedure for creating the base CF machines. However, in an environment with a lot of activity, the CPUs of the z/VM system may run close to one hundred percent. This will negatively impact the performance of the CF services machines. To reduce this impact, there are some updates to the CF machine definition that should be investigated.

Figure 5-13 provides an example of the updates to the CF definition. The first important modification is to the memory allocated to the CF machines. The recommendation is to upgrade the primary allocation to *1024M* and the maximum to *2048M*. In a z/VM environment running on real hardware, lower values may provide acceptable performance, but in a virtualized mainframe environment running on a PC, these larger values keep more data resident in memory and provide better performance.

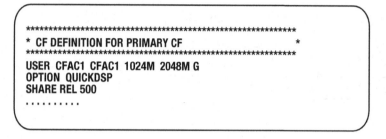

```
****************************************************************
* CF DEFINITION FOR PRIMARY CF                                *
****************************************************************
USER CFAC1 CFAC1 1024M 2048M G
OPTION  QUICKDSP
SHARE REL 500
. . . . . . . . . .
```

Figure 5-13. *CF definition*

The second modification is the *OPTION QUICKDSP* statement. This statement allows the CF machine to be dispatched quickly by the z/VM operating system without waiting in a queue. This allows the CF machine to quickly move data and reduce the possibility of causing performance problems.

The last statement is *SHARE REL 500*. This parameter controls the amount of CPU slices this machine gets relative to other machines. In this example, the value *500* is an arbitrary value and will vary from configuration to configuration. If this statement is added to the CF machine definition, then an appropriate value must be chosen based upon the share values for other z/VM guests.

User Definitions for z/VM Guest Systems

To easily allow the sharing of DASD between z/OS guest systems, there are two different user types that need to be defined. The first user is a proxy user that attaches DASD volumes that are to be shared. Any user that requires access to one of these volumes simply links to the proxy user. The second user defines the guest system that will be started. This user contains not only links to volumes attached to the proxy user, but other statements and links that are needed to create the appropriate configuration.

These users and their definitions in the user directory are discussed in this section. Their creation continues through the subsequent chapters of this book.

Proxy User

To enable flexibility and extensibility when sharing DASD volumes between z/VM guest systems, IBM has provided the ability to create a proxy user. This user defines and attaches volumes to itself. Normally the volumes are attached as multi read/write if the volumes are able to be updated. However, they can be attached as read-only if the data stored on the volume are needed by multiple systems but update authority is not required.

Figure 5-14 shows an example of a user directory entry for a proxy user. In this user definition, the proxy user is *ZPRXY*. There is a string of sixteen volumes *VOL000 - VOL00F* that are set up to share and are defined to the z/VM system as addresses *0C00 - 0C0F*. These volumes are attached as multiple write, *MWV*.

```
****************************************************************
* PROXY USER FOR SHARING DATA BETWEEN Z/OS GUEST SYSTEMS  *
****************************************************************
USER   ZPRXY   NOLOG  512M  512M G
MDISK  0C00    3390   0000 END  VOL000 MWV ALL ALL ALL
MDISK  0C01    3390   0000 END  VOL001 MWV ALL ALL ALL
MDISK  0C02    3390   0000 END  VOL002 MWV ALL ALL ALL
MDISK  0C03    3390   0000 END  VOL003 MWV ALL ALL ALL
. . . . . . . . . .

MDISK  0C0F    3390   0000 END  VOL00F MWV ALL ALL ALL
```

Figure 5-14. *Proxy user definition*

■ **Note**   For more information on the MDISK statement, refer to the IBM documentation.

---

z/OS Guest System User

The vendor documentation provides information on how to create the base user for a z/OS guest system. However, to maximize the potential of the environment that is being created, there are a few configuration changes that need to be made to the user.

The first change to the user is the memory allocation. In order to determine the appropriate value, the full virtualized mainframe environment must be analyzed. The physical hardware was built with a specific amount of memory. This memory is used by the Linux host, the emulator, the z/VM host, and the z/OS guest systems. The sum of all the allocations cannot exceed the physical memory installed in the PC.

Figure 5-15 illustrates a possible memory distribution for each component of the environment being created. In this example, the physical server has 64GB of memory installed. The emulator has 56GB assigned to it, leaving 8GB for the Linux host. The emulator is running a z/VM system that is managing three guest systems and several service machines. The memory allocated to the services machines totals 12GB (2GB each for the CF machines and 8GB for other service machines). The memory definitions for the z/OS guest machines are 12GB, 12GB, and 8GB, respectively, totaling 32GB. The sum of all these memory assignments is 44GB, leaving 12GB for the emulator and the z/VM operating system to use for their own requirements, or to allocate to new z/VM users.

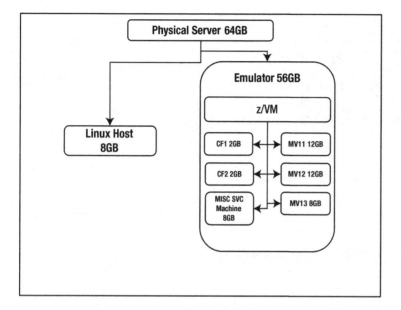

Figure 5-15. *Sample memory allocation for a virtualized mainframe environment with a z/VM host*

For the user MV11 illustrated in Figure 5-15, the memory allocation is 12GB. An example of a statement that defines the userid and the memory allocation for user MV11 is:

```
USER MV11 MV11 12000M 12000M ABCDEFG
```

The next modification connects the virtual machine to the virtual switch created as shown in Figure 5-7. The definition to add the network connection to the guest user and connect it to the virtual switch is shown in Figure 5-16. This statement defines a connection to the virtual switch *VMSWITCH*. The guest system will establish a connection to device address *0400*, and it will simulate a *QDIO* interface. It will also provide three NIC connections to the guest system that start at *0400*, and end at *0402*.

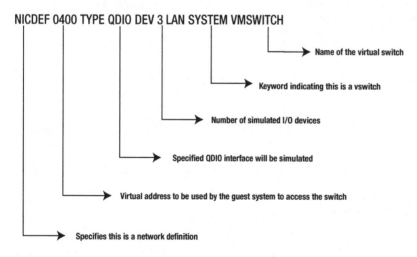

Figure 5-16. *Network definition for the z/VM guest user*

Many products that operate in a traditional mainframe environment still use CTC devices to communicate. The base user definition provided by the vendor may not provide statements to create CTC connections to other systems. As stated previously, the CTC capabilities of the z1090 software provide the ability for the systems in a virtual environment to communicate with systems in other virtual environments. In the following example, the CTC devices created are defined to communicate with other systems in the same mainframe virtual environment. Figure 5-17 shows an example of the *awsctc* statements that might be added to the device map for a three-z/OS guest system configuration that requires CTC communication between all systems. This device map defines two CTCs between each system. Notice that for this device map, the keyword *localhost* is used instead of an IP address. This tells the emulator to route the information locally instead of using a network connection to send the data to an external source. Each definition is also followed by a comment mapping out the connection to provide clarity for how the connections are created. While this is not required, it is recommended to aid in debugging connection problems.

```
[system]
memory 56000m                                    #Storage allocated to the emulator
3270port 3270                                    #3270 Port Number
processors 3  cp cp cp                            #Number and type of processors


. . . . . .
[manager]
name awsctc 0008                                 #awsctc device mgr  Control  Idx 0008
device 1E20 3088 3088 ctc://localhost:8000/2E40  #1E20 – 2E40
device 1E21 3088 3088 ctc://localhost:8001/3E40  #1E21 – 3E40
device 2E20 3088 3088 ctc://localhost:8002/1E40  #2E20 – 1E40
device 2E21 3088 3088 ctc://localhost:8003/3E41  #2E21 – 3E41
device 3E20 3088 3088 ctc://localhost:8004/1E41  #3E20 – 1E41
device 3E21 3088 3088 ctc://localhost:8005/2E41  #3E21 – 2E41
device 2E40 3088 3088 ctc://localhost:8000/1E20  #2E40 – 1E20
device 3E40 3088 3088 ctc://localhost:8001/1E21  #3E40 – 1E21
device 1E40 3088 3088 ctc://localhost:8002/2E20  #1E40 – 2E20
device 3E41 3088 3088 ctc://localhost:8003/2E21  #3E41 – 2E21
device 1E41 3088 3088 ctc://localhost:8004/3E20  #1E41 – 3E20
device 2E41 3088 3088 ctc://localhost:8005/3E21  #2E41 – 3E21
```

Figure 5-17. *CTC definition for the awsctc manager*

In the device map shown in Figure 5-17, each user will have four CTC definitions to create the virtual CTC paths that will be used. Each user will define a pair of CTCs to communicate with the other users in the z/VM guest environment.

Figure 5-18 shows an example of CTC statements that could be added to the user directory for user *MV11*. In this example the first address listed on the *DEDICATE* statement is the virtual address that will be given to the *MV11* user to use for accessing the CTC device. The second address is the real address that z/VM will use to communicate. After the virtual system has been started with the changes saved to the user directory, these devices can be used by the z/OS guest system controlled by user *MV11*.

```
**************************************************************
*  USER  DEFINITION  FOR  MV11                               *
**************************************************************
USER  MV11  MV11  12000M  12000M  ABCDEFG
- - - - - - - - -
DEDICATE   0E20   1E20
DEDICATE   0E21   1E21
DEDICATE   0E40   1E40
DEDICATE   0E41   1E41
```

Figure 5-18. *CTC definitions for user MV11*

A CF connection also needs to be added to the user definition. An example of a CF definition using the SPECIAL control to add a connection for user MV11 is shown in Figure 5-19. In this illustration, the CFAC1 and CFAC2 CF machines are added to the user definition for MV11. The next time the guest system is started, it will have access to the CF machines. Each guest that requires the use of the new CF machines will need updated to be able to communicate through the CF.

```
**************************************************************
*  USER  DEFINITION  FOR  MV11                               *
**************************************************************
USER  MV11  MV11  12000M  12000M  ABCDEFG

- - - - - - - - -
SPECIAL  1400  MSGP  CFAC1
SPECIAL  1500  MSGP  CFAC2
```

Figure 5-19. *CF connection for user MV11*

A proxy user was previously created to allow easy sharing of DASD volumes between guest systems. In order for one of the z/OS guest systems to use these volumes, a LINK statement must be created. Figure 5-20 shows an example of a LINK statement. In this example, volume 0C00 that is attached to user ZPRXY is being linked to this user at virtual address 0C00. A LINK statement must be added to the user for every volume currently attached to the proxy user that needs to be accessed by the guest system.

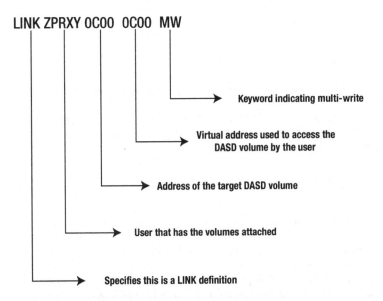

Figure 5-20. *Example of a LINK statement*

An MDISK statement is one of several methods that z/VM provides for adding DASD volumes to which only the user currently being defined is allowed access. Figure 5-21 shows a sample MDISK statement that might be used to define a volume that will only be used by the guest system being updated. This statement defines a full pack mini disk at device address 1AB0 for a DASD volume with a volume label of PAG100. The last three parameters in the definition are passwords for access to the volume. To help signify that this volume is intended for local system access only, the passwords have been set to the system name, MV11.

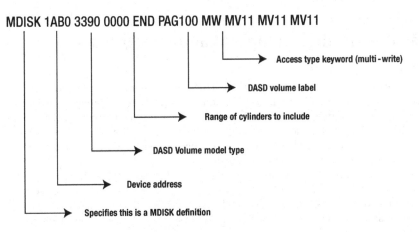

Figure 5-21. *Example of an MDISK statement*

Configuring the z/VM Performance Monitor

As part of a standard z/VM installation, IBM provides a performance monitor service machine. By default the service machine name is PERFSVM. This service machine delivers valuable information on the current activity on the z/VM system. It provides detailed information on current CPU usage, on memory usage, on I/O for both network and storage devices, and on individual users and service machines. The PERFSVM machine can also be configured to allow access to the data through a web interface.

Detailed information on how to install and customize the PERFSVM service machine can be found in IBM documentation. It is highly recommended that it be installed not only as a tool to solve performance problems but also as a mechanism to analyze system performance and anticipate problems.

Conclusion

The z/VM environment that is delivered by the vendor provides many advantages over a single first level system or multiple single processor environments running on single Linux host. However, it may not meet the demands of many use cases. To address the limitations of the base configurations, there are several modifications that can be made to the z/VM architecture to enable more scalability and flexibility.

By updating the supplied service machines such as the CF and virtual switch, the base system becomes more flexible in the use of hardware resources such as network connections and memory. Adding more paging and spool capacity avoids possible performance issues should the supplied volumes reach 100% utilization. By modifying the DASD volume allocations to the defined z/OS guest machines, sharing data becomes easier and management of the DASD volumes allocated to the guest systems is simplified.

Case Studies

Case 1: Single Laptop System for Mainframe Developer

This use case does not include the need for a z/VM host.

Case 2: Server Class Machine Hosting Multiple Mainframe Systems for Software QA Testing

Now that the Linux host and z1090 installation have been tested with a base z/OS environment, it is imperative to start building the environment dictated by the use case. The desired environment is a z/VM host running three z/OS guest systems. Most of the DASD volumes will need to be shared across systems to enable collaboration between team members. While not critical at this point, it is determined that a CCF should be created and CTCs defined for each system to provide the ability to quickly access these features if requirements change. As per design, a virtual switch will also be created to allow all three z/OS guest systems access to the network.

Before making changes, the existing z/OS configuration is moved to a temporary location on the Linux host in case any of the files are needed again. This includes the DASD files and the device map. After the z/OS environment has been moved, a new directory is created on the /zDATA file system and labeled */zDATA/zVM*. The z/VM DASD files supplied by the vendor are uncompressed and moved to the /zDATA/zVM file system. This will allow quick identification of any DASD files that are specific to the z/VM operating system.

A new device map is created based upon the new DASD files provided by the vendor and the requirements for the virtualized mainframe environment. The device map is placed at the root of the /zDATA file system and is created with the name *zuser1_map*, to match the userid that will be operating the virtual environment. Once the device map is created, the z/VM system is IPL'd and validated. The basic framework of the device map is as follows:

System Stanza

```
[system]
memory 56000m
3270port 3270
processors 3 cp cp cp
```

Device Manager aws3274 Stanza

```
[manager]
name aws3274 0002
device 0700 3279 3274 mastcon
device 0701 3279 3274
device 0702 3279 3274
device 0703 3279 3274
device 0704 3279 3274
device 0705 3279 3274
device 0706 3279 3274
device 0707 3279 3274
device 0708 3279 3274
device 0709 3279 3274
device 070A 3279 3274
device 070B 3279 3274
device 070C 3279 3274
device 070D 3279 3274
device 070E 3279 3274
device 070F 3279 3274
```

Device Manager awsckd Stanza

```
[manager]
name awsckd 0100
device 0200 3390 3990 /zDATA/zVM/v610res
device 0201 3390 3990 /zDATA/zVM/v610w01
device 0202 3390 3990 /zDATA/zVM/v610w02
device 0203 3390 3990 /zDATA/zVM/v610pag
device 0204 3390 3990 /zDATA/zVM/v610spl
device 0205 3390 3990 /zDATA/zVM/vprodpk
device 0206 3390 3990 /zDATA/zVM/vsbims1
device 0207 3390 3990 /zDATA/zVM/vsbims2
device 0208 3390 3990 /zDATA/zVM/vsbims3
device 0209 3390 3990 /zDATA/zVM/vvtampk
```

Device Manager awsosa Stanzas

```
[manager]
name awsosa 0300 --path=F0 --pathtype=OSD
device 0400 osa osa --unitadd=0
device 0401 osa osa --unitadd=1
device 0402 osa osa --unitadd=2

[manager]
name awsosa 0301 --path=F1 --pathtype=OSD
device 0500 osa osa --unitadd=0
device 0501 osa osa --unitadd=1
device 0502 osa osa --unitadd=2

[manager]
name awsosa 0302 --path=F2 --pathtype=OSD
device 0600 osa osa --unitadd=0
device 0601 osa osa --unitadd=1
device 0602 osa osa --unitadd=2
```

Device Manager awsctc Stanza

```
[manager]
name awsctc 0075
device 1E20 3088 3088 ctc://localhost:8000/2E40
device 1E21 3088 3088 ctc://localhost:8001/3E40
device 2E20 3088 3088 ctc://localhost:8002/1E40
device 2E21 3088 3088 ctc://localhost:8003/3E41
device 3E20 3088 3088 ctc://localhost:8004/1E41
device 3E21 3088 3088 ctc://localhost:8005/2E41
device 2E40 3088 3088 ctc://localhost:8000/1E20
device 3E40 3088 3088 ctc://localhost:8001/1E21
device 1E40 3088 3088 ctc://localhost:8002/2E20
device 3E41 3088 3088 ctc://localhost:8003/2E21
device 1E41 3088 3088 ctc://localhost:8004/3E20
device 2E41 3088 3088 ctc://localhost:8005/3E21
```

As a precaution for potential performance issues due to z/VM system resource issues, a secondary spool and paging volume are added to the system. The alcckd command is used to create the new 3390 model 9 DASD files and then the device map is updated to include the new volumes at the next emulator restart. The following commands create the DASD files:

```
alcckd /zDATA/zVM/PAG001 -d3390-9
alcckd /zDATA/zVM/SPOOL1 -d3390-9
```

The following entries are added to the awsckd manager stanza in the *zuser1_map* device map.

```
device 0220 3390 3990 /zDATA/zVM/PAG001
device 0221 3390 3990 /zDATA/zVM/SPOOL1
```

After the device map has been updated, the z/VM host machine is IPL'd. Using the IBM documentation for adding spool and paging volumes, the new devices are initialized and added to the z/VM system.

Once the new volumes have been successfully added to the z/VM system, the IPWIZARD is used to connect the z/VM system to the local network. The utility is run and the IP information and device information are updated based on the configuration data provided by the local IT team. The *system config* file is then updated to reflect the correct system name, *VM01*. The system is then restarted and the new configuration is validated.

The user directory is opened to confirm that the virtual switch service machines provided by IBM (DTCVSW1 and DTCVSW2) are defined and available for use. Once this has been confirmed, the following two lines are inserted at the end of the *system config* file to create a virtual switch with the label *VMSWITCH* and assign it a MAC prefix of *020001*:

```
DEFINE VSWITCH VMSWITCH RDEV 0500 0600
VMLAN MACPREFIX 020001
```

To complete the configuration of the z/VM virtual switching environment, the virtual switch service machines need to be autostarted at system startup, and the guest systems need to be given access to the new virtual switch. The following five lines are added to the profile exec of the autolog z/VM user to perform these tasks:

```
CP XAUTOLOG DTCVSW1
CP XAUTOLOG DTCVSW2
CP SET VSWITCH VMSWITCH GRANT MV11
CP SET VSWITCH VMSWITCH GRANT MV21
CP SET VSWITCH VMSWITCH GRANT MV31
```

Once the networking has been completed, the user directory is opened to define the CF machines. The two CF machine are labeled *CFAC1* and *CFAC2* and the console machine is created as *CFCON*. To optimize the flow of data between the systems utilizing the CF machines, the QUICKDSP and SHARE parameters are added to the machine definitions. The full CF configuration defined in the user directory is shown in Figure 5-22.

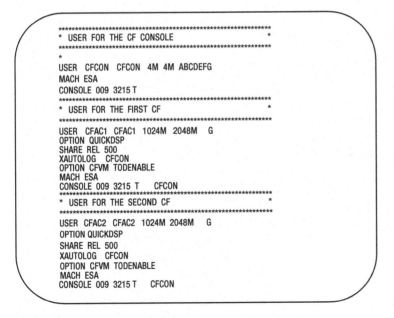

```
**********************************************************
* USER FOR THE CF CONSOLE                                *
**********************************************************
*
USER  CFCON  CFCON  4M 4M ABCDEFG
MACH ESA
CONSOLE 009 3215 T
**********************************************************
* USER FOR THE FIRST CF                                  *
**********************************************************
USER  CFAC1  CFAC1  1024M  2048M   G
OPTION QUICKDSP
SHARE REL 500
XAUTOLOG   CFCON
OPTION CFVM TODENABLE
MACH ESA
CONSOLE 009 3215 T    CFCON
**********************************************************
* USER FOR THE SECOND CF                                 *
**********************************************************
USER  CFAC2  CFAC2  1024M  2048M   G
OPTION QUICKDSP
SHARE REL 500
XAUTOLOG   CFCON
OPTION CFVM TODENABLE
MACH ESA
CONSOLE 009 3215 T    CFCON
```

Figure 5-22. *CF configuration for Case 2*

While the user directory is open for editing, the proxy user for sharing DASD is created. While there are currently no common DASD volumes that need to be shared between the guest systems, the base user is created for future expansion. The definition in the user directory is shown in Figure 5-23.

```
*******************************************************************
*     PROXY USER FOR SHARING VOLUMES BETWEEN Z/OS GUEST SYSTEMS   *
*******************************************************************
*
USER   ZPROXY  NOLOG  512M  512M  G
```

Figure 5-23. *Proxy user definition*

The next users to be defined are the z/OS guest systems. For this configuration, there are three z/OS guest systems planned for this environment: *MV11*, *MV21*, and *MV31*. Each of these systems will be allocated 10GB of memory, with a possible expansion to 12GB. Also, there is a full set of CTC definitions to connect all systems, and each system will have a connection to the virtual switch that is defined to the z/VM system. The base z/OS systems will be created and updated to have a network connection predefined. Each of these z/OS guest systems will have a network connection defined at address 0400, so it is important that the connection to the virtual switch be at 0400. While the base user definition defined by the vendor documentation is used to create much of each user for the z/OS guest system, the updates required by the design of this virtualized environment are shown below. The statements that need to be added or modified in the user directory are:

```
*************************************************
*   z/OS GUEST SYSTEM MV11                      *
*************************************************
*
USER MV11 MV11 10000M 12000M ABCDEFG
MACH ESA
OPTION CFUSER TODOENABLE
. . . . .
SPECIAL 1400 MSGP CFAC1
SPECIAL 1500 MSGP CFAC2
DEDICATE 0E20 1E20
DEDICATE 0E21 1E21
DEDICATE 0E40 1E40
DEDICATE 0E41 1E41
NICDEF 0400 TYPE QDIO DEV 3 LAN SYSTEM VMSWITCH
. . . . .
*************************************************
*   z/OS GUEST SYSTEM MV21                      *
*************************************************
*
USER MV21 MV21 10000M 12000M ABCDEFG
MACH ESA
OPTION CFUSER TODOENABLE
. . . . .
SPECIAL 1400 MSGP CFAC1
SPECIAL 1500 MSGP CFAC2
DEDICATE 0E20 2E20
```

```
DEDICATE 0E21 2E21
DEDICATE 0E40 2E40
DEDICATE 0E41 2E41
NICDEF 0400 TYPE QDIO DEV 3 LAN SYSTEM VMSWITCH

. . . . .
**************************************************
*    z/OS GUEST SYSTEM MV31                      *
**************************************************
*
USER MV31 MV31 10000MV 12000M ABCDEFG
MACH ESA
OPTION CFUSER TODOENABLE

. . . . .
SPECIAL 1400 MSGP CFAC1
SPECIAL 1500 MSGP CFAC2
DEDICATE 0E20 3E20
DEDICATE 0E21 3E21
DEDICATE 0E40 3E40
DEDICATE 0E41 3E41
NICDEF 0400 TYPE QDIO DEV 3 LAN SYSTEM VMSWITCH

. . . . .
```

CHAPTER 6

■ ■ ■

Establishing a DASD Repository for a Multi-Server Environment

This chapter discusses the use of a repository to provide software updates in a timely manner. The best practices detail how the DASD repository saves time and effort in providing updates in a large distributed platform lab running mainframe software.

Development teams require individual environments for testing products within a setting in which they are neither affecting nor being affected by other users. The capability for running mainframe software on a distributed platform presented in this book provides product development teams an ideal standalone environment for testing. Accessing current software levels of operating systems and subsystems via direct connectivity to the mainframe zEnterprise DASD would provide an even better setting for testing, but this level of connectivity is not yet available.

Once the mainframe zEnterprise software becomes available to the servers, testing with equivalent software levels becomes available regardless of the platform and the attraction of teams to the distributed environment increases dramatically. Environments with the same look and feel as a mainframe are desirable to those who can benefit from individualized environments.

As more teams gain access to mainframe software on a distributed platform, the environments become more diverse. Different teams have different requirements for operating system and subsystem versions and levels. Since the servers cannot share DASD, a solution to maintain the software levels on each server is necessary.

A DASD Repository Built on a Network File System Server

A repository provides a place to warehouse all of the software. A local repository is beneficial for providing software updates for individual servers. Without a repository, each software service level would need copied directly to each server.

The assimilation of software levels between the mainframe zEnterprise and server creates an environment familiar to development teams, whether they are developing on the mainframe or the server.

This chapter details how decisions to deploy solutions involving a repository come about.

Product Development Requirements

Software development requires the highest levels of operating system, subsystem, and integration software products. These are necessary for a product to be properly developed, tested, and certified. For example, if a customer has reported a problem at a specific operating system level, the product team can confirm whether the product testing was at the same level. It is critical to know and track the precise environment in which a product was developed and tested.

Research and development teams each have distinct environment requirements that are best suited to unique standalone settings in which product development and testing is uninhibited. In a large shared virtual environment there is too much competition for resources for development and testing to be meaningful and useful. Yet standalone environments are normally too costly to set up. These two constraints operate to inhibit effective and efficient product development.

zEnterprise Availability on a Distributed Platform

When zPDT technology became available, it provided the capability to run mainframe software on a distributed platform. This environment has the unique appearance of being a standalone mainframe processor, and the implementation of the technology is simple. Distributed platform servers provide development and testing environments in which the teams can have full control of the system, free of disruptions from other teams.

Current Software Levels

The availability of environments for developing and testing on a distributed platform entail the need to upgrade the provided software, as is normal for any operating system software whether it is for a mainframe or a distributed platform. Upgrading software must be easy to manage, yet there is no easy way to maintain the vendor-provided mainframe software on individual zPDT servers. Each server requires individual updating at different software levels. Even if there were only two servers, performing maintenance against the provided software poses an onerous task. The primary issue is that each server is independent and does not share any resources or have direct connectivity to DASDs hosted by the mainframe zEnterprise.

The need for current software levels creates the following concerns in relation to the support of a distributed platform:

1. How are disparate software levels on the servers to be managed?

2. How are software upgrades on each server to be handled?

3. How many people will be required to perform the updates and maintain the levels?

4. Will there be enough demand to requisition additional personnel?

5. Is there another solution?

6. Is a zEnterprise software license valid for the distributed server?

If the answer to the final question is yes, this solution resolves many of the other questions as well, for the following reasons:

- The IBM software on the mainframe is maintained at regular intervals with Recommended Service Upgrades (RSUs).

- The operating system levels (RSUs) can be the same on the distributed platform servers as on the mainframe zEnterprise.

- The demand for additional personnel to manage the individual software levels is negated by utilizing the mainframe zEnterprise RSUs.

Figure 6-1 shows how the operating system RSUs are the same on both the mainframe zEnterprise system and a distributed server.

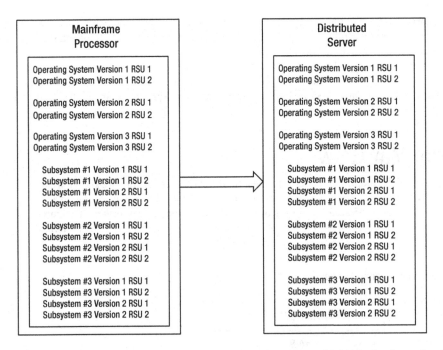

Figure 6-1. *Mainframe zEnterprise and distributed servers with identical software levels*

> ■ **Note** IBM Recommended Service Upgrades (RSUs) are preventive service and maintenance levels available at regular intervals.

Concerns associated with using RSUs maintained on the mainframe zEnterprise include the following:

- IBM utilities provide the capability to move volumes to the individual server. Although this process works well, it can be slow if the server lab is remote from the mainframe.

- The mainframe zEnterprise RSUs cannot replace the provided operating system volumes because there are many differences, including DASD volume and data-set naming conventions.

- The PARMLIB and catalog structuring need to be updated to accommodate the DASD volumes, data-set naming, and other items before the systems can start.

Process for Using zEnterprise Mainframe Software

The mainframe software provided for the distributed servers needs to be replaced from the zEnterprise mainframe software. This involves manipulating master and user catalogs from both environments to ensure that all data sets and products are available.

Once a server is reconfigured to use the mainframe zEnterprise operating system, the distributed lab environment can begin running the exact same operating system RSU as the mainframe. This server configuration can be backed up and used to build new servers as additional allocations of this environment are required, without needing to convert each server.

When a full conversion of the server environment is complete, the result is the infusion of a software currency model that produces a near-perfect environment for development and testing teams. The distributed platform servers can now be an extension of the mainframe zEnterprise environment.

The advantages of a standalone environment and well-maintained software environments can entice more teams to move critical development and testing to the distributed platform. From an operating system and subsystem standpoint, the available versions and RSU levels are the same whether testing on the mainframe or the distributed platform.

The Lab Environment May Grow

Enhanced environments encourage more development teams to request their own servers. Figure 6-2 shows z/OS contention among many systems competing for resources when running on a z/VM-based logical partition on a mainframe processor versus running a single z/OS system running under z/VM on a distributed server. This figure assumes that one development team with one system on the mainframe is in contention with many other systems for resources.

z/OS System Contention on Mainframe versus Distributed Server

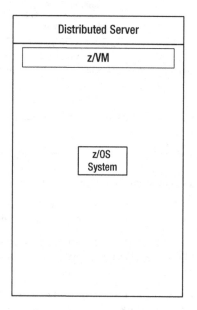

Figure 6-2. *z/OS system contention on a mainframe versus a distributed server*

A well-designed lab environment can quickly grow from only a few servers to a large farm containing a diverse mix of products, users, and maintenance requirements. Each product developed has unique qualities and requirements. Product dependencies and customer expectations determine features and requirements for each server. Individual product development teams might have one or more of the following requirements:

- Current operating systems and subsystems

- Current integration products

- All supported, generally available operating system versions

- All supported, generally available subsystem versions

- Limited dependency on operating system or subsystems

Service and Support Challenges

With the addition of more servers and teams, each its own software versions and RSU requirements and its distinctive look and feel, the lab environment can become heterogeneous and challenging to maintain.

The extent of the challenges depends on the answers to the following questions:

- How many operating system versions and RSU levels are required?

- How many subsystem versions and RSU levels are required?

- How many infrastructure/integration product versions and levels are required?

- Will all versions and levels be stored on each server in readiness for a possible future need?

Research and development teams on the mainframe may deploy disparate products and requirements. The products can range across facets of mainframe zEnterprise software and hardware technologies and the requirements of each can differ, whether slightly or significantly.

Development teams tend informally to refer to the servers as LPARs, but technically they are not LPARs. The servers do not share resources and therefore require individual attention for all software and hardware updates.

Service Methodology

Copying software to each server can raise the following concerns:

- If the mainframe and server lab are remote from each other, the copying of large data can be slow.

- Even when the mainframe and server lab are both local, the numerous copies can be cumbersome and network-intensive.

- With the diverse requirements of each development team, it is neither efficient nor practical to copy each new operating system and subsystem RSU to each server, causing clutter and incurring poor use of server storage.

■ **Example**   Each RSU for typical configuration of three generally available operating systems along with three subsystems, each with at least two or three generally available versions, entails with copying nine sets of software from the mainframe to each server. The expectation that each RSU typically needs to be performed nine times multiplied by the number of servers is complicated by the contingency that not every server necessarily requires each RSU when it is available.

Figure 6-3 depicts the possible number of RSUs with each update.

```
┌─────────────────────────────────────────┐
│           A Single Set of RSUs           │
│  ┌─────────────────────────────────────┐ │
│  │ Operating System Version 1 RSU x    │ │
│  │                                     │ │
│  │ Operating System Version 2 RSU x    │ │
│  │                                     │ │
│  │ Operating System Version 3 RSU x    │ │
│  │                                     │ │
│  │   Subsystem #1 Version 1 RSU x      │ │
│  │   Subsystem #1 Version 2 RSU x      │ │
│  │   Subsystem #1 Version 3 RSU x      │ │
│  │                                     │ │
│  │   Subsystem #2 Version 1 RSU x      │ │
│  │   Subsystem #2 Version 2 RSU x      │ │
│  │   Subsystem #2 Version 3 RSU x      │ │
│  │                                     │ │
│  │   Subsystem #3 Version 1 RSU x      │ │
│  │   Subsystem #3 Version 2 RSU x      │ │
│  └─────────────────────────────────────┘ │
└─────────────────────────────────────────┘
```

Figure 6-3. *A single set of RSUs*

Some development teams may require swift implementation of a current RSU immediately upon availability, while other teams can wait for the next testing cycle or product release. This bifurcation may cause the environments to become more diverse and complicate the provision of appropriate levels of support. The support needed to maintain all current software versions and RSUs available without transferring each one to all the servers is onerous. Although the methodology of transferring software from the mainframe to each individual server is not problematic, even a single-server environment needs to upgrade often and immediately. The copying of large data across the networks can be cumbersome and impedes vigorous updating of a server to meet on-demand needs. In some instances, a development team may need to retrofit at specific previous RSU levels. Retrofitting previous RSU levels on the distributed environment can be easier depending on the age of the RSU. It is unusual to maintain many RSU levels on active DASDs as the practice is wasteful of storage resources. A round-robin process of two or three versions may be common so that the same DASD volumes are continuously part of the cycle. The newest RSU will overlay the oldest RSU. It is also possible to back up the oldest RSU before updating with the new RSU. Thanks to lower cost of hard drives for a distributed platform, it is easy to maintain many previous versions for testing and certification.

Depending on specific development cycles, either an immediate need for current software presents or the cycle prevents the disruption from changing the service level, as in Figure 6-4.

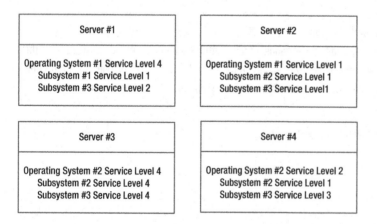

Figure 6-4. *Four distributed servers with disparate software versions and service levels*

Comparison of the four servers in Figure 6-4 yields the following observations:

- Server #2 is operating at the lowest possible service level for all software, even though three higher service levels are available. The need for current software levels is minimal.

- Server #3 is operating at the highest service level for all software. The need for current software levels is high.

- Server #1 and Server #4 have a mixture of service levels. The needs for software levels vary for operating systems and subsystems.

This scenario is typical, except that most server labs contain many more than just four servers. As product teams determine the current need for software versions and RSU levels and it becomes increasingly challenging to manage the contrasting levels of each server, a network file system server becomes an attractive solution.

Network File System Server

A local network file system sever can provide a solution for the varied requirements of software by imposing the structure for storing many versions of the operating systems, subsystems, and other products required by development teams utilizing the distributed servers. The copying of all of the software from the mainframe to a single point occurs only one time per RSU. If the repository is local within the same lab as the other development servers, it allows the copying of software to each server on-demand. The copying of software locally can takes minutes instead of hours if the mainframe is remote from the server.

In Figure 6-5, if each server required the latest version of an operating system, the transfer of the same DASD volume once per server over the network would be required—neither an economical nor a practical proposition.

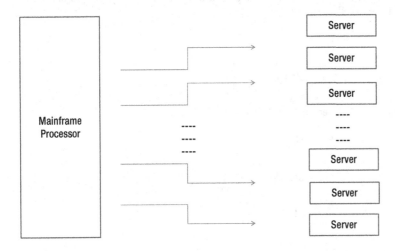

Figure 6-5. *Large data transfer from the mainframe to each server*

Provisioning many teams with different needs and requirement is facilitated by transferring new RSUs immediately to an interim repository that is local to the distributed platform lab (Figure 6-6).

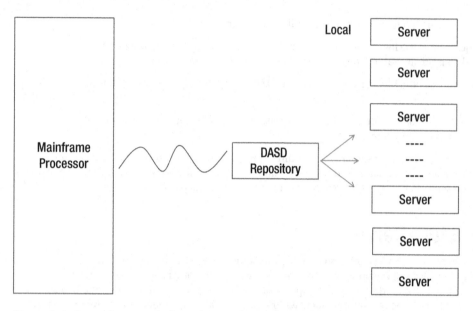

Figure 6-6. *Large data transfer from the mainframe to a DASD repository*

A network file system server can store the integration products and all the RSUs for generally available mainframe operating systems and subsystems. Some of the volumes may be full DASD volumes for a single operating system, and some may contain multiple products on a single DASD volume. Figure 6-7 is a partial rendering of possible data placed on the same local DASD repository as depicted in Figure 6-6.

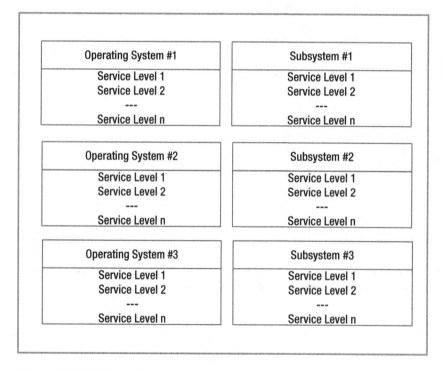

Figure 6-7. *DASD repository*

There are regularly scheduled updates of the operating systems and subsystems, and each version and RSU level on the mainframe is available on the DASD repository based on scheduled transfers. This arrangement allows for immediate updating of a server when requested by the product development teams.

The repository allows for the dissimilar server software versions and levels without requiring the maintenance of all levels on each server. This simplification of the maintenance and support of the distributed platform servers is effected by copying each RSU to the repository and then transferring directly to the individual servers on demand.

DASD Repository Efficiencies

DASD repository solutions drive efficiencies in terms of server storage, transfer on demand, individual product transfers, and fewer disruptions.

Server Storage Efficiency

By eliminating the need to warehouse the many versions and levels of software on each server, DASD repository solutions yield significant storage savings. The efficiency derives from the demand by development testing for many types of DASD and many DASD volumes. A facilitator understands that there can be no fixed rule for quantifying storage needs, because they vary with changes in testing and product directions.

Each generally available operating system and subsystem has multiple RSUs each year. Figure 6-8 shows the per-server storage requirements for just one year of RSUs. This assumes performing quarterly RSU updates. With the repository, the development team can request an RSU version whenever the need arises. This lessens the amount of processing, scheduling, and planning required each quarter to move RSUs to each server.

Operating System Version 1 RSU 1 Operating System Version 1 RSU 2 Operating System Version 1 RSU 3 Operating System Version 1 RSU 4	Subsystem #1 Version 1 RSU 1 Subsystem #1 Version 1 RSU 2 Subsystem #1 Version 1 RSU 3 Subsystem #1 Version 1 RSU 4	Subsystem #1 Version 2 RSU 1 Subsystem #1 Version 2 RSU 2 Subsystem #1 Version 2 RSU 3 Subsystem #1 Version 2 RSU 4
Operating System Version 2 RSU 1 Operating System Version 2 RSU 2 Operating System Version 2 RSU 3 Operating System Version 2 RSU 4	Subsystem #2 Version 1 RSU 1 Subsystem #2 Version 1 RSU 2 Subsystem #2 Version 1 RSU 3 Subsystem #2 Version 1 RSU 4	Subsystem #2 Version 2 RSU 1 Subsystem #2 Version 2 RSU 2 Subsystem #2 Version 2 RSU 3 Subsystem #2 Version 2 RSU 4
Operating System Version 3 RSU 1 Operating System Version 3 RSU 2 Operating System Version 3 RSU 3 Operating System Version 3 RSU 4	Subsystem #3 Version 1 RSU 1 Subsystem #3 Version 1 RSU 2 Subsystem #3 Version 1 RSU 3 Subsystem #3 Version 1 RSU 4	Subsystem #3 Version 2 RSU 1 Subsystem #3 Version 2 RSU 2 Subsystem #3 Version 2 RSU 3 Subsystem #3 Version 2 RSU 4

Figure 6-8. *Recommended service upgrades (RSUs) for a one-year period, representing the number of RSUs to be stored if all were saved for one year*

Transfer-on-Demand Efficiency

The time to transfer the DASD from the mainframe to the repository is the same as transferring the DASD to a server. Each transfer from the repository to a server is quick when on the local network, making the maintenance and support for each system easy. The transfer time to each server is only minutes, whereas it can be hours if the mainframe is remote. This efficiency has a direct relationship to Figure 6-6. The teams using the server can now request RSUs on demand knowing that they are readily available. Transfers from the repository are effected with less scheduling and contention than when transferring from the mainframe.

Individual Product Transfer Efficiency

Transfers for individual products housed on the repository do not always necessitate a full volume move to the server. The individual server can link to the DASD volume on the repository, allowing the requesting team to move only the required data sets for implementation of the product. This linking of DASD from a local repository remote to the server in turn enhances server storage efficiency.

Disruption Reduction Efficiency

The development teams now work independently and experience system disruptions only when they request additional software or RSUs. There is no need to transfer the latest software immediately when it becomes available. The software available on demand from a local repository, allowing teams to work without an interruption until a need arises for software updates.

Case Studies

Case 1: Single Laptop System for Mainframe Developer

The product developer requires an individualized system to verify a product against data-set structures. The simple requirements and tolerances are as follow:

- A place to test that will not affect or be detrimental to others

- A single z/OS system

- No requirements for specific operating systems RSU Levels

- No requirements for any subsystems

- No need for any infrastructure products

- Mobility (because the developer travels often)

- Backups not essential

- The product is simple to install and implement

For this scenario, a laptop is the best solution. There is no need for loading or updating the operating system levels once the initial environment is set. However, an initial backup will provide an easy rebuild of the system environment. Figure 6-9 shows the layout of a laptop with a single z/OS system.

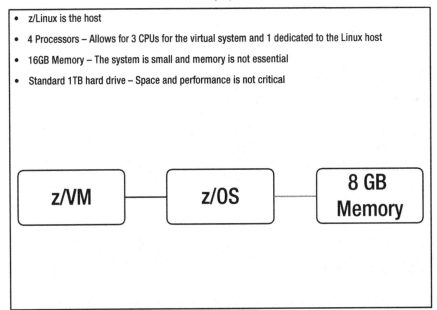

Figure 6-9. *Laptop with single z/OS system*

For this developer with a single system running on a laptop, there is no need for the updated software on a DASD repository. The development is not reliant on any software service levels.

Case 2: Server Class Machine Hosting Mainframe Systems for Software Quality Assurance Testing

In this use case, a development team requires a setting in which the systems are within a data-sharing environment. They require the use of multiple versions of the operating systems and regular updates as new RSU levels become available. The testing is to be a mix of operating systems and RSU service levels. The testing is to include the deliberate shutdown of individual systems to determine whether the products on the remaining system(s) recover appropriately and that no loss of essential data occurs. The mission consists of the following tasks:

- Certify the product against specific levels of the operating system and specific RSU levels.

- Determine product recoverability if one, two, or all three systems experience an unexpected crash.

Figure 6-10 represents the initial system setup.

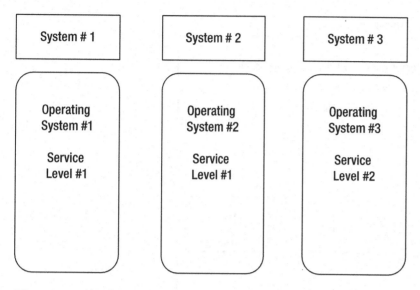

Figure 6-10. *z/OS layout of three systems on a single server*

This team of developers has solicited the QA team members to assist with the certification of the product with specific levels of all generally available operating systems. This certification is required for proof of concept that the product functions properly when running in a data-sharing environment with different operating system versions running at different RSU service levels. Figure 6-11 is a sample certification chart on which the checkmarks signify that the product was verified/certified at the stated operating system level.

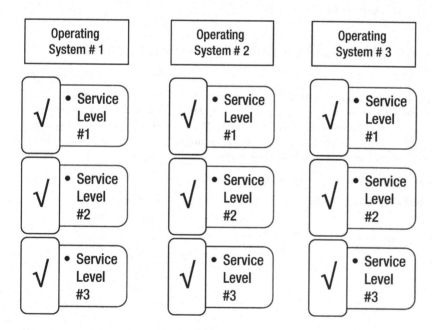

Figure 6-11. *Certification chart for product verification*

To be successful, the team will need a place where they can restart the systems in different configurations. The number of times the systems require restarting would be detrimental to other development and testing performed on shared systems or in shared environments. An isolated environment is required, as shown in Figure 6-12.

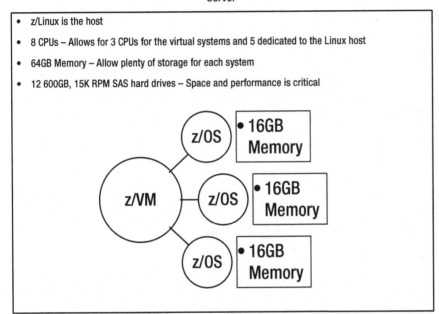

Figure 6-12. *Server layout*

Owing to the need to test continuously at the most current RSU levels, the server in Figure 6-12 requires regular updating from the DASD repository. Each time a new RSU is available, the team requests the RSU once they have finished the current testing. This is a good use of the DASD repository. The benefits of a DASD repository in a single server environment are tremendous when the need for regular software updates exists. In a larger lab environment, the benefits are even greater.

Summary

The ability to run mainframe zEnterprise software on a distributed platform is beneficial for product development. Thanks to an environment infused with a software upgrade schedule that matches and utilizes a process already in place on the mainframe, the usability has the potential to morph into a large farm of servers. Diverse products and differentiation of environments are no longer problematic and flexibility, usability, and maintainability are improved. Figure 6-13 depicts the scenario for interposing a DASD repository to serve as the intermediary to warehouse all new upgraded products and RSUs.

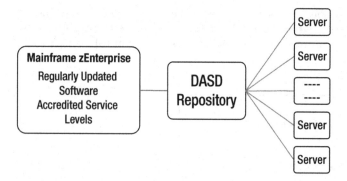

Figure 6-13. *DASD repository as intermediate warehouse of software upgrades*

Figure 6-14 depicts the scenario in which the software is warehoused in the cloud and readily available to all teams to perform their individual software upgrades.

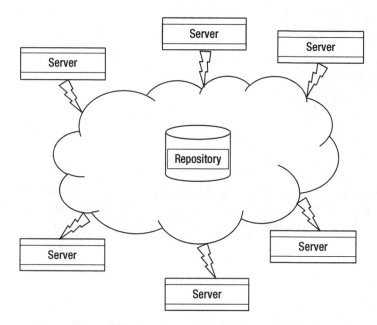

Figure 6-14. *DASD repository in a cloud*

CHAPTER 7

■ ■ ■

Staging for z/OS Optimization

The z/OS and z/VM DASD files supplied by the vendor to create the virtualized mainframe systems allow rapid implementation of mainframe operating systems. These systems provide users access to many of the software and hardware features available in a traditional mainframe environment. However, limitations to the provided base environment include the following:

- Delivered operating system and subsystem updates are
  - Provided infrequently
  - Updated are for the current IBM release only
  - Supplied with interim fixes that cannot be applied easily
  - Prone to destroy any customizations that have been made to the system when IBM operating system updates are applied
- It is complicated to start multiple operating systems in the same virtual environment.
- The operating systems and subsystems are provided as a bundle, and it is difficult to mix versions.
- Some use cases may require customizations to the virtualized mainframe environment that are not provided by the configurations delivered by the vendor.

By making some changes to the z/OS guest systems and by modifying the underlying z/1090 environment, many of these limitations can be mitigated.

To start the migration to a new virtualized mainframe configuration that will alleviate these limitations, several additions and modifications must be made to the existing environment. Once this process is completed, the z/OS systems that are used by the virtualized environment will be independent of the DASD files provided by the vendor. This will enable simplification of the management processes and increase the functionality that can be provided.

The first change is to create several new DASD files that will be used in the construction of the new virtualized z/OS systems. These new files must then be added to the device map, and the volumes must be added to the z/VM user directory. After the updates to the z/VM user director, the z/OS guest system must be IPL'd and the new volumes must be initialized.

Once the new DASD files have been initialized, the system volume must be updated with a new *input/output definition file* (IODF) so that the new virtual z/OS systems have access to the new device addresses that are available.

The last update needed to begin the migration is to configure access to the DASD repository, if one is available. This includes setting up the NFS mount points that are required, updating the device map to include any new DASD files, and then modifying the z/VM user directory to provide the z/OS guest systems access to any new volumes.

■ **Note** This chapter uses the naming conventions outlined in Appendix B when creating DASD files with the *alcckd* utility. All system and volume names also follow the conventions specified in the Appendix.

DASD Volume Updates to the Virtualized Mainframe Environment

To enable the creation of a virtualized mainframe environment that is not dependent on the vendor-supplied DASD volumes, it is necessary to create new files on the Linux operating system that can be used to build new volumes for the emulated mainframe environment. These DASD volumes will contain data that will allow the virtualized system to operate independently of the vendor-supplied operating systems.

Creation and Organization of New DASD Files

To begin migration of the virtual systems to an independent environment, the DASD files that will be used to create the new mainframe DASD volumes must be generated. The *alcckd* utility is used to create the DASD files on the Linux file system. Before the execution of the *alcckd* utility, a location must be selected for the new DASD files. Although it is not a requirement to do so, new DASD files are better placed in a different location than the files currently in use for the sake of organization and clarity.

The new DASD files can be organized several ways. One method is to segregate the new DASD files by function. For example, operating system DASD files might be in one location, product DASD files in another, and user DASD files in another. Another possible configuration is to place all DASD files associated with specific systems in a unique location, with common files all placed in the same location.

Figure 7-1 is an example of locating the DASD files according to function. In this example, */zDATA* is the root file system for the DASD files. Mounted under */zDATA* are other file systems that organize the DASD files by function. In this case, */zDATA/zVM* contains the z/VM DASD files, whereas */zDATA/zOS* contains the DASD files for the z/OS operating systems. The other file systems are also used to separate DASD files by based on functionality.

```
/zDATA                    root file system for z1090 DASD files
/zDATA/zVM                file system for z/VM DASD files
/zDATA/zOS                file system for z/OS DASD files
/zDATA/Subsystem          file system for IBM subsystem DASD files
/zDATA/Software           file system for OEM software DASD files
/zDATA/UserData           file system for general user DASD files
```

Figure 7-1. *Possible file system organizatation for the new virtual system configuration based on function*

Figure 7-2 is an example of locating the DASD files by function and virtual system association. In this example, */zDATA* is the root file system for the DASD files. As with Figure 7-1, */zDATA/zVM* contains the DASD files for the z/VM system, but in this example, the z/OS guest system DASD files are spread across */zDATA/MV1*, */zDATA/MV2*, */zDATA/MV3* and */zDATA/Common*. The DASD files associated to specific z/OS guest systems are located in */zDATA/MV1*, */zDATA/MV2* and */zDATA/MV3*. Any DASD files used by all guest systems are in */zDATA/Common*. The other file systems are also used to separate DASD files based on how they are used in the environment.

```
/zDATA                  root file system for z1090 DASD files
/zDATA/zVM              file system for z/VM DASD files
/zDATA/MV1              file system for the first z/OS guest DASD Files
/zDATA/MV2              file system for the second z/OS guest DASD Files
/zDATA/MV3              file system for the third z/OS guest DASD Files
/zDATA/Subsystem        file system for IBM subsystem DASD files
/zDATA/Common           file system for common DASD files
/zDATA/UserData         file system for general user DASD files
```

Figure 7-2. *Possible file system organization based on system association and function*

■ **Note**   The file system organization depicted in Figure 7-2 is used for the examples given in the rest of this chapter.

Once the correct file system organization has been built, the *alcckd* utility can be used to create the DASD files. Several required files and some optional files that need to be considered include the following:

- Page files for each z/OS guest system

- Spool files for each z/OS guest system

- JES2 checkpoint files for each z/OS guest system

- CF files to hold SYSPLEX structures

- A system configuration DASD file to be shared among all systems; containing the new IODF and shared parameter libraries

- Additional system DASD files

- Files to contain user data as specified in the use case

- Any additional files that might be required by the use case

Page Files

While it is recommended that each z/OS guest system be configured with enough real memory that paging will not occur, paging space still needs to be supplied for each z/OS system. Depending on the storage space available on the Linux file system, and the memory available to the z/OS guest, a single emulated 3390 volume should provide sufficient space. In the following example, 3390 model 9 devices are created for each guest system. However, based on the virtual environment requirements or constraints, other sizes may be appropriate.

```
alcckd /zDATA/MV1/PAG100 -d3390-9  -for system 1
alcckd /zDATA/MV2/PAG200 -d3390-9  -for system 2
alcckd /zDATA/MV3/PAG300 -d3390-9  -for system 3
```

Spool Files

As with z/VM, z/OS writes output to spool volumes. Depending on how much data is written to the spool on the z/OS guest, varying amounts of spool space may be required. The use case for the virtualized environment should provide insight into how much spool space is needed. Because spool shortages cause performance issues and possible system outages, it is recommended that adequate spool space be available at all times. In the present example of the new environment being created, a 3390 Model 9 device is used to contain the spool data. More can be allocated initially if required, but this is a suggested starting configuration. The following commands create three DASD files the size of a 3390 Model 9 device to be used for the spool volumes:

```
alcckd /zDATA/MV1/SPL100 -d3390-9  -for system 1
alcckd /zDATA/MV2/SPL200 -d3390-9  -for system 2
alcckd /zDATA/MV3/SPL300 -d3390-9  -for system 3
```

JES2 Checkpoint Files

In addition to the spool volumes, JES2 requires datasets to checkpoint data during normal operation. To provide the ability for the z/OS guest systems to checkpoint JES2 data, it is recommended that primary and secondary checkpoint DASD files be created to accommodate the JES2 checkpoint datasets. The size of the datasets is based upon the spool volumes and system activity. IBM documents a procedure to calculate precisely the size of the DASD volume needed to host the checkpoint datasets, but a 50-cylinder volume is sufficient for most z1090 environments. The *alcckd* commands that follow create primary and secondary DASD files to be used for the JES2 checkpoint datasets:

```
alcckd /zDATA/MV1/CKP10P -d3390 -s50  -for system 1
alcckd /zDATA/MV1/CKP10A -d3390 -s50  -for system 1
alcckd /zDATA/MV2/CKP20P -d3390 -s50  -for system 2
alcckd /zDATA/MV2/CKP20A -d3390 -s50  -for system 2
alcckd /zDATA/MV3/CKP30P -d3390 -s50  -for system 3
alcckd /zDATA/MV3/CKP30A -d3390 -s50  -for system 3
```

Couple Data Set Files

Most use cases that require multiple systems require that at least two of the z/OS systems be configured in a sysplex. To enable this configuration, *couple data sets* (CDSs) must be made available to the systems to hold information about the sysplex. The size for these data sets is determined by the number of systems in the sysplex, as well as the amount of data that is shared through the coupling structures. As for the JES2 checkpoint files, it is highly recommended that primary and alternate files be created. IBM documentation can be used to calculate the precise size of the file needed, but a 150-cylinder file should be adequate for most use cases of three z/OS guest systems. The following example illustrates how to create the primary and alternate CDS DASD files to be shared by the three z/OS systems:

```
alcckd /zDATA/Common/CPL00P -d3390 -s150
alcckd /zDATA/Common/CPL00A -d3390 -s150
```

System Configuration DASD Files

To migrate the z/OS guest systems from the vendor-provided DASD files to the new configuration, a DASD volume that will contain the new configuration data must be provided to the guest systems. A logical approach is to provide a common DASD volume that will allow the z/OS guest system to share the new system parameter data sets. The first step in creating the common system configuration volume is the creation of the DASD file. The space needed for the configuration data sets is minimal, so there is no need to allocate a large DASD file. The following command creates a DASD file the size of a 3390 Model 3 device to store the z/OS system configuration information:

```
alcckd /zDATA/Common/MVIPL1 -d3390-3
```

Additional System DASD Files

To complete the system migration, other DASD files may be needed to allow the z/OS system to function correctly. The following *alcckd* commands illustrate the creation of DASD files that might be desired:

```
alcckd /zDATA/Common/STG001 -d3390 -s65520
```

—Creates a 54GB file to be used as a storage volume by the z/OS systems

```
alcckd /zDATA/Common/WRK001 -d3390 -s65520
```

—Creates a 54GB file to be used as a work volume by the z/OS systems

```
alcckd /zDATA/Common/DMP001 -d3390 -s32760
```

—Creates a 27GB file to be used to hold dump data sets for the z/OS systems

User DASD Files

In addition to the files needed by the z/OS operating system to start and function properly, most use cases specify a requirement for additional storage. The number and size of DASD volumes required by each guest system must be determined before the DASD files can be created by the *alcckd* utility. Once the information for each volume has been identified the DASD files can be created in the appropriate file system on the Linux host. The following examples illustrate possible *alcckd* commands to create user files for system MV11:

```
alcckd /zDATA/UserData/TSO100 -d3390-9
alcckd /zDATA/UserData/TSO101 -d3390-9
. . . .
alcckd /zDATA/UserData/TSO10F -d3390-9
```

—Creates a full string of 3390 model 9 devices (approx 9 GB)

```
alcckd /zDATA/UserData/TSO110 -d3390 -s65520
alcckd /zDATA/UserData/TSO111 -d3390 -s65520
```

—Creates two 3390 model 54 devices (approx 54 GB)

Additional DASD Files Required by the Use Case

Depending on the use case for the virtualized mainframe environment, there may be other storage specifications for the z/OS systems. Once these requirements have been analyzed, the *alcckd* utility can be used to create the DASD files on the Linux host. Again, the placement of the DASD files needs to be considered when running the utility to ensure that the files are placed in the correct Linux file system. One example of such a file is a DASD volume that contains shared information used by all of the z/OS guest systems, but which is not part of the software required for system startup. This volume might contain system utility software. An example of *alcckd* command to create a DASD file the size of a 3390 Model 9 device for this software follows:

```
alcckd /zDATA/Common/MVSHR1 -d3390-9
```

Updates to the Device Map

Once the files have been created, they need to be added to the device map being built for the new environment. As with the file system structure, the device address organization for the new systems may require careful analysis to create an effective design. For future expansion, it is advantageous to organize device addresses for the new files on logical criteria. For example, DASD files that are associated with an individual system may be grouped together in a specific device address range, while DASD files that are common to all systems may be grouped together in a different address range.

The following exemplify updates to the device map for the files that have just been created:

```
. . . .
[manager]
name awsckd 0100
device 1A00 3390 3990 /zDATA/MV1/PAG100
device 1A01 3390 3990 /zDATA/MV1/SPL100
device 1A02 3390 3990 /zDATA/MV1/CKP10P
device 1A03 3390 3990 /zDATA/MV1/CKP10A
. . . .
[manager]
name awsckd 0200
device 2A00 3390 3990 /zDATA/MV2/PAG200
device 2A01 3390 3990 /zDATA/MV2/SPL200
device 2A02 3390 3990 /zDATA/MV2/CKP20P
device 2A03 3390 3990 /zDATA/MV2/CKP20A
. . . .
[manager]
name awsckd 0300
device 3A00 3390 3990 /zDATA/MV3/PAG300
device 3A01 3390 3990 /zDATA/MV3/SPL300
device 3A02 3390 3990 /zDATA/MV3/CKP30P
device 3A03 3390 3990 /zDATA/MV3/CKP30A
. . . .
[manager]
name awsckd 0400
device 0900 3390 3990 /zDATA/Common/MVIPL1
device 0901 3390 3990 /zDATA/Common/CPLOOP
device 0902 3390 3990 /zDATA/Common/CPLOOA
device 0903 3390 3990 /zDATA/Common/STG001
device 0904 3390 3990 /zDATA/Common/WRK001
device 0905 3390 3990 /zDATA/Common/DMP001
device 0906 3390 3990 /zDATA/Common/MVSHR1
. . . .
[manager]
name awsckd 0500
device 0D00 3390 3990 /zDATA/UserData/TSO100
device 0D01 3390 3990 /zDATA/UserData/TSO101
```

```
. . . .
device 0D0F 3390 3990 /zDATA/UserData/TSO10F
device 0D10 3390 3990 /zDATA/UserData/TSO110
device 0D11 3390 3990 /zDATA/UserData/TSO111
```

Updates to the User Directory

Once the device map has been updated, the user directory on the z/VM system needs updated to include the new volumes. As with most changes that are made to the virtual environment, there are several ways to implement updates to the user directory to utilize the new emulated DASD volumes.

For the volumes that will be used and shared by the z/OS guest systems, the logical decision is to define the new volumes to the proxy user that was created to manage shared volumes. The new shared volumes can be defined as minidisks to the proxy user with the MDISK statement. An example follows of defining some of the shared volumes using the MVIPL1, CPL00P and CPL00A volumes:

```
*****************************************************************
*    PROXY USER FOR SHARING VOLUMES BETWEEN Z/OS GUEST SYSTEMS *
*****************************************************************
*
USER ZPROXY NOLOG 512M 512M G
. . . .
MDISK 0900 3390 0000 END MVIPL1 MWV ALL ALL ALL
MDISK 0901 3390 0000 END CPL00P MWV ALL ALL ALL
MDISK 0902 3390 0000 END CPL00A MWV ALL ALL ALL
```

Not all the newly created DASD devices are shared among all z/OS systems. Several devices are intended to be used by only one z/OS guest system. There are a couple of common methods of attaching these to the correct z/OS guest system.

The first is simply to attach them to the correct system with an MDISK statement and provide a password. This ensures that only the intended system can access the emulated DASD device. An example of an MDISK statement for defining a device for access by only one system is as follows:

```
*****************************************************************
*    z/OS GUEST SYSTEM MV11                                    *
*****************************************************************
*
USER MV11 MV11 10000M 12000M ABCDEFG
. . . .
MDISK 1A00 3390 0000 END PAG100 MWV MV11 MV11 MV11
```

While attaching a device to a single system may provide some security to ensure that only the appropriate system uses the device, it does not provide much flexibility if there is a system failure and data on the device needs to be repaired. To allow more versatility in the configuration, it is recommended that even if a device is intended to be utilized by only one z/OS guest system, it should still be attached to the proxy user and then a link statement is used to connect the device to the intended z/OS guest. This enables the ability to link the device to another system to effect repairs, if needed. Possible MDISK and LINK statements are listed below for the new volumes:

```
**************************************************************
*    PROXY USER FOR SHARING VOLUMES BETWEEN Z/OS GUEST SYSTEMS *
**************************************************************
*
USER ZPROXY NOLOG 512M 512M G
. . . .
MDISK 1A00 3390 0000 END PAG100 MWV ALL ALL ALL
MDISK 1A01 3390 0000 END SPL100 MWV ALL ALL ALL
MDISK 1A02 3390 0000 END CKP10P MWV ALL ALL ALL
MDISK 1A03 3390 0000 END CKP10A MWV ALL ALL ALL
MDISK 2A00 3390 0000 END PAG200 MWV ALL ALL ALL
MDISK 2A01 3390 0000 END SPL200 MWV ALL ALL ALL
MDISK 2A02 3390 0000 END CKP20P MWV ALL ALL ALL
MDISK 2A03 3390 0000 END CKP20A MWV ALL ALL ALL
MDISK 3A00 3390 0000 END PAG300 MWV ALL ALL ALL
MDISK 3A01 3390 0000 END SPL300 MWV ALL ALL ALL
MDISK 3A02 3390 0000 END CKP30P MWV ALL ALL ALL
MDISK 3A03 3390 0000 END CKP30A MWV ALL ALL ALL
. . . .
**************************************************************
*    z/OS GUEST SYSTEM MV11                                  *
**************************************************************
*
USER MV11 MV11 10000M 12000M ABCDEFG
. . . .
LINK ZPROXY 1A00 0A00 MW
LINK ZPROXY 1A01 0A01 MW
LINK ZPROXY 1A02 0A02 MW
LINK ZPROXY 1A03 0A03 MW
. . . .
```

Initializing the New DASD Devices

At this point, the DASD files have been created on the Linux file system and have been defined to both the emulator and the z/VM virtual system. However, the files are not in a format that the z/OS guest systems can use. For the z/OS systems to use these DASD volumes they need to be attached to an active z/OS system and initialized.

IBM documentation provides details on the different options that can be employed when initializing a DASD volume. In addition to the IBM documentation, the local mainframe IT staff should be consulted to determine if there are any company standards that should be employed when initializing the volumes.

Since the systems are still in the process of being created, the base z/OS guest system provided by the vendor needs to be started to initialize the new DASD volumes. As each volume is initialized, it can be brought online to the vendor supplied system to validate the device.

System Volume

After the new volumes have been created and initialized, it is time to begin building the system volume. This volume will contain the information needed by the z/OS guest operating system to start. The first step in building the system volume is to create a new IODF. The IODF contains a list of all device addresses defined to the system, as well as the type of devices that are valid for each address.

Although the vendor-supplied IODF may be sufficient for small environments, it does not provide much capacity for growth. In addition, the IODF that is currently in use by the vendor-supplied system will not be available once the new system configuration is completed. For these reasons, it is important to create a new IODF on the system configuration volume.

At this point, the use case for the virtual systems being created needs to be consulted to determine how many of each device type is required. Once this list has been generated, the new IODF can be created. IBM documentation provides detailed information on how to create and/or update the IODF configuration for a system. The existing configuration can be used as a base for the new IODF, but ensure when saving the new definition file that is it placed on the new system configuration volume, *MVIPL1*.

DASD Repository

One key component of the new environment configuration is the DASD repository. The primary role of the DASD repository is to provide local access to DASD volumes that have been migrated from a traditional mainframe environment. These volumes can be comprised of the contents of any DASD volume that is hosted on the traditional mainframe environment. However, for this discussion, the volumes of interest are the volumes containing the IBM RSU maintenance for the z/OS operating system and the subsystems.

Three steps need to be taken to utilize the repository. The first is to create a process to access the emulated DASD volumes that are hosted on the repository. The second step is to add the DASD files to the device map. After the device addresses have been defined, the third step is to attach the new volumes to the z/OS guest systems. Once these steps have been completed, these volumes are available to the newly created z/OS guest systems.

Accessing the Emulated DASD Volumes on the Repository

When the DASD repository was created, the IBM RSU volumes should have been stored on a file system configured as a *network file system* (NFS) share. A mount point is created on the local machine for the share on the DASD repository, allowing the local machine to access the files on the DASD repository through the mount point as if they were on the local machine. The following command mounts the NFS share from a host machine *DASD_REPOSITORY* with a share name of *DASD* to */zDATA/NFS*:

```
mount DASD_REPOSITORY:/DASD /zDATA/NFS
```

This allows access to files on DASD_REPOSITORY as if they were on the local Linux host.

At this point, there are three options for configuring the virtual mainframe environment to access these emulated DASD volumes. The first is to configure the device map to access these files through the NFS share. The second option is to copy the files from the NFS share to a local file system. The third option is a combination of copying some files locally, and accessing some from the NFS mount point. The comparative advantages and disadvantages of each of these solutions are as follow:

1. *Using the emulated DASD files from the NFS mount point*

   • This option reduces storage requirements for the virtualized environment.

   • If the network connection to the DASD repository is lost, the virtualized environment could fail.

   • Response time from the files on the NFS mount point may be slow.

2. *Copying the files to a local file system*

   • This option increases the local storage requirements of the virtualized environment.

   • If the network connection is lost, there is no impact to access.

   • Depending on the local hardware configuration and the NFS connection speed, response times may be faster.

3. *Combination approach*

    •   Local storage requirements are reduced if some volumes are not copied locally.

    •   If the network connection is lost, there is no impact on access to important volumes that are stored locally.

    •   Access times can be evaluated to determine which location is optimal.

The third solution may be the best option for most situations. In many instances, information from a volume migrated from a traditional mainframe may be needed only for short periods of time or on an occasional basis. When this is the case, it is more efficient to store these volumes in a central location rather than consume storage on every Linux host.

For example, in many traditional mainframe environments, the RSU maintenance for IBM subsystems is stored on one volume. However, when the subsystem is installed and configured, the installation places only the data sets required for operation on new DASD volumes. In this scenario, it would be advantageous to keep the subsystem volumes on the NFS mount point. The z/OS system can access these volumes to install the subsystem to local emulated DASD volumes. The subsystem can then be run from the locally stored DASD volumes.

The use case and environment configuration need to be analyzed to determine which approach is desirable for the virtualized mainframe environment being constructed. In a situation in which the DASD repository is used to store z/OS, DB2, and CICS RSUs, the file system configuration to access the DASD volumes is illustrated in Figure 7-3.

/zDATA	root file system for z1090 DASD files
/zDATA/zVM	file system for z/VM DASD files
/zDATA/MV1	file system for the first z/OS guest DASD Files
/zDATA/MV2	file system for the second z/OS guest DASD Files
/zDATA/MV3	file system for the third z/OS guest DASD Files
/zDATA/Subsystem	file system for installed IBM subsystem DASD files
/zDATA/Common	file system for common DASD files
/zDATA/UserData	file system for general user DASD files
/zDATA/NFS/DB2	file system mount point for DB2 RSUs on DASD Repository
/zDATA/NFS/CICS	file system mount point for CICS RSUs on DASD Repository

Figure 7-3. Possible file system organizatation for the new virtual system configuration

In this configuration, the z/OS RSU files are copied to the local file system /zDATA/zOS. The DB2 and CICS subsystem RSU files remain on the DASD repository and are accessed through the NFS share.

Updating the Device Map

After the Linux host has been configured for access to the DASD files that are stored on the DASD repository, the emulator device map must be updated so that the virtual systems can access the information stored in these files. The definitions for these files can be added to existing *awsckd* device managers, or new device managers can be defined. In the following example, a new device manager is defined for the z/OS operating system volumes that are located on the local file system /zDATA/zOS. An additional *awsckd* device manager is also defined for the subsystem volumes that will be accessed from the NFS mounted file systems.

```
. . . .
[manager]
name awsckd 1000
device 0A80 3390 3990 /zDATA/zOS/ZOS1C0-RSU1209
```

```
device 0A81 3390 3990 /zDATA/zOS/ZOS1D0-RSU1209
device 0A82 3390 3990 /zDATA/zOS/ZOS1C1-RSU1212
device 0A83 3390 3990 /zDATA/zOS/ZOS1D1-RSU1212

. . . .
[manager]
name awsckd 1100
device 4AA0 3390 3990 /zDATA/NFS/DB2/DB2000-RSU1209
device 4AA1 3390 3990 /zDATA/NFS/CICS/CICS00-RSU1209
device 4AA2 3390 3990 /zDATA/NFS/DB2/DB2001-RSU1212
device 4AA3 3390 3990 /zDATA/NFS/CICS/CICS01-RSU1212

. . . .
```

In this example, note that the file names for the volumes obtained from the DASD repository are different than the other examples that have been used. As a standard convention, the file names for the DASD files on the Linux host are the same as the volume serial numbers for the DASD volumes that are attached to the virtual operating systems. An exception is made to this convention when working with RSUs or other service levels.

When new RSUs are made available by IBM, the updates may be installed on volumes that are reused. A given operating system version may have many RSUs before support is ended by IBM. In this case, it is inefficient to allocate DASD volumes to store all supported RSUs for this operating system version. To address this issue, a rotation of existing DASD volumes may be used so that the current version and a predetermined number of prior RSUs are retained. For example, volumes ZOS1C0, ZOS1C1 and ZOS1C2 may hold the desired RSUs in chronological order. When the next RSU is available from IBM, volume ZOS1C0 may be reused.

When a volume is reused on the traditional mainframe system, there is not a problem with data duplication because the old data stored on the volume is replaced. However, as the DASD volume is migrated to the DASD repository, a situation arises where there may be two DASD files with the same name that contain two different sets of data. This occurs when a volume on the traditional mainframe that was used for one RSU is reused to hold a different RSU. As the information is transferred to a DASD file on the DASD repository, this creates a situation where there is a duplicate file name, although the data within the file is unique. To address this issue, the RSU number is appended to the file name on the Linux host. This allows emulated DASD volumes with the same volume serial number to exist in the same Linux file system. This is important as older operating systems may need to be retained for compatibility testing.

■ **Note** Even though there may be several DASD files with the same mainframe volume serial number on the Linux host, z/OS does not allow devices with the same volume serial number to be online at the same time. For this reason, it is highly recommended that care is taken to ensure that only DASD volumes with unique volume serial numbers are added to the device map for each system.

Updating the User Directory

These newly created DASD files will be needed by all of the new z/OS guest systems. For this reason, it is recommended that all of the volumes be attached to the proxy user that was created to allow access to common volumes. The MDISK format for these volumes will be slightly different. With the previous MDISK statements, the DASD volumes were defined with Read/Write access (R/W). With these new volumes, the access is to be restricted to *read-only* (R/O).

The R/O access for these volumes is to ensure that the users of the z/OS systems do not make updates to volumes that will be replaced during an operating system upgrade. This process also helps protect data from being lost during an operating system upgrade, thus leaving the z/OS system in an unusable state.

The following example demonstrates how to create the MDISK statements for the proxy user so that the volumes from the DASD repository are accessed in R/O mode. These statements also define the volume serial number as the actual six digit serial number of the device, not the Linux file name. After the volume is defined to the proxy user, the LINK statement is added to the z/OS guest user.

```
***************************************************************
*   PROXY USER FOR SHARING VOLUMES BETWEEN Z/OS GUEST SYSTEMS *
***************************************************************
*
USER ZPROXY NOLOG 512M 512M G
. . . .
MDISK 0A80 3390 0000 END ZOS1C0 R    ALL ALL ALL
MDISK 0A81 3390 0000 END ZOS1D0 R    ALL ALL ALL
MDISK 0A82 3390 0000 END ZOS1C1 R    ALL ALL ALL
MDISK 0A83 3390 0000 END ZOS1D1 R    ALL ALL ALL
. . . .
MDISK 4AA0 3390 0000 END DB2000 R    ALL ALL ALL
MDISK 4AA1 3390 0000 END CICS00 R    ALL ALL ALL
MDISK 4AA2 3390 0000 END DB2001 R    ALL ALL ALL
MDISK 4AA3 3390 0000 END CICS01 R    ALL ALL ALL
. . . .
***************************************************************
*   z/OS GUEST SYSTEM MV11                                    *
***************************************************************
*
USER MV11 MV11 10000M 12000M ABCDEFG
. . . .
LINK ZPROXY 0A80 0A80 R
LINK ZPROXY 0A81 0A81 R
LINK ZPROXY 0A82 0A82 R
LINK ZPROXY 0A83 0A83 R
. . . .
LINK ZPROXY 4AA0 0AA0 R
LINK ZPROXY 4AA1 0AA1 R
LINK ZPROXY 4AA2 0AA2 R
LINK ZPROXY 4AA3 0AA3 R
. . . .
```

Progress and Prospectus

The updates to the environment that have just been outlined set the stage for changes that will be introduced in the next two chapters. It is critical to the success of the migration from the vendor-supplied environment that the information presented in this chapter be understood and the processes be correctly implemented as explained.

The new DASD volumes that have been created will be used to build new z/OS systems that are not dependent on the volumes provided by the vendor. These new volumes are currently empty, but will be configured to provide required functionality in Chapter 8. The information presented in the creation of these new emulated volumes provides an overview of what is needed to successfully migrate from the vendor-supplied z/OS environment. However, each virtualized mainframe environment will have different requirements, so implementation of these new volumes must be consistent with the requirements.

The system volume that was created (*MVIPL1*) will be populated with system parameter data sets that are crucial to the proper operation of the z/OS guest systems. It is critical that this volume be updated properly. At this point, only the new IODF has been placed on this volume. As it continues to be constructed, there are more data sets and libraries that will be copied and created on this volume. This one device will control the operational parameters for all of the z/OS guest systems.

The DASD repository built in Chapter 6 has now been integrated into the virtualized mainframe environment. This repository of emulated DASD volumes is an extremely powerful tool when implemented properly. If the repository is correctly maintained, it can enhance the virtualized mainframe environment by reducing the maintenance overhead of operating system and subsystem upgrades. It can also maintain a catalog of older DASD volumes that are no longer available on either the virtualized mainframe environment or the traditional mainframe system. The information provided in this chapter is instrumental in the construction of a z/OS guest environment that is not dependent on the DASD volumes delivered by the vendor. The environment supplied by the vendor is powerful and can be implemented quickly, but no mechanism is implemented by the vendor to perform system updates—the system is provided as-is. For some environments, this is not acceptable.

By migrating to an environment where the operating system and subsystem volumes are based on volumes currently in use in the traditional mainframe environment, the ability to update and upgrade the operating system software and subsystem software is available. Each z/OS guest system can be IPL'd with different operating system levels and software updates can be applied just as if these virtualized systems were running on traditional mainframe hardware rather than being emulated on a Linux host.

The process to migrate to this new environment has been started in this chapter and will be continued in Chapter 8. The next stage in this transformation is to create the framework that will allow the newly created z/OS guest systems to start from the OS volumes that have been migrated from the DASD repository.

Case Studies
Case 1: Single Laptop System for a Mainframe Developer

The virtualized mainframe environment has been configured and is running on the laptop. The software being developed is crucial to the success of the company, inasmuch as it is expected to control the billing processes for the company for many years. As such, the development environment will need the ability to upgrade to new operating systems as they are introduced. The software itself also requires substantial customization to the mainframe environment. There are significant updates to the security policies and system parameters. The need to make these changes every time there is a new set of updated files from the vendor would have a significant impact on the project. In addition, this project is also a proof of concept, because the company is considering adding more virtualized mainframe environments for other projects.

To reduce the impact of operating system upgrades, the decision is made to migrate from the vendor-supplied environment to an environment based on the current z/Enterprise configuration that is currently running in the company's data center. Because no funds have been allocated mainframe environment that to create a DASD repository, each OS upgrade will be migrated to the laptop on an as-needed basis.

To begin the migration, the following commands are issued on the laptop to create new DASD files:

```
alcckd /zDATA/OS/PAG000 -d3390-9
alcckd /zDATA/OS/SPL000 -d3390-9
alcckd /zDATA/OS/CKP00P -d3390 -s50
alcckd /zDATA/OS/CKP00A -d3390 -s50
alcckd /zDATA/OS/MVIPL1 -d3390-3
alcckd /zDATA/OS/STG001 -d3390 -s65520
alcckd /zDATA/OS/WRK001 -d3390 -s65520
alcckd /zDATA/OS/DMP001 -d3390 -s32760
alcckd /zDATA/UserData/USER00 -d3390-9
alcckd /zDATA/UserData/USER01 -d3390-9
```

```
alcckd /zDATA/UserData/USER02 -d3390-9
alcckd /zDATA/UserData/USER03 -d3390-9
alcckd /zDATA/UserData/USER04 -d3390-9
alcckd /zDATA/UserData/USER05 -d3390-9
alcckd /zDATA/UserData/USER06 -d3390-9
alcckd /zDATA/UserData/USER07 -d3390-9
```

Once these files have been created, the utility provided by the vendor to migrate DASD images from the traditional mainframe environment to the emulated environment is used to copy the current operating system volume to the Linux host. The volume serial number that is copied is *ZOS1D0*. This volume contains RSU 1309 so the Linux file that is created is named *ZOS1D0-RSU1309*. This file is located in */zDATA/OS*.

The device map is opened and the following updates are made to the existing device map:

```
. . . .
[manager]
name awsckd 1000
device 0AA0 3390 3990 /zDATA/OS/MVIPL1
device 0AA1 3390 3990 /zDATA/OS/PAG000
device 0AA2 3390 3990 /zDATA/OS/SPL000
device 0AA3 3390 3990 /zDATA/OS/CKP00P
device 0AA4 3390 3990 /zDATA/OS/CKP00A
device 0AA5 3390 3990 /zDATA/OS/STG001
device 0AA6 3390 3990 /zDATA/OS/WRK001
device 0AA7 3390 3990 /zDATA/OS/DMP001
device 0AA8 3390 3990 /zDATA/OS/ZOS1D0-RSU1309
. . . .
[manager]
name awsckd 1001
device 0AB0 3390 3990 /zDATA/UserData/USER00
device 0AB1 3390 3990 /zDATA/UserData/USER01
device 0AB2 3390 3990 /zDATA/UserData/USER02
device 0AB3 3390 3990 /zDATA/UserData/USER03
device 0AB4 3390 3990 /zDATA/UserData/USER04
device 0AB5 3390 3990 /zDATA/UserData/USER05
device 0AB6 3390 3990 /zDATA/UserData/USER06
device 0AB7 3390 3990 /zDATA/UserData/USER07
. . . .
```

The emulator and the virtualized z/OS system are then restarted. The IODF provided by the vendor is used as a base, and 64 more 3390 device addresses are added at 0C00 - 0C3F. The z/OS system is then restarted, and the new DASD volumes are initialized so that they can be used by the z/OS system.

After these changes have been completed, another file system is created in the root file system, */zbackup*. All the files located in /zDATA and its subdirectories are copied to */zbackup* so that if any mistakes are made during the rest of the migration, any corrupted volumes can be restored.

Case 2: Server Class Machine Hosting Multiple Mainframe Systems for Software QA Testing

The virtualized mainframe environment for the QA team has been configured and is running on the server. The z/VM environment with z/OS guest systems has been created and is functioning properly. However, the QA plans that have been developed for this environment include running tests with mixed operating systems. There is also a requirement that testing be performed with at least one z/OS system running the most current RSU maintenance provided by IBM. The environment not only needs to have access to the most current IBM software, but there may also be a need in the future to test older versions of z/OS.

To provide this flexibility, it is decided that the DASD repository will be used to host emulated DASD volumes of all IBM RSUs. As RSUs are delivered by IBM and the new z/OS volumes are built by the mainframe technical team, they will be installed on DASD volumes in the z/Enterprise environment and then transferred to the DASD repository using the provided vendor utility. The DASD file name for each transferred volume will be the volume serial number of the volume followed by the RSU number. All of the DASD files will be stored on the DASD repository and then transferred to the Linux machine hosting the virtualized mainframe systems.

To enable the use of these z/OS operating system volumes, the z/OS guest systems will be rebuilt so that they are no longer dependent on the DASD files supplied by the vendor. To begin this process, the *alcckd* utility is used to create DASD files to support migrating the z/OS environments to use the new z/OS volumes hosted on the DASD repository. The following *alcckd* commands are issued to create the DASD files in the appropriate locations:

```
alcckd /zDATA/MV1/PAG100 -d3390-9
alcckd /zDATA/MV1/SPL100 -d3390-9
alcckd /zDATA/MV1/CKP10P -d3390 -s50
alcckd /zDATA/MV1/CKP10A -d3390 -s50
alcckd /zDATA/MV2/PAG200 -d3390-9
alcckd /zDATA/MV2/SPL200 -d3390-9
alcckd /zDATA/MV2/CKP20P -d3390 -s50
alcckd /zDATA/MV2/CKP20A -d3390 -s50
alcckd /zDATA/MV3/PAG300 -d3390-9
alcckd /zDATA/MV3/SPL300 -d3390-9
alcckd /zDATA/MV3/CKP30P -d3390 -s50
alcckd /zDATA/MV3/CKP30A -d3390 -s50
alcckd /zDATA/Common/CPL00P -d3390 -s150
alcckd /zDATA/Common/CPL00A -d3390 -s150
alcckd /zDATA/Common/MVIPL1 -d3390-9
alcckd /zDATA/Common/STG001 -d3390 -s65520
alcckd /zDATA/Common/WRK001 -d3390 -s65520
alcckd /zDATA/Common/DMP001 -d3390 -s32760
```

In addition to creating the files for the migration of the operating systems, there are several files created to hold data that is needed by the QA team. The naming convention for these files is shown in Figure 7-4.

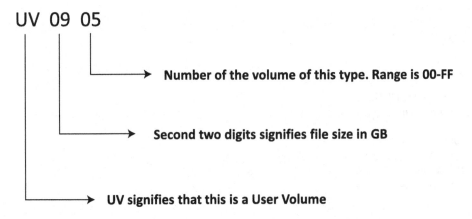

Figure 7-4. Naming convention for user volumes

The following *alcckd* commands are issued to create the user volumes for the new configuration. More may be added later as needed, following the same convention, but these are the base volumes to be used:

```
alcckd /zDATA/UserData/UV9000 -d3390-9                  *3390 model 9
alcckd /zDATA/UserData/UV9001 -d3390-9                  *3390 model 9
alcckd /zDATA/UserData/UV9002 -d3390-9                  *3390 model 9
alcckd /zDATA/UserData/UV9003 -d3390-9                  *3390 model 9
alcckd /zDATA/UserData/UV9004 -d3390-9                  *3390 model 9
alcckd /zDATA/UserData/UV9005 -d3390-9                  *3390 model 9
alcckd /zDATA/UserData/UV9006 -d3390-9                  *3390 model 9
alcckd /zDATA/UserData/UV9007 -d3390-9                  *3390 model 9
alcckd /zDATA/UserData/UV5400 -d3390 -s65520            *3390 model 9s 54GB
alcckd /zDATA/UserData/UV5401 -d3390 -s65520            *3390 model 9s 54GB
```

Once the system and user DASD files have been created, the current operating system volume, *ZOS1D0-RSU1312*, is copied from the DASD repository to the */zDATA/Common* file system on the Linux host.

The device map is opened, and the following updates are made to the existing device map:

```
. . . .
[manager]
name awsckd 1000
device 1AA0 3390 3990 /zDATA/MV1/PAG100
device 1AA1 3390 3990 /zDATA/MV1/SPL100
device 1AA2 3390 3990 /zDATA/MV1/CKP10P
device 1AA3 3390 3990 /zDATA/MV1/CKP10A
. . . .
[manager]
name awsckd 2000
device 2AA0 3390 3990 /zDATA/MV2/PAG200
device 2AA1 3390 3990 /zDATA/MV2/SPL200
device 2AA2 3390 3990 /zDATA/MV2/CKP20P
device 2AA3 3390 3990 /zDATA/MV2/CKP20A
. . . .
[manager]
name awsckd 3000
device 3AA0 3390 3990 /zDATA/MV3/PAG300
device 3AA1 3390 3990 /zDATA/MV3/SPL300
device 3AA2 3390 3990 /zDATA/MV3/CKP30P
device 3AA3 3390 3990 /zDATA/MV3/CKP30A
. . . .
[manager]
name awsckd 500
device 0A80 3390 3990 /zDATA/Common/MVIPL1
device 0A81 3390 3990 /zDATA/Common/STG001
device 0A82 3390 3990 /zDATA/Common/WRK001
device 0A83 3390 3990 /zDATA/Common/DMP001
device 0A84 3390 3990 /zDATA/Common/CPL00P
device 0A85 3390 3990 /zDATA/Common/CPL00A
device 0A86 3390 3990 /zDATA/Common/ZOS1D0-RSU1312
```

```
. . . .
[manager]
name awsckd 1001
device 0AB0 3390 3990 /zDATA/UserData/UV9000
device 0AB1 3390 3990 /zDATA/UserData/UV9001
device 0AB2 3390 3990 /zDATA/UserData/UV9002
device 0AB3 3390 3990 /zDATA/UserData/UV9003
device 0AB4 3390 3990 /zDATA/UserData/UV9004
device 0AB5 3390 3990 /zDATA/UserData/UV9005
device 0AB6 3390 3990 /zDATA/UserData/UV9006
device 0AB7 3390 3990 /zDATA/UserData/UV9007
device 0AB8 3390 3990 /zDATA/UserData/UV5400
device 0AB9 3390 3990 /zDATA/UserData/UV5401
. . . .
```

The emulator and the virtualized z/OS system are then restarted. The user directory is opened for editing, and the following statements are created to add the newly created DASD volumes for use:

```
*****************************************************************
*    PROXY USER FOR SHARING VOLUMES BETWEEN Z/OS GUEST SYSTEMS *
*****************************************************************
*
USER ZPROXY NOLOG 512M 512M G
. . . .
MDISK 0A80 3390 0000 END MVIPL1 MWV    ALL ALL ALL
MDISK 0A81 3390 0000 END STG001 MWV    ALL ALL ALL
MDISK 0A82 3390 0000 END WRK001 MWV    ALL ALL ALL
MDISK 0A83 3390 0000 END DMP001 MWV    ALL ALL ALL
MDISK 0A84 3390 0000 END CPLOOP MWV    ALL ALL ALL
MDISK 0A85 3390 0000 END CPLOOA MWV    ALL ALL ALL
MDISK 0A86 3390 0000 END ZOS1D0 R      ALL ALL ALL
. . . .
MDISK 0AB0 3390 0000 END UV9000 MWV    ALL ALL ALL
MDISK 0AB1 3390 0000 END UV9001 MWV    ALL ALL ALL
MDISK 0AB2 3390 0000 END UV9002 MWV    ALL ALL ALL
MDISK 0AB3 3390 0000 END UV9003 MWV    ALL ALL ALL
MDISK 0AB4 3390 0000 END UV9004 MWV    ALL ALL ALL
MDISK 0AB5 3390 0000 END UV9005 MWV    ALL ALL ALL
MDISK 0AB6 3390 0000 END UV9006 MWV    ALL ALL ALL
MDISK 0AB7 3390 0000 END UV9007 MWV    ALL ALL ALL
MDISK 0AB8 3390 0000 END UV5400 MWV    ALL ALL ALL
MDISK 0AB9 3390 0000 END UV5401 MWV    ALL ALL ALL
. . . .
MDISK 1AA0 3390 0000 END PAG100 MWV    MV11 MV11 MV11
MDISK 1AA1 3390 0000 END SPL100 MWV    MV11 MV11 MV11
MDISK 1AA2 3390 0000 END CKP10P MWV    MV11 MV11 MV11
MDISK 1AA3 3390 0000 END CKP10A MWV    MV11 MV11 MV11
. . . .
MDISK 2AA0 3390 0000 END PAG200 MWV    MV21 MV21 MV21
MDISK 2AA1 3390 0000 END SPL200 MWV    MV21 MV21 MV21
MDISK 2AA2 3390 0000 END CKP20P MWV    MV21 MV21 MV21
MDISK 2AA3 3390 0000 END CKP20A MWV    MV21 MV21 MV21
```

```
. . . .
MDISK 3AA0 3390 0000 END PAG300 MWV    MV31 MV31 MV31
MDISK 3AA1 3390 0000 END SPL300 MWV    MV31 MV31 MV31
MDISK 3AA2 3390 0000 END CKP30P MWV    MV31 MV31 MV31
MDISK 3AA3 3390 0000 END CKP30A MWV    MV31 MV31 MV31
. . . .
**************************************************************
*   z/OS GUEST SYSTEM MV11                                   *
**************************************************************
*
USER MV11 MV11 10000M 12000M ABCDEFG
. . . .
LINK ZPROXY 0A80 0A80 MW
LINK ZPROXY 0A81 0A81 MW
LINK ZPROXY 0A82 0A82 MW
LINK ZPROXY 0A83 0A83 MW
LINK ZPROXY 0A84 0A83 MW
LINK ZPROXY 0A85 0A83 MW
LINK ZPROXY 0A86 0A84 R
LINK ZPROXY 1AA0 0AA0 MW MV11
LINK ZPROXY 1AA1 0AA1 MW MV11
LINK ZPROXY 1AA2 0AA2 MW MV11
LINK ZPROXY 1AA3 0AA3 MW MV11
LINK ZPROXY 0AB0 0AB0 MW
LINK ZPROXY 0AB1 0AB1 MW
LINK ZPROXY 0AB2 0AB2 MW
LINK ZPROXY 0AB3 0AB3 MW
LINK ZPROXY 0AB4 0AB4 MW
LINK ZPROXY 0AB5 0AB5 MW
LINK ZPROXY 0AB6 0AB6 MW
LINK ZPROXY 0AB7 0AB7 MW
LINK ZPROXY 0AB8 0AB8 MW
LINK ZPROXY 0AB9 0AB9 MW
. . . .
```

Similar additions are made for users MV21 and MV31.

This environment has the potential to grow quickly; however, the IODF that is provided by the vendor does not provide much room for growth in the number of DASD unit addresses. To address this concern, the IODF provided by the vendor is used as a base and 128 more 3390 device addresses are added at 0C00 - 0C7F. After the IODF has been updated with the new addresses, the system is restarted and the new DASD volumes are initialized so that they can be used by the z/OS system.

After these changes have been completed, another file system is created in the root file system, */zbackup*. All the files located in */zDATA* and its subdirectories are copied to */zbackup* so that if any mistakes are made during the rest of the migration, any corrupted volumes can be restored.

CHAPTER 8

■ ■ ■

Migrating to Mainframe zEnterprise DASD

This chapter presents hints, tips, and general setup guidelines for establishing a virtualized environment using the operating system volumes from the mainframe zEnterprise. The chapter discusses and provides details for specific items that may require attention when migrating from the vendor-supplied system and DASD volumes to a new environment. Such items are not uniquely constrained. We highlight those that need to be considered generally, while omitting some items that vary with the diverse configurations within individual mainframe shops.

The vendor-provided systems use an excellent naming standard for system parameter members and volume serials. For example:

- The volumes may be prefixed with ZB, such as ZBRES1.

- Parameter members may be suffixed with CS, such as PROGCS.

To maintain consistency and not rely on the vendor-supplied standards, the prefixes/suffixes in this chapter are changed as follows:

- Lowercase "vl" is used for vendor volume serial prefixes.

- Lowercase "vs" is used for vendor system parameter library suffixes.

Backing Up the Base Environment

Before beginning the migration, ensure that a valid usable backup is available. The system manipulations and migration process may cause the system to fail in the event of an incorrect modification. It is easy to overlook a step or parameter change required to use a mainframe zEnterprise operating system volume. If a change to a system parameter causes the system to fail to start, then a restore of the server, system, or individual DASD volume may be enough to save time reworking the system changes from the beginning.

Starting the Vendor System

Before beginning the system manipulations, start the base system that has the entire vendor-supplied environment and new DASD volumes (Chapter 7). The system has additional paging, spool, and other DASD volumes attached. Starting the vendor system with the additional DASD volumes enables the start of the migration to using the operating system software from the mainframe zEnterprise environment.

Verify New DASD Volumes

Before beginning any work, ensure that all of the new DASD volumes are available to the system. If any volumes are not available, double-check previous work to determine what has caused the volume(s) to be missing. Enter the following command on the console:

```
D U,,,unit-addr,nn
```

The unit-addr is the starting address and the nn is the number of consecutive addresses to display the available volumes. This assumes that all of the new DASD volumes have sequential unit addresses. Multiple commands may be necessary, depending on the system setup for the new DASD.

Shared DASD Volume

A DASD volume—MVSHR1 (Chapter 7)—is part of the migration for eliminating the vendor volumes. Once fully populated with data sets necessary for the new z/OS system to start and run, it can be part of a shared data environment. MVSHR1 can be available to each system to facilitate data-set sharing. The migration in this chapter is for a single-system environment.

System Manipulations

The following sections provide an overview of several configuration changes required to start developing systems that are independent of the vendor-provided volumes. The experience level and methods of the systems programmer determine the frequency of system restarts to verify changes and the number of backups desired to create checkpoints. Multiple system restarts during system manipulations allow the systems programmer to verify changes at smaller intervals. System restarts after each major change will significantly reduce the time required to resolve any problems encountered.

The Storage Management Subsystem

An easy component to overlook is the *Storage Management Subsystem* (SMS). If there are plans to change the system name to a convention other than the one supplied by the vendor, it is good to add the names to SMS first. The changes for the system name are part of the Control Data Set in the *Interactive Storage Management Facility* (ISMF). A set of ISMF panels in ISPF allow changes to the system name(s).

SMS errors may cause the system to fail, so a backup of the system prior to updating parameters eliminates the need for a rebuild in the event of an error in configuration. Use MVS system utilities to copy the vendor-supplied SMS data sets into new data sets with a different name. The new data sets require SMS activation. Once SMS changes are complete, update the parameter library to reference the new data sets and SMS configuration.

Catalog Updates

The naming standards that are on the vendor-supplied setup may be different from the mainframe zEnterprise environment, complicating the simplicity of moving a mainframe zEnterprise operating system volume to replace the original volume. In some cases, changes are required before the volume is usable.

To move from the vendor-based volumes, create a new master catalog and multiple user catalogs, catalog the new operating system, and then clean up the catalog, as follows.

Create the Alternative Master Catalog

The new master catalog must retain the vendor-supplied master catalog entries to keep all original entries in sync while migrating from the vendor system. The process involves moving all of the objects from the vendor-supplied master catalog into the newly created master catalog.

Refer to IBM documentation for recommended parameters and settings for your environment when creating an alternate master catalog.

Create Multiple User Catalogs

Although a single user catalog could suffice for the system, user, and application data sets, most shops prefer to separate data sets by function and usage, entailing the creation of multiple user catalogs. This section describes the requirement of one user catalog for all user-defined data sets and a second user catalog for migrating the VSAM operating system data sets.

User Catalog for Aliases

It is a good practice to create alias definitions for all of the user data sets including parameter libraries to ensure they are in a user catalog. Create a user catalog specifically for all of these data sets. The first part of a data-set name (the characters before the first period) is the *high-level qualifier* (HLQ). The HLQ for user, product, and application data sets can have an alias associated with them and related to a user catalog. These are single-level HLQ alias definitions.

The following are defined aliases and a partial list of associated data sets:

- *KJB* (alias) for system-related data sets:
    - *KJB*.SYSTEM.CLIST
    - *KJB*.SYSTEM.ISPPLIB
    - *KJB*.SYSTEM.LINKLIB
    - *KJB*.USER.PARMLIB
    - *KJB*.USER.PROCLIB
- *KJBARR* alias for a user with data sets:
    - *KJBARR*.ISPF.ISPPROF
    - *KJBARR*.SPFLOG1.LIST
    - *KJBARR*.SRCHFOR.LIST
- *product1* alias for a product with data sets:
    - *product1*.PROCLIB
    - *product1*.PARMLIB
    - *product1*.LINKLIB
    - *product1*.MACLIB

A multi-level alias facility allows the use of more than the first-level HLQ for definitions.

User Catalog for Migrating the Operating System VSAM Data Sets

In a data center with many virtual systems, the operating system volume may be shared among environments. These environments may be disparate where there are several LPARs on the mainframe zEnterprise and multiple distributed servers running virtual z/OS guests.

A caveat when moving the same operating system volume between environments: Some data-set structures such as VSAM require special handling for cataloging on the new environment. An example of VSAM data sets is the zFS file structure for *UNIX system services* (USS). A solution for handling VSAM is to catalog the data sets into a user catalog on the originating system.

A few steps are necessary to migrate the USS data sets between environments:

1. Create a user catalog on the receiving system with the same name as the originating system.

2. Use the *IMPORT CONNECT* command of IDCAMS to import the new user catalog.

3. Define an alias for the high-level qualifier of the data sets relating it to the new user catalog.

Catalog the New Operating System

Cataloging the operating system data sets requires two processes:

- Catalog the VSAM data sets.

- Catalog the non-VSAM data sets.

The Operating System VSAM Data Sets

To catalog the operating system VSAM data sets, use the IDCAMS DEFINE CLUSTER statement to catalog the data sets in the catalog described in the preceding section. The DEFINE CLUSTER command creates new VSAM data sets. In this solution, the DEFINE CLUSTER command catalogs a VSAM data set that already exists. To use this technique, the following IDCAMS parameters must be specified:

- *VOLUME*

- *RECATALOG*

- *CATALOG*

The Operating System Non-VSAM Data Sets

When a new version of z/OS is available in this environment, a recatalog of all the data sets needs to be performed to ensure that all existing and any new data sets are available to the operating system. This is also true for the first-time migration. With each new z/OS version or release, the data-set names do not usually change; however, there is a possibility of introducing new data sets.

The data sets are indirectly cataloged using six asterisks (******) for the volume serial. Normally, data sets are associated with a specific volume serial, such as *MVSDR1*. When the six asterisks are used in place of a valid volume serial, z/OS will attempt to locate each data set on the operating system volume that starts the system. Indirect cataloging allows each operating system to start using the correct system data sets without the need to recatalog them.

Example 1

Assume that SYS1.NUCLEUS and all operating system data sets are using indirect cataloging (******). The operating system volumes are:

- *MVSBR1* operating system release 11
- *MVSCR1* operating system release 12
- *MVSDR1* operating system release 13

If *MVSCR1* is the volume used to start the system, then the system will use SYS1.NUCLEUS on volume *MVSCR1*. This action is true for all of the operating system data sets.

Example 2

Assume that SYS1.NUCLEUS and all operating system data sets are using direct cataloging to *MVSBR1*. The operating system volumes are:

- *MVSBR1* operating system release 11
- *MVSCR1* operating system release 12
- *MVSDR1* operating system release 13

If *MVSDR1* is the volume used to start the system, then the system will use SYS1.NUCLEUS on volume *MVSBR1*. This action is true for all of the operating system data sets. This will cause unpredictable results owing to starting the system with release 13 and using operating system data sets that are on the release 11 operating system DASD volume.

Clean Up the Catalog

At some point, depending on the processes used by the IT technical staff, many data-set aliases point to the correct mainframe zEnterprise volume (*MVSxR1*), but also point to the vendor catalog. The issue is that the vendor-supplied configuration has alias pointers for system data sets. For example:

- The data set TCPIP.SEZATCP catalog entry points to the mainframe zEnterprise volume *MVSDR1*.
- When the system starts, it will find the data set on *MVSDR1*.
- An alias TCPIP exists in the vendor-supplied user catalog (USERCAT.Zxxx.PRODS) and master catalog (CATALOG.Zxxx.MASTER). Both catalogs are on the vendor-supplied volumes.

The alias pointers need to be resolved so that the alias exists in a new user catalog and the new master catalog. To this end, check each operating system data set to determine where the alias catalog entry resides. For each data set alias pointing to the vendor catalogs, the following steps are required to keep a similar setup:

1. Uncatalog each data set. This can be done manually via ISPF option 3.4.
2. Delete the associated alias using the IBM utility *IDCAMS*—e.g., *DELETE alias-name ALIAS*.
3. Define the alias and relate it to the catalog created for the new environment using the IBM utility *IDCAMS*—e.g., DEF ALIAS(NAME(alias-name) REL(KENB.UCAT)) CATALOG(CATALOG.NEW.MASTER).
4. Catalog each data set associated with the alias. This can be done manually via ISPF option 3.4.

Procedure Libraries

It is sensible and practical to create procedure libraries based on function. The various procedure libraries fall into a number of categories. Here are three examples:

- System procedure libraries
- User procedure libraries
- Product procedure libraries

A procedure library is commonly called a PROCLIB. The data-set naming convention normally has the low-level qualifier (the characters after the last period) PROCLIB. For example:

- SYS1.PROCLIB for the system procedure library
- user.PROCLIB for the user procedure library
- product.PROCLIB for a product procedure library

The following data sets may be necessary for the creation of three z/OS systems in a shared environment:

- system.SHARED.PROCLIB
- system.MV1.PROCLIB
- system.MV2.PROCLIB
- system.MV3.PROCLIB
- SYS1.PROCLIB
- user.SHARED.PROCLIB
- user.MV1.PROCLIB
- user.MV2.PROCLIB
- user.MV3.PROCLIB

This structure supports the separation of procedures by system and user, which results in a smaller number of members in each procedure library and keeps the shared procedures separate from the individual system procedures.

Procedure Library Concatenations

The procedure library concatenation is set up in the JES2-started task. Within JES2, the default PROCLIB concatenation is PROC00. From the JES2-started task:

```
//PROC00    DD DISP=SHR,DSN=user.MV1.PROCLIB,VOL=SER=MVSHR1,UNIT=3390
//          DD DISP=SHR,DSN=user.SHARED.PROCLIB,VOL=SER=MVSHR1,UNIT=3390
//          DD DISP=SHR,DSN=system.MV1.PROCLIB,VOL=SER=MVSHR1,UNIT=3390
//          DD DISP=SHR,DSN=system.SHARED.PROCLIB,VOL=SER=MVSHR1,UNIT=3390
//          DD DISP=SHR,DSN=SYS1.PROCLIB
```

The concatenation of data sets is critical to how the system searches for tasks and members. For example, a search for a member begins with the first library and continues to the last. The search ends when the member is found in a library. There is no further search for a duplicate member in another library downstream in the concatenation.

Procedure Library Members

The JES2 PROC00 concatenation displayed in the previous section specifies five procedure-library members:

- The two user libraries are first in the concatenation. These are for user procedures set up for specific needs or that override system procedures further down in the concatenation. The first user library is specific to the individual system. The second user library is for procedures that may be common across two or more systems.

- The next two libraries in the concatenation are for the system. These are normally for system procedures. However, they can also override system procedures further down in the concatenation. The first system library is specific to the individual system. The second system library is for procedures that may be common across two or more systems.

- The last library is the IBM procedure library (SYS1.PROCLIB). This contains all of the default procedures supplied for the system. Any system procedure that is not in a user or system library higher in the concatenation starts from here.

Some vendor-supplied system procedures are required on the new system and will need moved from the vendor volumes to the new environment. A couple of examples are TN3270 and ZFS. Carefully review the vendor PROCLIBs to determine the system procedures that require movement to the new environment.

Parameter Libraries

A parameter library is a PARMLIB. The data-set naming convention normally has the low-level qualifier (the characters after the last period) PARMLIB. For example:

- SYS1.PARMLIB System parameter library
- user.PARMLIB User parameter library
- product.PARMLIB Product parameter library

It is sensible and practical to create parameter libraries based on function. The various parameter libraries fall into many categories. Here is a sampling:

- IPL libraries
- System libraries
- User libraries
- Product libraries

The following data sets may be necessary for the creation of three z/OS systems:

- SYS1.IPLPARM - LOAD and NUCLST members
- system.SHARED.PARMLIB - Shared system members and parameters
- system.MV1.PARMLIB - System-specific members and parameters
- system.MV2.PARMLIB - System-specific members and parameters
- system.MV3.PARMLIB - System-specific members and parameters
- user.SHARED.PARMLIB - .Contains shared user members and parameters
- user.MV1.PARMLIB - User-created system-specific members and parameters
- user.MV2.PARMLIB - User-created system-specific members and parameters
- user.MV3.PARMLIB - User-created system-specific members and parameters

This structure supports separation of parameters by system and user, which results in a smaller number of members in each parameter library and keeps the shared parameters separate from the individual system parameters.

The parameter libraries concatenation list can be setup in the LOAD member.

Parameter Library Concatenations

The concatenation of data sets is critical to how the system searches for parameters and members. For example, a search for a member begins with the first library and continues to the last. The search ends when the member is found in a library. There is no further search for a duplicate member in another library in the concatenation.

A sample partial LOAD member follows:

```
VMUSERID MV11
PARMLIB  system.SHARED.PARMLIB                      MVSHR1
PARMLIB  system.MV1.PARMLIB                          MVSHR1
PARMLIB  user.SHARED.PARMLIB                         MVSHR1
PARMLIB  user.MV1.PARMLIB                            MVSHR1
PARMLIB  SYS1.PARMLIB
IODF     FF SYS1
SYSCAT   MVIPL1113CCATALOG.NEW.MASTER
*
VMUSERID MV21
PARMLIB  system.SHARED.PARMLIB                      MVSHR1
PARMLIB  system.MV2.PARMLIB                          MVSHR1
PARMLIB  user.SHARED.PARMLIB                         MVSHR1
PARMLIB  user.MV2.PARMLIB                            MVSHR1
PARMLIB  SYS1.PARMLIB
IODF     FF SYS1
SYSCAT   MVIPL1113CCATALOG.NEW.MASTER
*
VMUSERID MV31
PARMLIB  system.SHARED.PARMLIB                      MVSHR1
PARMLIB  system.MV3.PARMLIB                          MVSHR1
PARMLIB  user.SHARED.PARMLIB                         MVSHR1
PARMLIB  user.MV3.PARMLIB                            MVSHR1
PARMLIB  SYS1.PARMLIB
IODF     FF SYS1
SYSCAT   MVIPL1113CCATALOG.NEW.MASTER
*
```

In this LOAD member, the concatenation is set up so that the operating system startup parameters are in the first two libraries. The system installers create these for system-related parameters.

- The SHARED parameter library holds all of the system startup members that are common to two or more systems. These can be new or may override those provided by system default. For example, if the default system is using IEASYSvs, a new member IEASYSKB could be a replacement for IEASYSvs to start the system. On the other hand, a member named IEASYSvs may be in the SHARED parameter library that will override IEASYSvs in SYS1.PARMLIB.

- The MVn PARMLIB contains system startup parameters that pertain only to the system started (refer to the preceding LOAD member example). These parameters can be new or may override the parameters provided by system default.

■ **Note** The system libraries can override the system defaults specified in the IBM PARMLIBs by creating same-name members, because the system libraries are before the IBM-supplied default library in the concatenation. Owing to the concatenation, the user libraries (unlike the system libraries) cannot contain same-name members to override the system libraries. This concatenation ensures consistency and the ability to start the system. The user may create individual system startup members by copying the system member(s) as a base and modifying and renaming the member(s) in the user library. The user members may override the system defaults. If the user modifications fail, the system libraries contain the proper parameters to start the system.

The next two libraries in the concatenation are set up for the user-specified parameters. These libraries may contain parameters that are system-related or may be for user products and tasks that are not system-related. For example, a developer working on a specific product may place parameters for the product in the user parameter library. If the product is available on many systems and the parameters are not system specific, the developer may place them in the user SHARED parameter library. For some products, the parameters cannot be shared. In this situation, the parameters are in a system-specific user parameter library.

- The SHARED parameter library contains all of the user members that can be common to all systems.

- The MVn PARMLIB contains user parameters that pertain only to the system started.

The final parameter library (SYS1.PARMLIB) is IBM-supplied as part of the operating system installation. It is the last in the concatenation to provide any system members that are required at startup, but it is not tailored by the installation or user.

Parameter Library Members

Figure 8-1 is a sampling of what members may be in each parameter library:

system.SHARED.PARMLIB

IEASYSxx   –   Shared startup parameters
CLOCKxx   –   Shared parameters for clock setting
COMMNDxx –   Shared startup commands

system.MV1.PARMLIB

CLOCKxx – A system may have users in a different time zone

user.SHARED.PARMLIB

product1 – A product that runs on any system using the same parameters

user.MV1.PARMLIB

COMMNDxx – Commands specific for this system setup by the user

SYS1.PARMLIB

Will pick up any members not overridden by same-name members earlier
in the concatenation

Figure 8-1. *Parameter library members sampling*

System Migration Considerations

The process to enable migration from the vendor-supplied configuration to a new architecture depends on many system environmentals.

The following information is for fundamental mainframe components that may need created or modified in order to enable the migration from the vendor-supplied environment to a traditional mainframe zEnterprise based environment. The migration presented is not all-inclusive, but rather a guide for system configuration changes to enable migrating from the vendor-supplied configuration to a more flexible and sustainable environment.

Build the Page and Spool Data Sets

Prior to the parameter library manipulations, the page and spool data sets need to be created on the new paging and spool volumes. Refer to the IBM documentation for guidance in creating these data sets. Depending on the naming conventions, the volumes could be:

- PAGnxx for the page data sets

- SPLnxx for the SPOOL data sets

- CKP10P for SPOOL checkpoint 1 data set

- CKP10A for SPOOL checkpoint 2 data set

In the bulleted items above, the lower case n represents the system number and the xx represents an incremental volume sequence.

Parameter Library Manipulations

There are many techniques for updating the parameter libraries. Proprietary software for data-set management can expedite the changes by searching all data sets and libraries at the same time. The software can make all the changes at the same time.

When the vendor system starts, the operating system data sets have catalog entries on the vendor volumes. In addition to recataloging the system data sets and building the new parameter libraries, more changes are required to finalize the new environment.

■ **Note**   The following manipulations do not contain all of the changes required for replacing the vendor-based operating system with the mainframe zEnterprise-based DASD volumes.

Create New LOAD and IEASYS Members

New LOAD and IEASYS members allow the original vendor system setup to remain intact during this part of the migration. They should have a unique suffix and be placed in libraries that are not associated with the vendor system. The following process creates the new LOAD member:

1.   Ensure that the SYSn.IPLPARM data set is on the same volume as the IODF that has the modifications for the new system. According to the standards presented in Chapter 7, this volume is *MVIPL1*.

2.   Copy the vendor LOAD member into the SYSn.IPLPARM data set.

3.   Rename the LOAD member with a new unique suffix.

4. Update the LOAD member as follows:

   a. New master catalog name, DASD volume, and other items as necessary

   b. New suffix for the IEASYS member that represents the new system environment

   c. Parameter library concatenation., such that all systems can be defined now if multiple systems are desired or planned for the future

   d. New IODF suffix

Copy the vendor-supplied IEASYS member into the system's shared parameter library and rename it with a unique suffix. The suffix must match the SYSPARM statement in the LOAD member. The new IEASYS member sets the system parameters for each subsequent system startup. At this point, the PAGE parameters need to be changed to reflect the new page data-set names.

Depending on the mainframe zEnterprise system environment, there may be more or fewer members to be moved and shared. It is important to ensure that, with all these changes, the IEASYS member reflects the proper suffix for each member.

Update the Symbols

The vendor provides within its parameter libraries symbols that represent their operating system volumes and system volumes. The symbols are:

- &SYSR1 for the vendor system resident volume

- &SYSR2 for the vendor system resident volume #2

- &SYSS1 for the vendor system user libraries

A complete search of the parameter libraries should reveal the members that have these symbols. All of the member statements that have these symbols need to be changed to the actual volume serial. There are several reasons for doing this:

- Once the mainframe zEnterprise volume is used to start the system, &SYSR1 refers to the zEnterprise volume, not the vendor volume.

- Depending on the mainframe zEnterprise installation of the operating system and the size of the volume, &SYSR2 may also refer to the same volume or a secondary volume. The data sets that had &SYSR2 will point to a zEnterprise DASD volume, not the vendor DASD volume.

- With the possibility of data-set naming standards being different and the potential to miss a change, some data sets that are critical to startup may be required temporarily. The operating system version is the same, but the service level is likely to be different, so this may create a mismatch in module levels and needs to be remedied immediately, lest unpredictable results occur.

Depending on future versions of the vendor system, this part of the migration might not be necessary.

At the end of the migrations process, a new IEASYM member removes the vendor symbols. In this supplied system, the following are no longer valid:

```
SYMDEF(&SYSP1.='vlPRD1')
SYMDEF(&SYSP2.='vlPRD2')
SYMDEF(&SYSP3.='vlPRD3')
SYMDEF(&SYSR2.='vlRES2')
SYMDEF(&SYSS1.='vlSYS1')
```

Create the New MSTJCL Member

The MSTJCL member is for the master scheduler subsystem. The master scheduler establishes communication between the job entry subsystem (JES) and the operating system.

The MSTJCL member should have a unique suffix. Copy the vendor-supplied MSTJCL member into the system shared parameter library and rename it with a new suffix. The suffix must match the suffix for the MSTRJCL statement in the IEASYS member. If using MSTJCL00, no entry is required in the IEASYS member.

It is necessary to update the IEFPDSI section of MSTJCL to ensure that the procedure libraries are correct. Prior to restarting the system, verify that the procedure names are correct. For any procedure libraries not in the master catalog, the VOL=SER=parameter is required for the operating system to find the data sets. The VOL=SER=parameter specifies the volume serial where the data set resides. For example, the MSTJCL member may contain the following statements:

```
//MSTJCLKB JOB MSGLEVEL=(1,1),TIME=1440
//         EXEC PGM=IEEMB860,DPRTY=(15,15)
//STCINRDR DD SYSOUT=(A,INTRDR)
//TSOINRDR DD SYSOUT=(A,INTRDR)
//IEFPDSI  DD DSN=user.MV1.PROCLIB,DISP=SHR,VOL=SER=MVSHR1,UNIT=3390
//         DD DSN=user.SHARED.PROCLIB,DISP=SHR,VOL=SER=MVSHR1,UNIT=3390
//         DD DSN=system.MV1.PROCLIB,DISP=SHR,VOL=SER=MVSHR1,UNIT=3390
//         DD DSN=system.SHARED.PROCLIB,DISP=SHR,VOL=SER=MVSHR1,UNIT=3390
//         DD DSN=SYS1.PROCLIB,DISP=SHR
//SYSUADS  DD DISP=SHR,DSN=SYS1.UADS.KJB
//SYSLBC   DD DISP=SHR,DSN=SYS1.BRODCAST
//SYSRACF  DD DISP=SHR,DSN=SYS1.KJB.ICH01
```

The IEFPDSI DD statement defines the data set or data-set concatenation that contains the procedure source JCL for the started tasks.

Create the New BPXPRM Member

The BPXPRM member contains parameters for the USS environment and the associated file systems. Copy the vendor-supplied BPXPRM member into the system shared parameter library and rename it with a unique suffix. The suffix must match the OMVS= statement in the IEASYS member.

It is necessary to update this member to reflect the system-related USS data sets residing on the mainframe zEnterprise version of the operating system volume.

Create the New VATLST Member

The *volume attribute list member* (VATLST) defines the usage of the DASD volumes. The volumes specified are either permanently resident or reserved and can have one of the following three use attributes.

1. *Storage*: Job control language does not need to specify the volume; primarily for nontemporary data sets.

2. *Public*: Job control language does not need to specify the volume; used for temporary or scratch data sets.

3. *Private*: Job control language must specify VOL=SER= to reference the volume.

Copy the vendor-supplied VATLST member into the system shared parameter library and rename it with a unique suffix. The suffix must match the VAL= statement in the IEASYS member.

If there are volumes initialized with WRK001 and STG001, then the volumes should be in the VATLST to allow for proper utilization for work and storage. For these volumes, the VATLST would have the following entries:

```
VATDEF IPLUSE(PRIVATE),SYSUSE(PRIVATE)
WRK001,1,1,3390    ,N
STG001,1,0,3390    ,N
```

(The highlighted *0* indicates that the volume is defined as storage; the highlighted *1* indicates that the volume is defined as public; and a third option, *2,* would indicate that a volume is defined as private.)

Specifying the N allows for multiple work and storage volumes in a shared member even when the volumes are not associated with each system. The N signifies that the volume does not need to be available during startup. Assume an installation has:

- STG001 and WRK001 are only available on system 1

- STG002 and WRK002 are only available on system 2

- STG003 and WRK003 are only available on system 3

In this case, using N in the VATLST member allows for sharing the member. If there is a Y in place of the N, the system stops and requests the volume to be mounted. A response to the mount request allows the system startup to continue, but this is not necessary when using the N. An example of a shared member follows:

```
VATDEF IPLUSE(PRIVATE),SYSUSE(PRIVATE)
WRK001,1,1,3390    ,N
WRK002,1,1,3390    ,N
WRK003,1,1,3390    ,N
STG001,1,0,3390    ,N
STG002,1,0,3390    ,N
STG003,1,0,3390    ,N
```

Dynamic Dump Data Sets

Dynamic dump data sets allow each dump data-set allocation to be system-managed to reduce the system inefficiency that stems from predefining the size of data sets to be unnecessarily large.

Commands similar to the following can be in a shared COMMND member in the shared parameter library:

```
COM='DD ALLOC=ACTIVE'
COM='DD ADD,VOL=DMP001'
COM='DD NAME=SYS1.SYSDUMP.&SYSNAME..&JOBNAME..D&YYMMDD..S&SEQ'
COM='D D,STATUS'
```

The dump command includes the system name (&SYSNAME), which allows sharing across systems. This also permits sharing of common DASD volumes across multiple systems. There is no need to segregate the volumes by system, thereby allowing more flexibility in the event that a single system is having an application problem. If the volumes are segregated, then the chance of a volume's filling is greater than when multiple volumes are shared across the systems.

Resource Access Control Facility

The *Resource Access Control Facility* (RACF) data sets need to be moved to a non-vendor-provided volume, such as MVIPL1 (defined in Chapter 7). It is important to keep the vendor-supplied volumes and data sets separate from the new environment.

RACF generally has two databases: primary and backup. The RACF utility IRRUT400 can be used to copy these databases to a new volume and new name. Once the new databases are ready, the templates need to be updated to the level of RACF residing on the new mainframe zEnterprise operating system volumes. There are two choices to update the database:

- Immediately: Update the job control language to point to the proper data set on the mainframe zEnterprise volume serial.

- After system restart with the new mainframe zEnterprise volumes: The system is now referencing the correct data sets.

The RACF utility IRRMIN00 updates the RACF templates. It also updates other areas of RACF and has safeguards to prevent downgrading the database.

Depending on the version of RACF that is running and the specific setup, the RACF module ICHRDSNT may need to be assembled to reflect the new RACF database names (*Primary* and *Backup*).

■ **Note**   The MSTJCL member requires an update to the DD SYSRACF statement to reflect the new RACF database name.

Add Users

After the RACF database has been migrated to the new volumes, define any new users who will require access to the systems. Depending on the system requirements, there are two considerations for adding users:

- Define the users to RACF and TSO/E using RACF

- Define the users to RACF; then add the users to TSO/E using UADS

The choice of using either RACF or UADS should be made after consulting the IT staff to ensure consistent corporate practices.

System Data Sets

Several system data sets may require movement or rebuilding to be migrated from the vendor system. Carefully review the startup and data sets to determine which need attention. Data sets that may require attention include the following:

SYS1.UADS: The *user attributes data set* (UADS) defines users who may log in to TSO/E. The UADS information may reside in the RACF database. If it does not, then the system will use the SYS1.UADS data set. If RACF is not available for any reason, having a SYS1. UADS data set offers the advantage of being able to log in to TSO/E. In a good security environment, RACF will regularly require new passwords; the same is not true for the UADS data set. Therefore, you need to know the user ID and password to use the UADS database. It is not likely that the passwords required for RACF and UADS match.

SYS1.LOGREC: Moving to a different non-vendor-supplied volume will suffice. After relocating, format the data set to start the record collection anew.

SYS1.STGINDEX: Building a new SYS1.STGINDEX data set on a non-vendor-supplied volume will suffice.

SYS1.BRODCAST: Moving to a non-vendor-supplied volume wil l suffice.

SYS1.DAE: Moving to a non-vendor-supplied volume will suffice.

JES2 Migration Considerations

Copy the vendor-supplied JES2-started task member into the system procedure library on volume *MVIPL1*. In preparation for sharing the member, it can reside in the system shared procedure library. There is no need to change the name because the vendor-supplied system procedure library should not be in the concatenation for the new system configuration. A few items require changing in the started task.

The following is an example of a JES2-started task:

```
//JES2     PROC VERSION=20,MEMBER=JES2SS
//IEFPROC EXEC PGM=HASJES&VERSION,DPRTY=(15,15),TIME=1440,PERFORM=9
//PROC00   DD DISP=SHR,DSN=user.&ZSYS..PROCLIB,VOL=SER=MVSHR1,UNIT=3390
//         DD DISP=SHR,DSN=user.SHARED.PROCLIB,VOL=SER=MVSHR1,UNIT=3390
//         DD DISP=SHR,DSN=system.&ZSYS..PROCLIB,VOL=SER=MVSHR1,UNIT=3390
//         DD DISP=SHR,DSN=system.SHARED.PROCLIB,VOL=SER=MVSHR1,UNIT=3390
//         DD DISP=SHR,DSN=SYS1.PROCLIB
//HASPPARM DD  DSN=system.SHARED.PARMLIB(&MEMBER),DISP=SHR
//HASPLIST DD  DDNAME=IEFRDER
```

The following changes are required for this JES2-started task:

- The **PROC** statement: The JES2 parameter member needs to be updated to reflect the JES2 parameter member for the new system environment; in this sample, member JES2SS has the parameters for JES2.

- **PROC00:** This requires updates for the new procedure libraries.

The JES2 parameter member should have a unique suffix. Copy the vendor-supplied JES2 parameter member into the system shared parameter library, and rename it with a new suffix. The suffixed member name must match the name specified in the JES2-started task.

Changes are required to pick up the new SPOOL and checkpoint data sets. It is possible to share this member, depending on the system installation environment and requirements. Update the member specified for MEMBER=; in the sample, it is member JES2SS.

Check for the following statements in the JES2 parameter member placed in a new system parameter library for changes, as follows:

- SPOOLDEF: Defines the spool data set, DASD volume, and other items relating to SPOOL

- CKPTDEF: Defines the JES2 checkpoint data sets, DASD volume, and other items relating to the checkpoints

Other items may need to be changed depending on the environment. This includes items such as network nodes, connections, destinations, and applications.

The next system start will require JES2 to "cold start." A cold start of JES2 formats the SPOOL and checkpoint data sets. Update the COMMND member that is specified in the IEASYS member to ensure the proper JES2 started task and JES2 parameters are set appropriately.

Virtual Telecommunications Access Method (VTAM)

Virtual Telecommunications Access Method (VTAM) supports System Network Architecture (SNA) and provides an application-programming interface (API), as well as other features.

VTAM will require new data sets and started tasks. The following items need to be considered:

- New system VTAMLIB(s) data set, copied from the vendor-supplied data set(s) and created on a new volume such as *MVSHR1*

- New system VTAMLST(s) data set, copied from the vendor-supplied data set(s) and created on a new volume such as *MVSHR1*

- New VTAM-started task placed in a non-vendor-supplied procedure library; it may be possible to share the VTAM-started task

The goal is to ensure that there are no requirements for the vendor-supplied volumes. This will eliminate the need for the vendor volumes while also making changes for the new environment.

The started task will require changes to place the new VTAMLST and VTAMLIB data sets into the appropriate concatenations for the VTAMLST and VTAMLIB DD statements. For simplicity, make no changes to the network until after a system or VTAM restart occurs, so as to ensure that the new setup is correct. At this point, the entire vendor networking is still in effect. The difference is that the started task and the data sets now reside on new non-vendor-supplied volumes.

Internet Protocol Activity

TCP/IP drives the *internet protocol* (IP) activity. There are likely to be many changes, and—as with the other tasks—the recommendation is to copy the started tasks, data sets, and supporting members to new data sets on the new volumes. Some of the items and data sets that need to be reviewed are listed below. There may be more items depending on the system environment and requirements.

- OSA parameter definitions in VTAMLST

- TCPPARMS parameters for device definitions and routing

- PROFILE data set for device definitions, Ethernet, routing

- DATA parameters for HOSTNAME, DOMAIN, NAMESERVER

- /etc/hosts file for IP address and name

- HOSTS LOCAL data set for hosts and net

At some point, the MAKESITE TSO command will need execution. It will create two data sets suffixed ADDRINFO and SITEINFO. These will replace existing TCP/IP data sets. The names should be different from the ones that are in use by the vendor-supplied system. The TCP/IP-started task will also need to be updated in order to use the new data sets created by this command.

Interactive System Productivity Facility (ISPF)

Once logged onto TSO/E, *Interactive System Productivity Facility* (ISPF) should be available. It provides an editor, browser, and utilities.

ISPF will require updating to move the logon procedures and CLISTs from the vendor-supplied volumes. Copy the members to new libraries using the same member names. If modifications are required, then copy the members to a new name and modify the new members. Note that all users who will use a new logon procedure need to be authorized to use it.

During verification, have a userid defined by the original system logged into TSO/E and ISPF while testing the new user and logon procedure. This will allow one user to handle modifications in the event of errors. Once the new logon procedure is working, ensure that the data sets are properly set. The following TSO command will list the concatenation: **TSO ISRDDN.** This command can verify that the vendor-supplied data sets are no longer in use by the logon procedure.

Many users will use the default logon procedure to sign on to TSO/E and use ISPF. However, some users have applications with panels and menus that interface with the ISPF panels. Those application panels have various options for implementation, including the following:

- Update existing menus

- Create new menus

- Create new menus that are selected from existing menus

For example, an ISPF panel may look like this:

```
0   Settings      Terminal and user parameters
1   View          Display source data or listings
2   Edit          Create or change source data
3   Utilities     Perform utility functions
4   Foreground    Interactive language processing
5   Batch         Submit job for language processing
6   Command       Enter TSO or Workstation commands
7   Dialog Test   Perform dialog testing
9   IBM Products  IBM program development products
10  SCLM          SW Configuration Library Manager
11  Workplace     ISPF Object/Action Workplace
M   More          Additional IBM Products
```

A user application may need to be added to the menu. The application can either create all of its menu items here or create a link to another panel. Here is an example:

```
0   Settings      Terminal and user parameters
1   View          Display source data or listings
2   Edit          Create or change source data
3   Utilities     Perform utility functions
4   Foreground    Interactive language processing
5   Batch         Submit job for language processing
6   Command       Enter TSO or Workstation commands
7   Dialog Test   Perform dialog testing
9   IBM Products  IBM program development products
10  SCLM          SW Configuration Library Manager
11  Workplace     ISPF Object/Action Workplace
C   application 1 Application description
M   More          Additional IBM Products
```

The menu item "C" takes the user to another panel that contains items related only to application 1. If there are many menu selections for application 1, then moving the application to another panel eliminates the clutter on the main screen.

Coupling Facility

If data sharing across systems is required, then a CF and SYSPLEX need to be defined to the system. The CF may contain the following:

- Structures

- Policies

- Logstreams

- Workload Manager (WLM)

IBM documentation provides information on how to determine the best fit and setup for each unique environment. As hardware and software advances, enhancements provide better ways to perform the same function. There is also the possibility of new commands and parameters.

Use caution when establishing the SYSPLEX/coupling facility. It is good practice to create a new IEASYS member for this part to ensure that the system will restart. If the system does not start, then revert to the previous IEASYS member.

If the CF is not a requirement, then specify COUPLE SYSPLEX(LOCAL) in the COUPLE member. Refer to the IBM documentation for more information.

Sharing Data Sets and Volumes

If the systems are in an environment where data sharing is required, using system management software can ensure data integrity. Problems can occur in an unprotected environment that leads to corruption of data. For example, simultaneous update access to a data set from different systems can cause corruption of the data set. System management software can alleviate and manage the data set to disallow simultaneous update.

There are software product solutions that provide a safe data-sharing environment. These solutions provide data integrity by serializing access to data which creates a much safer environment for protecting data.

Starting the New System Environment

Many changes to the initial virtualized environment have been made. To verify each modification, perform system restarts at regular intervals to verify and validate those changes. At this point, with the system running with the mainframe zEnterprise operating system volume, verification should begin. To complete the validation process, use the following steps:

1. Shutdown the operating system.

2. Detach all of the vendor-supplied volumes.

3. Restart the system.

    a. If there are errors and the system started, correct them.

    b. If there are errors and the system start fails, diagnose and add only the vendor volume(s) required to start the system.

4. Repeat steps 1–3 until the system starts with no errors regarding the vendor volumes.

The purpose of this process is to determine whether there are any vendor-supplied volumes still required. The verification may require attaching some of the vendor volumes until appropriate changes can eliminate the need for them.

Verifying the New System

When the system starts with no vendor volumes attached, system validation can begin. In addition to the following list of steps that can assist with the validation, there may be other tasks necessary to determine that all changes are correct. When these validation tests are completed successfully, and there are no vendor-supplied volumes attached to the system, a user can log on to TSO/E and ISPF—at which point any other changes or remedies needed are much easier to make.

1. *Verify DASD*

   a. *Q DASD*: Entered from z/OS guest machine before starting the guest operating system, to verify the required DASD volumes are attached to the guest

   b. *d u,dasd,online,,64*: Entered from the MVS console to verify the DASD attached to guest operating system are online after the guest operating system has been started

2. *Verify master catalog*: Check *MVS syslog* for message showing the master catalog name.

3. *Verify user catalog*: from *ISPF 3.4,*: Enter the aliases defined to the user catalog. The resulting screen will display the catalog name;. Each alias is entered individually.

4. *Verify IODF*: Check *MVS syslog* for message showing the IODF name with the suffix.

5. *Verify SMS*: From MVS console, enter *D SMS* to verify the data sets.

6. *Verify dynamic dump data sets*: From MVS console, enter *D D* to verify the information.

7. *Verify VATLST changes*: From MVS console, enter *d u,,,,nnnn,1*. Use this command for each unit in the VATLST or enter a number greater than 1 to list all the volumes within the range of the VATLST assignments.

8. *Verify page data sets*: From the MVS console, enter *D ASM* to verify the page data set names.

9. *Verify OMVS/USS file systems*: From the MVS console, enter *D OMVS,MF* to list any mount failures.

10. *Verify SYSPLEX*: From the MVS console, enter *D XCF* to verify the name.

11. *Verify coupling facility*: From the MVS console, enter *D XCF,COUPLE* to verify the couple data-set names.

12. *Verify WLM*: From the MVS console, enter *D WLM* to verify information.

13. *Verify IPL information*: From the MVS console, enter *D IPLINFO* to verify the information.

14. *Verify JES2 SPOOL*: From the MVS console, enter *$DSPL* to verify the information.

15. *Verify JES2 Checkpoints*: From the MVS console, enter *$DCKPTDEF* to verify the information.

16. *Verify Started Tasks*: From the MVS console, enter *D A,L* to verify that all expected tasks are listed.

Summary

This chapter focused on the migration from the vendor-supplied environment setup to a new advanced setup based on the mainframe zEnterprise volumes. This environment provides more flexibility including the ability to apply system maintenance and configure customized test environments.

The next chapter will discuss some system management techniques and the use of symbols and naming conventions to create simple, easy-to-modify system startups.

Case Studies

Case #1: Single Laptop System for Mainframe Developer

A developer using a laptop for the mainframe environment has a new requirement to validate the software product against each new operating system update. However, the vendor-supplied system does not allow for easy updating. The developer verifies with the IT staff that migrating licensed operating systems from the zEnterprise server to the laptop is permissible. The IT staff informs the developer that the solution is not so simple; it will require many system modifications to migrate the volume into the environment.

The developer is determined to set up the system so that the vendor-based z/OS is not required and starts on a quest to make it happen. He wants to be the first to make this happen and does not request assistance from the technical support staff. To perform the required validation, the developer begins the process of converting the system to run the same operating system volumes currently used on the zEnterprise server.

■ **Note** The first step in this process is to copy the volumes from the zEnterprise server to the laptop.

After all the required volumes transfer and the resultant DASD files are properly placed, then update the device map on the laptop to access the new DASD files. One of the volumes transferred to the laptop is ZOS1D0, which is the operating system volume containing release 13. The remaining 86 steps to complete the migration from the vendor-supplied operating system volumes to the volumes created by the corporate IT team are enumerated below.

■ **Note** As part of the migration process, system backups of the Linux DASD files at logical points of the conversion process will minimize the effort required to recover in the event of an error.

The vendor-provided systems use an excellent naming standard for system parameter members and volume serials. In this case study, the prefixes/suffixes are changed:

- Lowercase "vl" for vendor-supplied volume serial prefixes

- Lowercase "vs" for vendor-supplied system parameter library suffixes

The following steps migrate the vendor-supplied volumes to a new environment running from the operating system volumes created by the corporate IT team:

1. ***Start the z/OS system***

   ```
   IPL A80 LOADP 0A82vs        Vendor IPL command
   ```

2. ***Display the system information from z/OS***

   ```
   D IPLINFO
   IEE254I  04.40.54 IPLINFO DISPLAY 786
    SYSTEM IPLED AT 07.59.19 ON 10/26/2013
    RELEASE z/OS 01.11.00    LICENSE = z/OS
    USED LOADvs IN SYS1.IPLPARM ON 0A82
   ```

```
ARCHLVL = 2   MTLSHARE = N
IEASYM LIST = 00
IEASYS LIST = vs (OP)
IODF DEVICE: ORIGINAL(0A82) CURRENT(0A82)
IPL DEVICE: ORIGINAL(0A80) CURRENT(0A80) VOLUME(v1RES1)
```

3. **Review the LOAD member**

```
IODF     99 SYS1
SYSCAT   v1SYS1113CCATALOG.Zxxx.MASTER
SYSPARM  vs
IEASYM   00
PARMLIB  USER.PARMLIB                    v1SYS1
PARMLIB  vendor.Zxxx.PARMLIB             v1RES1
PARMLIB  SYS1.PARMLIB                    v1RES1
NUCLEUS  1
SYSPLEX  VENDPL
```

4. **Create a new master Catalog**

Merge the vendor master catalog into the new master catalog. This keeps all the existing data sets cataloged and available.

If any data sets in the vendor catalog are not found on the volumes use the "delete noscratch" parameters with the IDCAMS utility to remedy this.

5. **Create a new LOAD member in the vendor data set**

```
LOADvs is in SYS1.IPLPARM
LOADKB is created by copying LOADvs
```

6. **Update new LOAD member.** Changed

```
SYSCAT   v1SYS1113CCATALOG.Zxxx.MASTER
```

to

```
SYSCAT   MVIPL1113CCATALOG.NEW.MASTER
```

7. **A new system start is performed** using the new LOAD member

```
IPL A80 LOADP 0A82KB
```

8. **Build a user catalog KENB.UCAT**

Verify the user catalog by performing a IDCAMS LISTCAT

9. **Create alias definition for system data sets HLQ.** Create KJB

10. **Build new data sets for establishing system startups** separate from the vendor system

```
KJB.USER.PARMLIB
KJB.SYSTEM.PARMLIB
KJB.vendor.PARMLIB
```

11. ***Copy the vendor parameter library to a new library*** to keep all of the existing system parameters in place

```
Copy vendor.Zxxx.PARMLIB to KJB.vendor.PARMLIB
```

12. ***Create a back out for the LOADKB member,*** then update

```
PARMLIB   KJB.SYSTEM.PARMLIB                         MVIPL1
PARMLIB   KJB.USER.PARMLIB                           MVIPL1
PARMLIB   KJB.vendor.PARMLIB                         MVIPL1
PARMLIB   SYS1.PARMLIB                               v1RES1
```

13. ***IPL*** to verify the recent changes

IPL A80 LOADP 0A82KB

Verify via the syslog; search for KJB.vendor.PARMLIB and member selections

14. ***Determine how JES2 is being started*** by searching syslog

```
S JES2,PARM='COLD,NOREQ'

JES2 WAS EXPANDED USING SYSTEM LIBRARY vendor.Zxxx.PROCLIB

JES2      PROC MEMBER=JES2PARM,ALTMEM=JES2BACK
```

15. ***Create PROCLIBs***

```
KJB.vendor.PROCLIB
KJB.SYSTEM.PROCLIB
KJB.USER.PROCLIB
```

16. ***Copy JES2 STC to KJB.SYSTEM.PROCLIB*** and update

```
//ALTPARM   DD    DSN=KJB.SYSTEM.PARMLIB(&ALTMEM),DISP=SHR
//HASPPARM  DD    DSN=KJB.SYSTEM.PARMLIB(&MEMBER),DISP=SHR
//PROC00    DD    DSN=KJB.USER.PROCLIB,DISP=SHR
//          DD    DSN=KJB.vendor.PROCLIB,DISP=SHR
//          DD    DSN=EUV.SEUVPRC,DISP=SHR
//          DD    DSN=IOE.SIOEPROC,DISP=SHR
//          DD    DSN=EOY.SEOYPROC,DISP=SHR
//          DD    DSN=HLA.SASMSAM1,DISP=SHR
//          DD    DSN=SYS1.PROCLIB,DISP=SHR
```

17. ***Copy from vendor.Zxxx.PARMLIB to KJB.SYSTEM.PARMLIB***

```
JES2PARM & JES2BACK - kept same names
MSTJCL00 – renamed to MSTJCLKB
```

18. ***Update MSTJCLKB*** to add KJB.SYSTEM.PROCLIB

```
//IEFPDSI   DD DSN=KJB.SYSTEM.PROCLIB,DISP=SHR
//          DD DSN=vendor.Zxxx.PROCLIB,DISP=SHR
//          DD DSN=SYS1.PROCLIB,DISP=SHR
```

19. **Search for the IEASYS members** in syslog

```
IEASYS00 FOUND IN KJB.vendor.PARMLIB
IEASYSvs FOUND IN KJB.vendor.PARMLIB
```

20. **Update KJB.SYSTEM.PARMLIB**

    Copied IEASYS00 & IEASYSvs to KJB.SYSTEM.PARMLIB

    Renamed IEASYSvs to IEASYSKB and updated

    Changed CMD=vs to CMD=KB in IEASYSKB
    Changed MSTRJCL=00 to MSTRJCL=KB - for previous step creating MSTJCLKB

    Updated COMMNDKB

    COM='S JES2' – Allow for warm or cold start
    COM='DD ADD,VOL=DMP001' - to point dumps to the new dump volume

21. **Create IPLPARM**

    Create SYS0.IPLPARM (system will find before SYS1.IPLPARM). Load members must be here now.

    Copied LOADvs,LOADKB,LOADKO

    Updated LOADKB -- SYSPARM   KB

22. **Move vendor IODF** to the same volume as SYS0.IPLPARM

    Copy IODF99 to IODF11

23. **SYS0.IPLPARM(LOADKB)** - Updated

    ```
    IODF      11 SYS1
    ```

24. **IPL** to verify the changes

    ```
    IPL A80 LOADP OAA0KB - New volume replaces vendor volume
    ```

■ **Note**   The developer stopped to check and verify changed members to this point.

---

25. **Check log to see where vendor.Zxxx is still used**

    MSTJCL

    JES2

```
ZFS - vendor.Zxxx.PARMLIB(IOEFSPRM)

TCPPARMS
```

26. ***Check to see all started tasks:*** Enter D A,L on console

```
LLA  -- SYS1.PROCLIB (no changes-will use MF version later)
JES2 -- KJB.SYSTEM.PROCLIB
VLF  -- SYS1.PROCLIB (no changes-will use MF version later)
VTAM -- KJB.vendor.PROCLIB - no changes needed at this point
DLF  -- SYS1.PROCLIB (no changes-will use MF version later)
RACF -- vendor.Zxxx.PROCLIB - Needs fixed
TSO  -- KJB.vendor.PROCLIB
SDSF -- KJB.vendor.PROCLIB
TCPIP -- KJB.vendor.PROCLIB
TN3270 -- KJB.vendor.PROCLIB
HTTPD1 WEBSRV1 -- KJB.vendor.PROCLIB
PORTMAP PMAP -- KJB.vendor.PROCLIB
INETD4 OMVSKERN -- SYS1.PROCLIB (no changes-will use MF version later)
FTPD1 FTPD -- SYS1.PROCLIB (no changes-will use MF version later)
SSHD4 START2 -- SYS1.PROCLIB (no changes-will use MF version later)
```

27. ***Update RACF***

Copy RACF procedure member to KJB.SYSTEM.PROCLIB

Update MSTJCL
```
Add -      //SYSRACF   DD DISP=SHR,DSN=SYS1.KJB.ICHO1
Update - //SYSUADS   DD DISP=SHR,DSN=SYS1.UADS.KJB
Leave -   //SYSLBC    DD DISP=SHR,DSN=SYS1.BRODCAST
```

The vendor system requires ***ICHRDSNT*** to be assembled to set the RACF database names

```
lu IBMUSER - verify RACF is running
```

28. ***Run batch jobs to copy and place data sets on new volumes***

```
Copy SYS1.RACFDS to SYS1.KJB.ICHO1

Copy SYS1.BRODCAST to SYS1.BRODCAST

Create SYS1.UADS.KJB

SYS1.UADS  - COPY SYS1.UADS TO SYS1.UADS.KJB and sync with SYS1.BRODCAST
   This job must have TYPRUN=HOLD and have all users signoff TSO
   Release the job via the console $AJ(jobname)
```

29. ***Restart the system*** to verify the recent changes

```
IPL A80 LOADP OAAOKB
```

Verify via syslog
```
//SYSUADS  DD DISP=SHR,DSN=SYS1.UADS.KJB
//SYSLBC   DD DISP=SHR,DSN=SYS1.BRODCAST
//SYSRACF  DD DISP=SHR,DSN=SYS1.KJB.ICHO1
```

Verify within TSO - lu IBMUSER or the vendor supplied userid if not IBMUSER

30. **Update VATLST**

Create VATLSTKB from VATLST00 and *update VATLSTKB*
```
Remove - vlSYS1,0,0,3390     ,Y
Add    - WRK001,1,1,3390     ,N
Add    - STG001,1,0,3390     ,N
```

Update IEASYSKB -- VAL=KB,

31. **Restart the system** to verify the recent changes

IPL A80 LOADP OAAOKB

Verify using D U,,,devaddr,1 - do this for each volume
```
OAA6 3390 A           WRK001      PUB/RSDNT
OAAB 3390 O           STG001      STRG/RSDNT
```

32. **Update JES2 SPOOL and CHECKPOINT**

```
Volumes
   SPL100
   CKP10A
   CKP10P

Run batch jobs
   Define spool space -  SYS1.KJB.HASPACE
   Define Checkpoint 1 - SYS1.JES2.KJB.CKPT
   Define Checkpoint 2 - SYS1.JES2.KJB.CKPT2

Update JES2PARM - KJB.SYSTEM.PARMLIB (must cold start next IPL)
   SPOOLDEF
     DSNAME=SYS1.KJB.HASPACE,
     VOLUME=SPL1
   CKPTDEF
     CKPT1=(DSNAME=SYS1.JES2.KJB.CKPT,
     VOLSER=CKP10P,
     CKPT2=(DSNAME=SYS1.JES2.KJB.CKPT2,
     VOLSER=CKP10A,
```

33. **Restart the system** to verify the recent changes

IPL A80 LOADP OAAOKB

```
Verify via syslog
   $HASP423 SPL100 IS BEING FORMATTED  - large volume will take some time

   *$HASP436 CONFIRM z11 MODE COLD START ON 155
     CKPT1 - VOLSER=CKP10P DSN=SYS1.JES2.KJB.CKPT
     CKPT2 - VOLSER=CKP10A DSN=SYS1.JES2.KJB.CKPT2
     SPOOL - PREFIX=SPL1   DSN=SYS1.KJB.HASPACE
```

34. *Update the page data sets*

Run batch job to build page data sets

```
IEASYSKB - replace PAGE= with: -- based on the names in the batch job
  PAGE=(PAGE.PLPA,
        PAGE.COMMON,
        PAGE.LOCALA,
        PAGE.LOCALB,
        PAGE.LOCALC,L),
```

35. *Restart the system* to verify the recent changes

IPL A80 LOADP 0AA0KB

```
Verify via syslog -- Command D ASM - the names should match the previous step
PLPA      68%   OK   0AB2  PAGE.PLPA
COMMON    0%    OK   0AB2  PAGE.COMMON
LOCAL     0%    OK   0AB2  PAGE.LOCALA
LOCAL     0%    OK   0AB2  PAGE.LOCALB
LOCAL     0%    OK   0AB2  PAGE.LOCALC
```

36. *Create RACF users*

Create all required userids
Create an alias for each userid
Add userids to UADS and authorize logon procedures $userid and PROCKJB

37. *Update ISPF*

```
Create KJB.SYSTEM.CLIST

Create KJB.vendor.CLIST

Copy vendor.Zxxx.CLIST to KJB.vendor.CLIST

Create KJB.SYSTEM.ISPPLIB - copy in vendor.Zxxx.ISPPLIB

Copy vendor.Zxxx.PROCLIB(ISPFPROC)  TO  KJB.SYSTEM.PROCLIB(PROCKJB) and update:
  Comment out all vendor data sets
  Update for KJB data sets
  Update for UADS,BRODCAST,CLIST and other data sets
  Update PARM on EXEC statement to call ISPFKJB
```

152

```
Copy vendor.Zxxx.PROCLIB(ISPFCL)  TO  KJB.SYSTEM.PROCLIB(ISPFKJB) and update

Update JES2 to add KJB.SYSTEM.PROCLIB to PROC00 - These are the 1st 3 libraries
  //PROC00    DD   DSN=KJB.USER.PROCLIB,DISP=SHR
  //          DD   DSN=KJB.SYSTEM.PROCLIB,DISP=SHR
  //          DD   DSN=KJB.vendor.PROCLIB,DISP=SHR
```

38. **Restart the system** to verify the recent changes

    IPL A80 LOADP 0AA0KB

Verify that one of the vendor supplied userids and one of the new userids can successfully logon to TSO.

■ **Note**   Steps 39 and 40 are the final preparations for replacing the vendor operating system volume with the mainframe zEnterprise operating system volume.

---

39. **Copy KJB.vendor.PARMLIB(PROGxx) to KJB.SYSTEM.PARMLIB(PROGKB)**

    Change the volume for all vendor.** data sets from &SYSR1/2 to vlRES1/2, respectively

    Change all &SYSR2 to &SYSR1 since the mainframe operating system is 1 volume

    Change &SYSS1 to vlSYS1

    Check vendor supplied IEASYM member for other possible changes

    Change IEASYSKB - PROG=xx to PROG=KB

40. **Catalog entries for mainframe zEnterprise volume**

    Create user catalog with same name as mainframe zEnterprise system alias for the VSAM zFS operating system data sets

    Create alias for the VSAM zFS

    Run batch job to catalog zFS data sets

    Run job to catalog all mainframe zEnterprise operating system data sets indirectly to volume ******. This allows the data sets to be automatically cataloged to the operating system volume that starts the system

41. **IPL AA4 LOADP 0AA0KB - Both vendor volumes are now replaced during IPL**

■ **Note**   System starts with the mainframe zEnterprise operating system volume.

Now that the system is using the mainframe zEnterprise volume, the process to eliminate using vendor-based volume begins.

42. ***Search syslog for data sets that did not resolve or have different naming standards*** between the two operating system volumes. There is a possibility that some required system parameter members are still in the vendor system or point to the vendor system. For example, on this system, NFS.NFSLIBE is changed to SYS1.NFSLIBE for the mainframe zEnterprise volume

43. ***The IBM naming convention was vendor.Z***

Search the following PARMLIB/PROCLIB data sets for vendor.Z:

```
KJB.vendor.PROCLIB
KJB.SYSTEM.PROCLIB
KJB.vendor.PARMLIB
KJB.SYSTEM.PARMLIB
```

Review the members to determine which are relevant to the system.

Update the members by removing the data sets or moving some/all contents to a different or new data set. The developer process will show examples as the process continues.

44. ***Update TCPIP/FTP and others***

```
Create KJB.vendor.TCPPARMS and copy vendor.Zxxx.TCPPARMS

Copy these members from KJB.vendor.PROCLIB to KJB.SYSTEM.PROCLIB
  FTPD
  NFSC
  NFSS
  PORTMAP
  TCPIP
  TN3270

Update each - change vendor.Zxxx.TCPPARMS to KJB.vendor.TCPPARMS
```

45. ***Restart the system*** to verify the recent changes

```
IPL AA4 LOADP OAAOKB
```

46. ***Other tasks copied*** from KJB.vendor.PROCLIB to KJB.SYSTEM.PROCLIB with vendor.Zxxx

```
TSO
Copy TSOKEY00 from vendor.Zxxx.PARMLIB to KJB.SYSTEM.PARMLIB

Update the TSO task with KJB.SYSTEM.PARMLIB

VTAM
VTAMLST - create KJB.SYSTEM.VTAMLST - copy in vendor.Zxxx.VTAMLST
VTAMLIB - create KJB.SYSTEM.VTAMLIB - copy in vendor.Zxxx.VTAMLIB

Add   KJB.SYSTEM.VTAMLIB to PROGKB for APF authorization
```

Update VTAM with the new data sets

VTAMAPPL
STEPLIB - Create KJB.SYSTEM.LINKLIB - copy in vendor.Zxxx.LINKLIB

PARMLIB - copy vendor.Zxxx.PARMLIB(VTAMAPPL) to KJB.SYSTEM.PARMLIB

Add   KJB.SYSTEM.LINKLIB to PROGKB for APF authorization

Update VTAMAPPL with the new data sets

Rename each in KJB.vendor.PROCLIB with a 2 at the end for backup (TSO2/VTAM2/VTAMAPPL2)

47. **Restart the system** to verify the recent changes

    IPL AA4 LOADP OAAOKB

48. **KJB.SYSTEM.PROCLIB** changes

    ISPFPROC & PROCKJB
      Update SYSPROC
        Replace vendor.Zxxx.CLIST with KJB.vendor.CLIST
        Replace vendor.Zxxx.PROCLIB with KJB.vendor.PROCLIB
      Update ISPPLIB - vendor.Zxxx.ISPPLIB with KJB.SYSTEM.ISPPLIB

Test by having two persons logged on to TSO so that the procedures can be fixed if a change is not correct.

49. **KJB.SYSTEM.PARMLIB** changes

    MSTJCLKB - Replace vendor.Zxxx.PROCLIB with KJB.vendor.PROCLIB

50. **Restart the system** to verify the recent changes

    IPL AA4 LOADP OAAOKB

51. **Backup IEASYSKB** into IEASYSKO

52. **LPALST**

    Create KJB.vendor.LPALIB from vendor.Zxxx.LPALIB

    Build LPALSTKB in KJB.SYSTEM.PARMLIB - copy in KJB.vendor.PARMLIB(LPALSTxx)

    Update IEASYSKB - LPA=xx, to LPA=KB,

53. **BPXPRM**

    Create BPXPRMKB in KJB.SYSTEM.PARMLIB from BPXPRMvs

Ensure that the correct /dev /etc /var /etc is properly cataloged for mainframe zEnterprise volume such as:
```
KJB.TMP
KJB.DEV
KJB.VAR
KJB.VARWBEM
KJB.ETC
KJB.U
```

Update IEASYSKB - OMVS=vs, to OMVS=KB,

54. *Restart the system* to verify the recent changes

IPL AA4 LOADP OAAOKB

55. *Backup IEASYSKB* into IEASYSKO

56. *Remove Coupling Facility / SYSPLEX (IEASYSKB)*; the developer has no need for a multi-system sysplex.

57. Change *COUPLE=00* to *COUPLE=KB*

Create COUPLEKB with 1 line -- COUPLE SYSPLEX(LOCAL)

```
Leave GRS=NONE
Add GRSCNF=00,
Add GRSRNL=00,
```

Backup LOADKB to LOADKO - Remove SYSPLEX   vendorPL

58. *Restart the system* to verify the recent changes

IPL AA4 LOADP OAAOKB

59. *Backup IEASYSKB* into IEASYSKO

60. *SMS*

Copy acds,scds,commds to KJB.acds,scds,commds

Copy IEFSSN00 to KJB.SYSTEM.PARMLIB as IEFSSNKB

Update IEASYSKB - SSN=00, to SSN=KB,

Update IEFSSNKB - SMS INITPARM - ID=00 to ID=KB

```
Copy KJB.vendor.PARMLIB(IGDSMS00) to KJB.SYSTEM.PARMLIB(IGDSMSKB)
  ACDS(SYS1.ACDS)      to ACDS(KJB.ACDS)
  COMMDS(SYS1.COMMDS) to COMMDS(KJB.COMMDS)
```

Enter: SET SMS=KB command on console

Did not specify SCDS .., The developer needed to have the Source defined and corrected it here:
  SETSMS SCDS(KJB.SCDS) on MVS console to set SCDS

```
Enter D SMS command on console
  SCDS = KJB.SCDS
  ACDS = KJB.ACDS
  COMMDS = KJB.COMMDS
```

61. ***Restart the system*** to verify the recent changes

```
IPL AA4 LOADP OAAOKB
```

62. ***Depending on configuration – SYS1.PARMLIB*** should be cataloged on new configuration

May need to uncatalog SYS1.PARMLIB

```
Copy SYS1.IBM.PARMLIB on mainframe zEnterprise volume to SYS1.PARMLIB on new volume

Ensure new SYS1.PARMLIB is cataloged in new environment
```

Update LOADKB for SYS1.PARMLIB   Change volume serial

63. ***Check for SYS1 data sets*** and remedy as appropriate

SYS1.LOGREC - this data set can be copied (then cleared) after system restart

```
SMF logging
  These data sets can be created and formatted with a different name
  Create SMFPRMKB member and update

Disable SMF logging if not required
  Create SMFPRMKB member and update
    NOACTIVE
    NOPROMPT
    JWT(0100)
```

Update IEASYSKB - SMF=KB

SYS1.STGINDEX - This data set can be recreated

64. ***Restart the system*** to verify the recent changes

```
IPL AA4 LOADP OAAOKB
```

65. ***USER libraries can be removed*** from members – they are all empty

```
USER.CLIST     - ISPFPROC
USER.ISPPLIB   - ISPFPROC
USER.LINKLIB   - PROGKB
USER.LPALIB    - LPALSTKB
USER.PARMLIB
USER.PROCLIB   - ISPFPROC
```

```
USER.VTAM.SOURCE
USER.VTAMLIB    - PROGKB, VTAM
USER.VTAMLST    - VTAM
USER.WLM.INPUT
```

66. ***Search for vlRES*** to determine more data sets that require attention

    LPALSTKB - not pointing to system volume &SYSR1 (verify catalog is correct before changing to &SYSR1) - this is an inconsistency since these data sets are pointing to the vendor volume directly.
    ```
    ISF.SISFLPA(vlRES1),
    EOY.SEOYLPA(vlRES2),
    ISP.SISPLPA(vlRES1),
    TCPIP.SEZALPA(vlRES1),
    ```

    PROGKB - replace with KJB.vendor data sets and the correct volume serial
    ```
    DSNAME(vendor.Zxxx.LINKLIB)                          VOLUME(vlRES1)
    DSNAME(vendor.Zxxx.VTAMLIB)                          VOLUME(vlRES1)
    LNKLST ADD NAME(LNKLST00) DSN(vendor.Zxxx.LINKLIB)   VOLUME(vlRES1)
    ```

    ISPFPROC - this is strictly vendor based - no changes required

67. ***Restart the system*** to verify the recent changes

    IPL AA4 LOADP OAAOKB

68. ***Double-check all vendor.Z data sets*** in members

    ZFS - Replace vendor.Zxxx.PARMLIB with KJB.vendor.PARMLIB

    TCPIP - Replace vendor.Zxxx.VTAMLIB with KJB.SYSTEM.VTAMLIB

    TN3270 - Replace vendor.Zxxx.VTAMLIB with KJB.SYSTEM.VTAMLIB

    PROGKB
    ```
    replace vendor.Zxxx.LINKLIB  with KJB.SYSTEM.LINKLIB
    replace vendor.Zxxx.VTAMLIB  with KJB.SYSTEM.VTAMLIB
    ```

    Ensure KJB. Libraries are authorized in PROGKB

69. ***Restart the system*** to verify the recent changes

    IPL AA4 LOADP OAAOKB

70. ***SYS1.PROCLIB is incorrect***

    SYS1.PROCLIB on vlRES1 - follow same process as used for SYS1.PARMLIB to use the zEnterprise SYS1.PROCLIB

71. ***Verify all members*** for SYS1.PARMLIB & PROCLIB

72. ***Restart the system*** to verify the recent changes

    IPL AA4 LOADP OAAOKB

73. ***SYS1.DAE*** - copy this data set from the vendor volumes

74. ***SYNC RACF***

75. ***Create IEASYMKB*** from IEASYM00 and then remove:

```
SYMDEF(&SYSP1.='vlPRD1')
SYMDEF(&SYSP2.='vlPRD2')
SYMDEF(&SYSP3.='vlPRD3')
SYMDEF(&SYSR2.='vlRES2')
SYMDEF(&SYSS1.='vlSYS1')
```

76. ***Move SYS1.SMS.CNTL*** from vendor volume

77. ***Move KJB.vendor.PARMLIB(MMSLST00)*** to KJB.SYSTEM.PARMLIB

```
Copy SYS1.APPCMSG.CLUSTER to SYS1.APPCMSG.CLUSTER.KJB
    Update MMSLST00 in KJB.SYSTEM.PARMLIB
```

78. ***Move TCPIP.FTP.DATA (FTPD)*** from vendor volume

79. ***Assembler data set name*** changed from HLA to ASMA

```
Update JES2 PROC00 & PROGKB
```

80. ***Fix LNKLST (PROGKB)***

```
FFST.SEPWMOD2 should be FFST.V120ESA.SEPWMOD2
FFST.SEPWMOD4 should be FFST.V120ESA.SEPWMOD4
HLA.SASMMOD1 should be ASMA.SASMMOD1
IOA.SIOALMOD should be SYS1.SIOALMOD
```

81. ***Restart the system*** to verify the recent changes

```
IPL AA4 LOADP 0AA0KB
```

82. ***VTAM***—Move the following from vendor volume:

```
SYS1.DSDBCTRL
SYS1.DSDB1
SYS1.DSDB2
SYS1.TRSDB
```

83. ***Restart the system*** to verify the recent changes

```
IPL AA4 LOADP 0AA0KB
```

84. ***Clean up the catalog***

■ **Note** Many data-set aliases are now pointing to the correct mainframe zEnterprise volume, but they have the alias relating to the vendor catalog. Therefore, the data set seems fine, but when the vendor volume is detached, the system cannot find it.

---

85. *Check each HLQ*

Check all volumes where the data sets reside
Uncatalog each data set - this can be done in ISPF using option 3.4
Delete the alias
Define the alias to the new catalog created at the beginning
Manually catalog the data sets via 3.4
HLQs found on this system that required immediate attention:

```
ISF - Cataloged on volume ZOS1D0
CSF - Cataloged on volume ZOS1D0
EOY - Cataloged on volume ZOS1D0
GIM - Cataloged on volume ZOS1D0
CEE - Cataloged on volume ZOS1D0
CBC - Cataloged on volume ZOS1D0
ISP - Cataloged on volume ZOS1D0
IOE – Cataloged on volume ZOS1D0
TCPIP - Cataloged on volumes ZOS1D0 and MVIPL1
```

86. *Detach the vendor DASD and start the system*

■ **Note**   Depending on problems, the vendor resident and system volumes may require reattachment until all problems are resolved.

After completing these changes, the developer is able to start his virtual environment with no dependence on the vendor-supplied DASD volumes.

Case #2: Server Class Machine Hosting Mainframe Systems for Software Quality Assurance Testing

A QA Team has been successful in their adoption of the virtual environment running on a Linux host. However, the team now requires regular updates of the operating system, as the testing requires certification for each operating system update that is available.

The IT staff informs the team that quarterly operating system updates are available. The QA team confirms that quarterly updates are adequate for the testing requirements.

The IT staff developed a streamlined approach for making updates using the information received from the developer in Case#1. The staff creates a method to utilize two z/OS guest systems. The first system is to make the changes required to migrate away from the vendor-supplied operating system volumes. The second system is available to attach volumes from the first system in the event of erroneous changes. If a change is incorrect and the system will not start, it is possible to attach the volume(s) to the second system and remedy the error. While this will work for most corrections, changes to catalogs may require a restore of the system. In this case, all changes made prior to the previous backup will need to be performed again.

The migration of the QA systems from the vendor-supplied environment to a mainframe zEnterprise based environment will use the procedure created in Case #1. The only exceptions to the procedure involve starting a z/VM system first and performing the procedure from a z/OS guest system.

CHAPTER 9

■ ■ ■

Customizing the z/OS Environment with Symbols

This chapter is a technical overview of techniques for running multiple systems utilizing:

- Shared Parameter Libraries
- Symbol Substitutions

The systems represented are running as virtual guests under z/VM. It is not necessary that they be running as virtual guests to utilize the optimizations presented here, although some parameters relate to a virtual environment. Although a general knowledge of MVS parameters and symbol usage will make the chapter easier to follow, it is not required.

■ **Note** Refer to Appendix B, "Setting the Standards and Conventions," for an explanation of standards and conventions.

Reserved Symbols

To avoid unexpected and unpredictable results, be careful when setting symbols not to define symbols that are IBM-reserved, such as the following:

- &DATE
- &DAY
- &HHMMSS
- &JOBNAME
- &SEC
- &SID
- &SYSCLONE
- &SYSNAME
- &SYSPLEX

- &SYSR1

- &SYSUID

- &TIME

Refer to IBM's manual "MVS Initialization and Tuning Reference" to learn more about static symbols.

MVS Operating System Management

There are many components to operating system management. For the discussion of symbol usage, the following three parameter library members play an important part and are considered in turn in the next sections:

- **LOADxx**: Specifies system-related items such as I/O configuration, master catalog, parameter library concatenation, and others

- **IEASYMxx**: Defines system static symbols that can be used as substitutions within other members such as IEASYS to allow sharing of members while maintaining individual system uniqueness

- **IEASYSxx**: Specifies system parameters for the customized system startup and operation

LOADxx

The LOAD member specifies many items for system initialization, such as:

- I/O Definition File (IODF)

- Parameter library concatenation

- System symbol members (IEASYM)

The LOAD member can reside in a number of system parameter data sets. A common practice is to place it in SYS**n**.IPLPARM, where n can be 0 through 9, such as:

- SYS0.IPLPARM

- SYS3.IPLPARM

- SYS9.IPLPARM

The LOAD member may also exist in SYS1.PARMLIB. Be careful when placing the LOAD member and creating the parameter library setup. The concern is that the operating system will attempt to locate the LOAD member, but will not search all SYSn.IPLPARM or SYS1.PARMLIB for the specified LOAD member. When the system locates the first SYSn.IPLPARM or SYS1.PARMLIB, the specified LOAD member must exist in that parameter library. If it is not located in the first parameter library, the system will stop in a wait state.

The parameters in the LOAD member to be considered in relation to the operating system management are:

```
SYSPARM   AA
```

The SYSPARM parameter identifies the suffix for the IEASYS member. The member name in the parameter library is IEASYSAA.

```
IEASYM    AA
```

The IEASYM parameter identifies the suffix for the IEASYM member. The member name in the parameter library is IEASYMAA.

```
PARMLIB  xxx.xxxx.PARMLIB
PARMLIB  yyy.yyyy.PARMLIB
```

The PARMLIB statements identify the concatenation of parameter libraries searched for members that are required for system startup.

```
VMUSERID VM11
```

The VMUSERID statement identifies a system that is running as a virtual guest. The load parameters after this statement apply to this guest.

```
SYSCAT   RESP01113CICF.VRESP01
```

The SYSCAT statement identifies the MASTER catalog on volume RESP01 with name ICFVRESP01.

```
IODF    AA SYS1
```

The IODF parameter identifies the name of the IODF configuration data set. This data set must exist at system startup. The name of the data set is SYS1.IODFAA.

Figure 9-1 is a partial LOAD member representing a sample of the parameters.

```
SYSPARM   AA
IEASYM    AA
PARMLIB   xxx.xxxx.PARMLIB
PARMLIB   yyy.yyyy.PARMLIB
VMUSERID  VM11
SYSCAT    RESP01113CICF.VRESP01
IODF      AA SYS1
```

Figure 9-1. Partial LOAD member

IEASYMxx

This parameter member defines static system symbols that enable the enforcement of naming standards for the system. It allows controlling such things such as:

- System names
- Product versions
- Product service levels
- Parameter library member selection
- Parameter library member overrides

Several symbols supplied by IBM are reserved. A couple of these reserved symbols are:

- &SYSCLONE - By default, the last two positions of SYSNAME

- &SYSNAME - The system name

- &SYSPLEX - The MVS sysplex name

A couple of definitions that could be in an IEASYM member are:

```
SYSDEF VMUSERID(MV11) SYSNAME(MV11)
```

This defines the system name to be *MV11* whenever a virtual system named *MV11* logs onto VM and starts the z/OS system.

```
SYSDEF SYMDEF(&SYSR2='&SYSR1')
```

&SYSR2 will be the same name as &SYSR1. These are IBM-supplied symbols. &SYSR1 represents the DASD volume serial that contains the operating system used when the system starts. Depending on the amount of space required for the operating system and the size of the DASD volumes, it may be necessary to utilize more than one volume. When this symbol definition is set, the operating system volume is large enough to contain the entire operating system, so the secondary volume is not required. For example, if the operating system volume is ZOSDR1, then &SYSR1 and &SYSR2 are set to ZOSDR1.

```
SYSDEF SYMDEF(&PRODUCT1='R11SL8')
```

In the above statement the symbol &PRODUCT1 is set to R11SL8. This symbol assists in starting the proper product version. It can enable the segregation of version, release, and service levels of a product. If two versions of PRODUCT1 are available for testing, then this static symbol can decide which version starts. For example, assume that there are a series of data sets prefixed as follows:

- PRODUCT1.*R11SL8.*

- PRODUCT1.*R10SL5.*

The naming convention is the high-level qualifier for a product followed by the release and service level. In this example, the product has two releases available:

- Release 11 Service Level 8

- Release 10 Service Level 5

At startup for the product, you can select the release started by using the symbol &PRODUCT1 in the job control language (JCL) for the product.

An example of a statement that uses this method is:

```
//STEPLIB  DD  DISP=SHR,DSN=PRODUCT1.&PRODUCT1..LOADLIB
```

This STEPLIB translates to data set PRODUCT1.R11SL8.LOADLIB based on the setting for the symbol &PRODUCT1. This is just one statement in the startup of the product. It is possible that more job control statements will provide additional overrides.

IEASYSxx

Essentially, the IEASYS members provide the system parameters for startup. With good naming standards and member placement, this member is easy to manage and maintain.

A good use of member IEASYS00 (IEASYS suffixed with 00) is to define all default system parameters. Advantages of using IEASYS00 for default parameters include the following:

- IEASYS00 is always picked up first in the parameter library concatenation.

- IEASYS00 does not need to be specified in a concatenation because it will picked up automatically.

- Routine use of IEASYS00 standardizes system startups.

Parameters that might appear in IEASYS00 include the following:

```
CLPA,
LOGCLS=L,
LOGLMT=999999,
MAXUSER=500,
SQA=(12,24M),
VRREGN=64
```

IODF

The IODF is a data set that contains the input/output configuration for the system. This data set must exist. The data set selection is in the LOAD member using the IODF parameter. For example:

```
IODF    AA SYS1
```

This defines the IODF data set as SYS1.IODFAA. Therefore, a data set with this precise name must be available when the system starts. The data set SYS1.IODFAA has all of the input and output definitions required to successfully start the system.

Establishing Shared Parameter Libraries

When building a group of systems, whether they are connected and sharing data or not, it is essential to create an environment that is easy to maintain. One element that makes this much easier is a shared parameter library. When system startup parameters are shared, each system shares system components that create commonality among systems. At the same time, when set up properly, each system can remain independent by having the capability to override the default system parameters. This provides the ability to create unique systems by overriding the parameters that do not apply to an individual system or to add unique system parameters that apply to the individual system. For example, here are a couple members where this might occur:

- LNKLST

  - Contains program libraries concatenated to system library SYS1.LINKLIB

  - Other system libraries are also concatenated - SYS1.MIGLIB, SYS1.CSSLIB, SYS1. SIEALNKE, and SYS1.SIEAMIGE

- LPALST

  - Contains read-only reenterable programs added to the pageable link pack area (PLPA)

- IEALPA

  - Modified LPA (MLPA)

  - Contains reenterable modules added as a temporary extension to the pageable link pack area (PLPA)

Parameter Overriding

This section contains examples of how to handle system and user parameter requirements.

Example #1 - Shared IEASYS Member Sets System Standards

A parameter library shared by all systems has an IEASYS member (IEASYSSH) that contains the default parameters for all systems. The **SH** suffix does not relate to a system; it represents the fact that it is shared among the systems.

On each system, there is a unique parameter library available only with that system. The parameter library concatenation is this:

```
system.SHARED.PARMLIB          where IEASYSSH resides
user.MV1.PARMLIB               where IEASYS01 resides
SYS1.PARMLIB                   default operating system members
```

On system MV11 is IEASYS member (IEASYS01) which contains parameters that are not in IEASYSSH. No parameters in the individual system override any parameter in IEASYSSH. For example, the IEASYSSH member may have these parameters (partial representation):

```
CLPA,
CMB=(UNITR,COMM,GRAPH,250),
LOGCLS=L,
LOGLMT=999999,
MAXUSER=255,
PAGE=(PAGE.&ZSYS..PLPA,
      PAGE.&ZSYS..COMMON,
      PAGE.&ZSYS..LOCALA,
      PAGE.&ZSYS..LOCALB,
      PAGE.&ZSYS..LOCALC,L),
VRREGN=64
```

The individual member, IEASYS01, may contain these parameters (partial representation):

```
CMD=(DD,01,SS),
CLOCK=(SS,L),
CON=SS,
```

This example allows a common IEASYS member to contain all pertinent common parameters that make each system similar while allowing each system to be independent.

The LOAD member that starts system 01 contains a SYSPARM statement such as:

```
SYSPARM (SH,01,L)
```

This statement tells the system to use members IEASYSSH and IEASYS01. It also tells the system to display the contents of IEASYS at the operator console. The IEASYS concatenation is:

- IEASYS00

- IEASYSSH

- IEASYS01

Example #2 - Shared IEASYS Member Is Overridden by Systems

A parameter library shared by all systems uses the IEASYS00 member for default parameters for all systems. IEASYS00 is always first in the concatenation. This is the default.

On each system, there is a unique parameter library available only with that system. In this library is an IEASYS member which contains statements that are unique to the system. The parameter library concatenation is this:

```
system.SHARED.PARMLIB          where IEASYS00 resides
user.MV1.PARMLIB               where IEASYS01 resides
SYS1.PARMLIB                   default operating system members
```

In this case, IEASYS01 uses some parameters that are the same as IEASYS00, with different options. For example, member IEASYS00 contains these parameters (partial representation):

```
CMD=ZD
LPA=ZD
PROG=ZD
```

Member IEASYS01 contains these parameters (partial representation):

```
CMD=(ZD,01)
LPA=(ZD,01)
PROG=(ZD,01)
```

The ZD suffixed parameters of member IEASYS00 are for the system startup and contain no additional modifications.

In IEASYS01, the development team wants to use the same system startup and add additional parameters. Since IEASYS00 is first in all concatenations, any parameter values found for subsequent IEASYS members will override IEASYS00. In a situation where many IEASYS members are in a concatenation, the parameter values found in IEASYS members closest to the bottom of concatenation will be the values used.

This allows a common IEASYS member to contain all parameters required to start a system successfully. It also allows an individual system to override those parameters. In the event that the development team has overridden a parameter that causes the system to fail, the development team can revert to the system default that uses IEASYS00 to successfully start the system and remedy the failure.

The LOAD member that starts system 01 contains a SYSPARM statement such as:

```
SYSPARM  (01,L)
```

This statement tells the system to use member IEASYS01. It also tells the system to display the contents of IEASYSxx at the operator console. The IEASYS concatenations are:

- IEASYS00

- IEASYS01

It is essential to determine all the requirements for the systems that will be utilizing the distributed platform servers. Once all of the requirements are gathered, the default system parameters can be set in a shared parameter library. The shared parameter library may establish many functions for the starting of MVS, JES, and system products.

The following sections analyze the interlocking of the parameters at system startup.

LOADxx Members

When running z/OS in a virtualized environment, many techniques are used that distinguish the systems. These techniques are easy to implement. Figure 9-2 shows a partial LOAD member that will permit its use as a shared member for multiple systems.

```
IODF      FF SYS1
SYSCAT    MVIPL1113CCATALOG.NEW.MASTER
SYSPARM   SS
IEASYM    SS
NUCLEUS   1
SYSPLEX   PLEXZPDT
*
VMUSERID MV11
PARMLIB   system.SHARED.PARMLIB                      MVSHR1
PARMLIB   system.MV1.PARMLIB                         MVSHR1
PARMLIB   user.SHARED.PARMLIB                        MVSHR1
PARMLIB   user.MV1.PARMLIB                           MVSHR1
PARMLIB   SYS1.PARMLIB
IODF      FF SYS1
SYSCAT    MVIPL1113CCATALOG.NEW.MASTER
*
VMUSERID MV21
PARMLIB   system.SHARED.PARMLIB                      MVSHR1
PARMLIB   system.MV2.PARMLIB                         MVSHR1
PARMLIB   user.SHARED.PARMLIB                        MVSHR1
PARMLIB   user.MV2.PARMLIB                           MVSHR1
PARMLIB   SYS1.PARMLIB
IODF      FF SYS1
SYSCAT    MVIPL1113CCATALOG.NEW.MASTER
```

Figure 9-2. *Partial shared LOAD member*

A brief explanation of select statements from Figure 9-2 follows. Refer to the IBM manual "MVS Initialization and Tuning Reference" for a more detailed explanation of each parameter.

SYSPARM Statement

The SYSPARM statement specifies the suffix(es) for the IEASYS member(s) to concatenate during the system startup. In this instance, it is specifying only one member (IEASYSSS). The suffix may represent that the IEASYS member is common among a group of *shared* *systems* (SS).

At system startup, the SYSPARM statements process as follows:

- IEASYS00

- SYSPARM statement in the LOAD member

- SYSPARM statement in the IEASYM member

- Operator overrides

It is possible in the parameter library concatenation to have IEASYS members with the same suffix. IEASYS00 is always first, and if there are no specifications in any of the members or by the operator, the system will use IEASYS00 as the only member at startup. To verify the correct IEASYS members are used, review the system console during the system startup. The console displays messages for all of the members selected and the data sets where they reside.

There is a specific method for how the system determines the IEASYS concatenation with many possibilities. Please refer to IBM documentation to determine the method used for a given configuration.

IEASYM Statement

The IEASYM parameter specifies the suffixes for the IEASYM members that contain static symbols used for the system. More than one suffix, separated by commas, concatenates the members specified.

This LOAD member example specifies one member, *IEASYMSS, with the definition "IEASYM SS".*

VMUSERID Statements

The individual parameters after the first VMUSERID statement are for the system specified on that parameter. This is true until it reaches the next VMUSERID statement or the end of the load member. The VMUSERID statement indicates that the name listed to the right is a virtual z/OS guest system.

PARMLIB Statements

The PARMLIB statements identify the concatenation for the search order for members when a system starts. Members such as IEASYS can be in any of the parameter libraries in the concatenation.

If SYS1.PARMLIB is not in the concatenation, then, by default, the system places it at the end of the concatenation. When SYS1.PARMLIB is in the concatenated list, then it will be in the order listed by the PARMLIB statements.

IBM requires the SYS1.PARMLIB data set. Its primary use is for supplying system startup members. The SYS1. PARMLIB data set is where the IBM system members reside.

IODF Statements

The IODF parameter designates the IODF data set. The IODF definition is the same for all systems represented here. The IODF data set name that the system searches for is SYS1.IODFFF. It is possible for systems to use different IODF configurations. Some systems may require specific special hardware while others do not. In a small environment, sharing all hardware configurations is easier than creating a separate configuration for special requirements.

SYSCAT Statements

The SYSCAT parameter identifies the master catalog for the system. The first six characters (columns 10-15) identify the DASD volume serial where the master catalog resides. The last part of the parameter identifies the name of the master catalog. The master catalog name begins in column 20. Its name is CATALOG.NEW.MASTER.

The systems represented in the portions of the LOAD member shown are utilizing a shared master catalog. The name and location are the same for each SYSCAT specification.

IEASYS Members

In a development environment where multiple operating system versions and releases are used, it is essential to develop standards that allow for ease of introducing new versions into the environment. Figure 9-3 details a partial IEASYS member.

```
CMD=(DD,01,SS),
LNK=(ZD,01,SS,L),
LPA=(ZD,01,SS,L),
MLPA=(ZD,SS),
OMVS=(ZD,01),
PROG=(ZD,01),
SSN=(SS,01),
PAGE=(PAGE.MV1.PLPA,
      PAGE.MV1.COMMON,
      PAGE.MV1.LOCALA,
      PAGE.MV1.LOCALB,
      PAGE.MV1.LOCALC,L),
```

Figure 9-3. *Partial IEASYS member*

This member contains many naming standards. The following are part of a naming standard:

- 01 — The "1" represents "system 1" in each occurrence. The suffix is two characters, so there is a leading zero.

- ZB — The "B" represents the operating system release in each occurrence. The "Z" represents "z/OS."

- MV1 — Represents a partial system name in each occurrence. The "1" represents "system 1."

A discussion of these items is in the "Start to Finish with Symbols" section of this chapter.

Creating Shared Master Catalog

In the multisystem environment discussed here, a shared master catalog is required to permit the sharing of parameter libraries and other essential data sets.

It is important to review the recommendations set forth by IBM for the proper definitions when creating a master catalog for sharing across systems. As software advances, a review of current documentation will result in a better overall environment.

Manipulating with System Symbols

The manipulation of system parameters with symbols is critical in systems management. Creating naming standards enables the ability to share members such as LOAD and IEASYS.

Assume the following symbols are set:

```
SYSDEF  VMUSERID(MV11) SYSNAME(MV11)
SYSDEF  SYMDEF(&SYSR2='&SYSR1')
        SYMDEF(&ZSYS='MV&SYSCLONE(1:1)')
```

The following values are assigned to the symbols:

```
&ZSYS = MV1
&SYSCLONE = 11  - by default, &SYSCLONE is the last two positions of SYSNAME
```

Operating System DASD Volume Serial

Assume that the operating system DASD volume is using the naming convention outlined in Appendix B. For this example, the DASD volume serial number is ZOS*D*R1. The fourth position, D, is the release of z/OS.

A user wants to start a system using release 13 of the operating system and he is starting system MV11. When the user checks the setting of LNKLST and LPALST, this is what he discovers:

- LNK=(ZD,01,SS,MM,L),

    - The ZD refers to z/OS (Z) release 13 (D)

- LPA=(ZD,01,MM,L),

    - The 01 refers to system 1 with a leading zero to create the two-character suffix

The setup is valid and the user is satisfied that the correct operating system members are in effect. When the user views the IEASYS member, the representation is:

```
LNK=(Z&SYSR2(4:1),0&ZSYS(3:1),SS,MM,L),
LPA=(Z&SYSR2(4:1),0&ZSYS(3:1),SS,MM,L),
```

The system symbol &**SYSR2** represents the DASD volume used to start the system. The **4:1** tells the system to pull the fourth position of the volume serial and use just one position, which is the letter **D**. The "D" represents operating system release 13. Figure 9-4 shows these relationships.

The "D" is the operating system release:

```
Operating System Volume
        ZOSDR1
```

The symbol &SYSR1(4:1) represents "D"; it is the fourth position:

```
    IEASYS Parameters (partial list)
LNK=(Z&SYSR1(4:1),&SYSCLONE,SS,MM,L),
LPA=(Z&SYSR1(4:1),&SYSCLONE,SS,MM,L),
```

Substituting "D" for &SYSR1(4:1):

```
IEASYS Parameter partial Translation
    LNK=(ZD,&SYSCLONE,SS,MM,L),
    LPA=(ZD,&SYSCLONE,SS,MM,L),
```

The parameter members selected:

```
Parameter Library Members
        LNKLSTZD
        LPALSTZD
```

Figure 9-4. DASD volume serial relationships through library member selection

Page Data Set Naming Standard

Figure 9-5 shows the page data set parameters within an IEASYS member and the symbol translation. This figure demonstrates that the data set naming convention for page data sets easily translates into a common shared setup when using a unique system-naming standard.

Assume &SYSNAME is MV23.

IEASYS Parameters for Page Data Sets

```
PAGE=(PAGE.P&SYSNAME(3:2)..PLPA,
      PAGE.C&SYSNAME(3:2)..COMMON,
      PAGE.L&SYSNAME(3:2)..LOCAL1,
      PAGE.L&SYSNAME(3:2)..LOCAL2,
      PAGE.L&SYSNAME(3:2)..LOCAL3,L)
```

IEASYS Parameters Translation

```
PAGE=(PAGE.P23.PLPA,
      PAGE.C23.COMMON,
      PAGE.L23.LOCAL1,
      PAGE.L23.LOCAL2,
      PAGE.L23.LOCAL3,L)
```

Figure 9-5. Page data set names and translation

In this example, each system has similar requirements for page data sets. However, the example does not assume that the data sets are the same size. Since the data sets are predefined, it allows for larger or smaller data sets as long as the number of LOCAL data sets is the same. The size depends on the use case for the system environment. The types of page data sets are:

- PLPA - This represents the pageable link pack area

- COMMON - Common area paging plus PLPA if it overflows

- LOCAL - Private Area and VIO pages

The following is an example of the naming conventions concerning the PLPA data set:

- PAGE.P01.PLPA --- name for system 01

- PAGE.P08.PLPA --- name for system 08

- PAGE.P16.PLPA --- name for system 16

- PAGE.P23.PLPA --- name for system 23

The data set naming structure is the same for the other page data sets for COMMON and LOCAL. This demonstrates symbol usage for page data sets on multiple systems. It also simplifies system management.

Starting a z/OS Virtual Guest

The following command starts the z/OS operating system when entered from within the virtual z/VM guest:

```
IPL 21BF CLEAR LOADP 2099SDM
```

The *IPL* command is how the system starts. IPL stands for *Initial Program Load.*
21BF is the address for the operating system volume.
CLEAR resets the guest's storage to zeros before IPL; this parameter is not a requirement for starting a system.
LOADP short for LOADPARM specifies that the LOAD information follows:

> *2099* is the address for the DASD volume that contains the IODF and SYSx.IPLPARM data sets. In this environment, the LOAD members reside in a SYSx.IPLPARM data set (specifically SYS1.IPLPARM). It is possible for the LOAD members to reside in the SYS1. PARMLIB data set.

> *SD* identifies the LOAD member to use. This translates to be LOADSD.

> *M* is the IMSI character (initialization message suppression indicator). IMSI values control message suppression and system prompts during IPL. IBM manages the IMSI values and their related controls. Refer to IBM documentation for full details on the IMSI values and their individual controls.

■ **Note**   The IODF data sets and the SYSn.IPLPARM data sets reside on MVIPL1.

Start to Finish with Symbols

This section details the critical concept of symbol substitutions within system management. The details provide an understanding of how naming standards and conventions can translate into an easy-to-manage multisystem environment.

It is the intention of the authors that readers will understand the techniques presented and potentially implement more symbol usage depending on their systems' installation(s) and requirements.

The distributed environment is much smaller than the mainframe zEnterprise and the number of systems created for any server is normally only a few depending on the use case for each server.

The discussions with symbols are for an environment with only three systems being available. Descriptions of some alternative methods for use in a larger environment are also part of the following sections.

Symbol Substitutions

The relationship among all of the parameters starts with the IPL command. Two important items exist within the command for symbol translation.

IPL String

```
IPL 21BF CLEAR LOADP 2099SDM
```

The first is the LOAD member referenced for use when the system starts. In the sample IPL command it is the suffix SD. It calls LOAD member LOAD**SD**.

The second part is the address of the operating system DASD volume. In the sample command, the address is 21BF. See Figure 9-6 for a depiction of the IPL string and the first part of the system standardization.

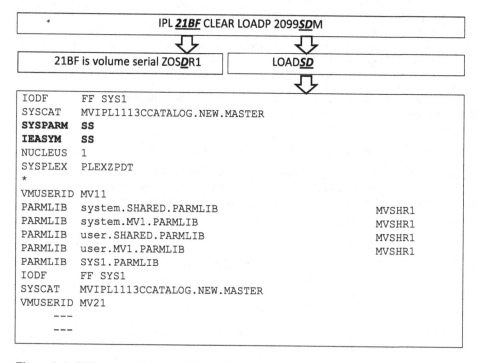

Figure 9-6. *IPL command and the relationships*

LOAD Member Relationships

The next two figures depict the relationship of the LOAD member to the IEASYM and IEASYS members used in Figure 9-6. The IEASYM member contains symbols that are in effect for the system that is running and the IEASYS member will show symbol substitutions. From Figure 9-6, the members are IEASYMSS and IEASYSSS.

An explanation of some symbols from Figure 9-7 follows:

- &SYSR2 - Defined to be equal to &SYSR1, which is the operating system volume serial ZOSDR1.

- &ZSYS - The system installer created this symbol to be "MV" plus the first position of &SYSCLONE, which is the system number. For example:

  - MV11 sets &ZSYS to MV1

  - MV21 sets &ZSYS to MV2

```
          Parameter library member IEASYMSS

SYSDEF   SYMDEF(&SYSR2='&SYSR1')
         SYMDEF(&ZSYS='MV&SYSCLONE(1:1)')
SYSDEF   VMUSERID(MV11) SYSNAME(MV11)
SYSDEF   VMUSERID(MV21) SYSNAME(MV21)
    ---
    ---
SYSDEF   VMUSERID(MV11) SYSCLONE(11)
SYSDEF   VMUSERID(MV21) SYSCLONE(21)
    ---
    ---
```

Figure 9-7. Partial IEASYM member

The IEASYS member is where a majority of the symbol substitution comes into play. Figure 9-8 depicts a partial representation of the IEASYSSS member with symbols and the translation.

```
                  Parameter member IEASYSSS

CMD=(DD,0&ZSYS(3:1),SS),

LNK=(Z&SYSR2(4:1),0&ZSYS(3:1),SS,L),

LPA=(Z&SYSR2(4:1),0&ZSYS(3:1),SS,L),

UNI=(1&SYSR2(4:1)),
```

```
                IEASYSSS member Translation

CMD=(DD,01,SS),

LNK=(ZD,01,SS,L),

LPA=(ZD,01,SS,L),

UNI=(1D),
```

Figure 9-8. *IEASYS example and translation*

Parameter Library Members

Figure 9-9 shows the translation into parameter library member selection. The parameters in IEASYS, along with the two-character suffixes listed after each, translate into member names.

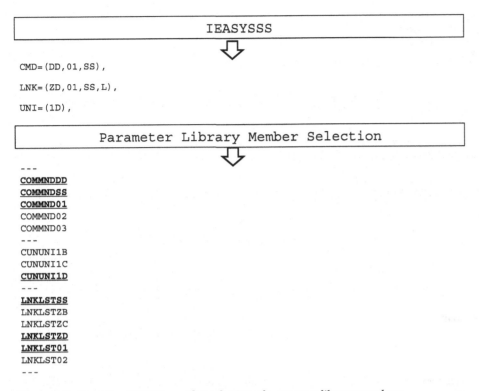

```
                              IEASYSSS

CMD=(DD,01,SS),

LNK=(ZD,01,SS,L),

UNI=(1D),

                Parameter Library Member Selection

---
COMMNDDD
COMMNDSS
COMMND01
COMMND02
COMMND03
---
CUNUNI1B
CUNUNI1C
CUNUNI1D
---
LNKLSTSS
LNKLSTZB
LNKLSTZC
LNKLSTZD
LNKLST01
LNKLST02
---
```

Figure 9-9. *Depicting IEASYS member selection of parameter library members*

Based on the sample provided, here are some translations:

- CMD is COMMND followed by a prefix such as DD - COMMNDDD
- LNK is LNKLST followed by a prefix such as ZD - LNKLSTZD
- UNI is CUNUNI followed by a prefix such as 1D - CUNUNI1D

The underlined members in Figure 9-9 are the ones chosen by the operating system at startup based on the IEASYS partial example. The figure is representative of many members in a system parameter library.

This completes the discussion of symbols deployed in starting the MVS system. The following sections present additional usages for symbols.

Job Entry Subsystem

This section describes the use of symbols with JES2. Knowledge of JES2 setup is required to understand this section.

The JES2 component of the operating system provides job, data, and task management. Essentially, JES receives jobs for the operating system, schedules them, and manages their output.

Once again, naming standards creates the opportunity for shared parameter library members. Figure 9-10 is a partial JES2 member.

```
SPOOLDEF  BUFSIZE=3992,
          DSNAME=SYS1.&ZSYS..HASPACE,
          FENCE=(ACTIVE=YES,VOLUMES=1),
          LARGEDS=ALLOWED,
          SPOOLNUM=32,
          TGSIZE=30,
          TGSPACE=(MAX=65152,WARN=75),
          TRKCELL=3,
          VOLUME=SPL&ZSYS(3:1)

CKPTDEF   CKPT1=(DSN=SYS1.JES2.&ZSYS..CKPT,
          VOL=CKP&ZSYS(3:1)00,INUSE=YES),
          DUPLEX=OFF,
          CKPT2=(DSN=SYS1.JES2.&ZSYS..CKPT2,
          VOL=CKP&ZSYS(3:1)01,INUSE=YES),
          DUPLEX=OFF

NJEDEF    DELAY=120,
          LINENUM=200,
          JRNUM=3,
          JTNUM=3,
          SRNUM=3,
          STNUM=3,
          NODENUM=200,
          OWNNODE=&SYSCLONE,
          PATH=4,
          RESTTOL=0,
          RESTNODE=125

N&SYSCLONE    NAME=US&SYSCLONE.xx,
          AUTH=(NET=YES,DEV=YES,JOB=YES,SYS=YES)

LOGON(1)  APPLID=A&SYSCLONE.JS2

INCLUDE  MEMBER=JES2IN&SYSCLONE
```

Figure 9-10. *Partial JES2 parameter member used for sharing*

For deploying systems across servers, each of the statements using &ZSYS is for all servers when you consider a good system-naming convention:

- MV11 is system 1 on server 1

- MV21 is system 2 on server 1

- MV35 is system 3 on server 5

Each virtualized mainframe environment normally does not share any data or resources with another environment. Therefore, the same volume serials may appear in multiple virtualized mainframe environments. This enables the ability to build a new server without changing volume serials or data set names.

A brief explanation of the bolded statements from Figure 9-10 follows. In Figure 9-10, assume that the system name is MV11, making the system number 1. The following information confirms the usefulness of appropriate naming standards.

SPOOLDEF

The standard naming convention for spool data sets allows sharing of this parameter. For the DSNAME= parameter of SPOOLDEF:

```
SYS1.&ZSYS..HASPACE translates to
SYS1.MV1.HASPACE
```

For three systems, the names are:

- SYS1.MV*1*.HASPACE - for system *1*
- SYS1.MV*2*.HASPACE - for system *2*
- SYS1.MV*3*.HASPACE - for system *3*

This naming convention allows for the usage of the same names across any number of servers since the naming standard using the first three positions includes the system number and excludes the server number.

In a larger environment, symbol &SYSCLONE may replace symbol &ZSYS in the following manner:

```
SYS1.Z&SYSCLONE..HASPACE
```

The translation for multiple systems is exemplified as follows:

- SYS1.Z*01*.HASPACE for system *01*
- SYS1.Z*13*.HASPACE for system *13*
- SYS1.Z*22*.HASPACE for system *22*

The standard for the SPOOL DASD volume serial allows sharing of this parameter. For the VOLUME= parameter of SPOOLDEF:

```
SPL&ZSYS(3:1)  translates to
SPL1 - for system 1
```

If there is more than one spool volume, this sets the prefix for all spool volumes. JES2 searches for all DASD volume serials with the prefix SPL1. For example:

- SPL*1*00 - first SPOOL volume for system *1*
- SPL*1*01 - second SPOOL volume for system *1*
- SPL*1*02 - third SPOOL volume for system *1*

For three systems, the names for a single volume are:

- SPL*1*00 - single volume for system *1*
- SPL*2*00 - single volume for system *2*
- SPL*3*00 - single volume for system *3*

Adding additional volumes to any system also works fine.

In a larger environment, symbol &SYSCLONE may replace symbol &ZSYS in the following manner:

```
SPL&SYSCLONE
```

The translation for multiple systems is exemplified as follows:

- SPL*01* for system 01

- SPL*13* for system 13

- SPL*22* for system 22

CKPTDEF

For the naming standard for the two data sets on the CKPTDEF statement:

```
SYS1.JES2.&ZSYS..CKPT
SYS1.JES2.&ZSYS..CKPT2
```

These translate as:

```
SYS1.JES2.MV1.CKPT - for system 1
SYS1.JES2.MV1.CKPT2 - for system 1
```

For three systems the translation is:

- SYS1.JES2.MV*1*.CKPT - for system *1*

- SYS1.JES2.MV*2*.CKPT - for system *2*

- SYS1.JES2.MV*3*.CKPT - for system *3*

For checkpoint 2, the data set names are:

- SYS1.JES2.MV*1*.CKPT2 - for system *1*

- SYS1.JES2.MV*2*.CKPT2 - for system *2*

- SYS1.JES2.MV*3*.CKPT2 - for system *3*

In a larger environment, symbol &SYSCLONE may replace symbol &ZSYS in the following manner:

```
SYS1.JES2.Z&SYSCLONE..CKPT
SYS1.JES2.Z&SYSCLONE..CKPT2
```

The translation for multiple systems is:

- SYS1.JES2.Z*01*.CKPT for system *01*

- SYS1.JES2.Z*09*.CKPT for system *09*

- SYS1.JES2.Z*19*.CKPT for system *19*

For checkpoint 2, the data set names are:

- SYS1.JES2.Z*01*.CKPT2 for system *01*

- SYS1.JES2.Z*09*.CKPT2 for system *09*

- SYS1.JES2.Z*19*.CKPT2 for system *19*

```
VOL=CKP&ZSYS(3:1)00 translates to volume serial
VOL=CKP100 - for system 1
```

For VOL= for CKPT2 of CKPTDEF:

```
VOL=CKP&ZSYS(3:1)01 translates to volume serial
VOL=CKP101 - for system 1
```

For the three systems the translation is:

- VOL=CKP*1*00 - for system *1*

- VOL=CKP*2*00 - for system *2*

- VOL=CKP*3*00 - for system *3*

For checkpoint 2 volume serials are:

- VOL=CKP*1*01 - for system *1*

- VOL=CKP*2*01 - for system *2*

- VOL=CKP*3*01 - for system *3*

In a larger environment, symbol &SYSCLONE may replace symbol &ZSYS in the following manner:

```
VOL=CKP0&SYSCLONE
VOL=CKP1&SYSCLONE
```

The translation for multiple systems is:

- CKP0*01* for system *01*

- CKP0*12* for system *12*

- CKP0*21* for system *21*

For checkpoint 2 volume serials are:

- CKP1*01* for system *01*

- CKP1*12* for system *12*

- CKP1*21* for system *21*

NJEDEF

When defining NJE, definition standards are essential to sharing a common JES2 member. In the area of networking, using &SYSCLONE suffices. There are no data sets or volume serial naming conventions to be concerned with this. For example:

```
OWNNODE=&SYSCLONE translates to
OWNNODE=02 - for system 2 in the distributed environment; O2 in a large environment
```

This allows each system to define its node as the last two positions of the system name. Here are further examples for multiple systems:

- OWNNODE=*03* for system *03*
- OWNNODE=*14* for system *14*
- OWNNODE=*23* for system *23*

DNS Host Naming

This section shows how to use symbols for sharing the parameters for the DNS host name. In the area of networking, using &SYSCLONE may be sufficient. However, a strong naming convention is required when communicating between systems to ensure distinct DNS host names. For a larger environment, the following recommendation may prove valuable:

```
N&SYSCLONE    NAME=US&SYSCLONE.xx, translates to
NO2                          NAME=USO2xx,
```

For multiple systems, it is:

- N*12*   NAME=US*12*xx, for system 12
- N*15*   NAME=US*15*xx, for system 15
- N*36*   NAME=US*36*xx, for system 36

LOGON

This section shows how to use symbols for sharing the parameters for the APPLID statement. This name must match the name defined to VTAM. In the area of networking, using &SYSCLONE works fine. For example:

```
APPLID=A&SYSCLONE.JS2 translates to
APPLID=A02JS2
```

For multiple systems:

- APPLID=A*01*JS2 for system *01*
- APPLID=A*10*JS2 for system *10*
- APPLID=A*17*JS2 for system *17*

INCLUDE additional JES2 members

This section demonstrates that when there are unique requirements for systems beyond the single shared member, the shared concept can continue to function by calling subsequent members for the unique items. The uniqueness can be printers, special networking, or other items. For example:

```
INCLUDE MEMBER=JES2IN&SYSCLONE calls member JES2IN02 - for system 02
```

The JES2IN02 member may consist of only one blank line when a system requires no special items or may contain an item such as:

```
PRT(1) DRAIN,UNIT=OOE,CLASS=AJ
```

Another option may be for the JES2IN02 member to call other members that contain special items segregated for ease of maintaining JES2. For example:

```
INCLUDE DSN=user.PARMLIB(JES2ENF)
INCLUDE DSN=user.PARMLIB(JES2EXIT)
INCLUDE DSN=user.PARMLIB(JES2NJE)
```

In this example, the JES2 members are in a specific parameter library. This allows the unique members to reside in parameter libraries unique to the individual system. The shared JES2 member is in a shared parameter library, while the unique members are in unique parameter libraries only available to the individual system. This technique provides sharing of the common JES2 parameters while allowing each individual system to add any unique requirements. The individual system requirements are in a parameter library only available to the individual system.

Summary

Our intent in this chapter has been to demonstrate how using proper naming standards and conventions along with symbols makes it easy to move from one operating system to another without making any changes to the startup members. The only requirement when introducing a new operating system is to supply the new parameter members that relate to the operating system.

The next chapter presents methods for updating the environment. The standards and conventions presented in this chapter play a role in easing the creation of a new distributed server from scratch.

Case Studies

Case 1: Single Laptop System for Mainframe Developer

A developer using a laptop for the mainframe environment has a new requirement to test two products with multiple versions of the z/OS operating system. It is important that the two products can function on all supported operating systems versions. There is a need to change between the operating systems to verify the product features.

The developer implements many DASD, data set, and networking standards, and uses symbols to distinguish between the operating systems. The symbol usage and standard naming convention for the system parameter data sets allow their use independent of the operating system started. Once the symbols are properly in place, the system can start with any operating system volume without other modifications.

The critical update to ensure that the new configuration will function properly with the new operating system volumes is to configure all of the operating system data sets to use indirect cataloging. Any data set indirectly cataloged must reside on the system IPL volume (such as *ZOSDR1*). This ensures that no matter which operating system starts, the data sets on that volume will be the ones chosen for the operating system. Unpredictable results will occur if the data set cataloging is incorrect.

With the setup of these standards and conventions, the developer verifies the system by starting two versions of the operating system. The difference in starting the two operating systems lies in the operating system DASD volume unit addresses; no other changes are necessary.

Start the system with Operating System Release 13

This IPL command:

```
IPL 21BF CLEAR LOADP 2099SHM
```

Points to volume *21BF* and LOAD member *LOADSH*

21BF is volume ZOSDR1 where D is the operating system release 13

LOADSH is shared and refers to shared IEASYS member (IEASYSSH)

IEASYSSH has members that are IBM supplied for the operating system

LPA=(Z&*SYSR2(4:1)*),0&ZSYS(3:1),SS,L) is just one example - LPALSTZ*D*

Figure 9-11 shows relationships with this command and a single member selection based on this example:

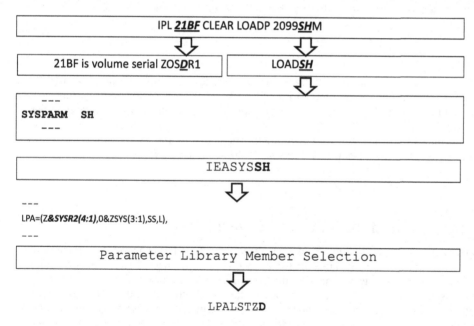

Figure 9-11. System startup member selection based on volume serial

Start the system with Operating System Release 12

This IPL command:

```
IPL 21AA CLEAR LOADP 2099SHM
```

Points to volume **21AA** and LOAD member **LOADSH**

21AA is volume ZOS**C**R1 where C is the operating system release 12

LOADSH is shared and refers to shared IEASYS member (IEASYSSH)

IEASYSSH has members that are IBM supplied for the operating system

LPA=(Z&**SYSR2(4:1)**,0&ZSYS(3:1),SS,L) is just one example - LPALSTZ**C**

Figure 9-12 shows relationships with this command and a single member selection based on this example:

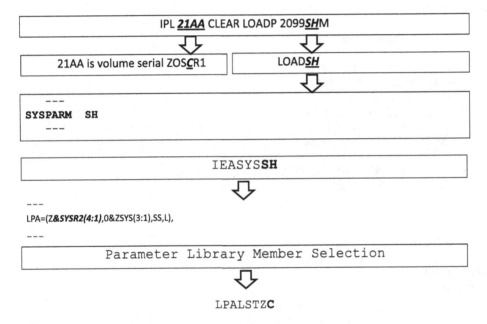

Figure 9-12. *System startup member selection based on volume serial*

Conclusion

The only changes that are required to use different operating systems are to change the operating system volume that is starting the system. The naming conventions and symbols take care of the rest.

When introducing a new operating system, the IBM-supplied members for items such as LNKLST and LPALST need to be moved to the shared system library. The member's suffix for each member is set according to the naming standard.

Figures 9-11 and 9-12 have only one change made between starting different releases of an operating system: the unit address of the volume serial. The symbols and naming standards performed automatic selection of the correct members for starting and using the correct data sets and parameters.

Case 2: Server Class Machine Hosting Multiple Mainframe Systems for Software QA Testing

A QA team has a new requirement to test with multiple z/OS operating systems simultaneously. The current virtual system configuration provided does not easily support this requirement. It is necessary to migrate from the current environment to one that uses the same configuration as the zEnterprise system that resides in the corporate data center. In order to implement this in a sustainable format, proper naming conventions and the use of symbols are essential. The IT staff assists with system parameter naming conventions and a systematic use of symbols to enable rapid deployment of new operating systems. The requirement to test different operating systems simultaneously raises the concern that many systems may be required. With the potential for many new systems, the QA team recognizes more ways to implement symbols to ease the introduction of new systems in the environment.

The following PARMLIB/PROCLIB changes for various components were updated on each system to utilize symbols to reduce the effort required when introducing new systems:

- System parameter library *(AXR00)* - Alternate Rexx

```
CPF('REXX&SYSCLONE.',SYSPLEX)
```

- *BPXPRM* - (Unix System Services) parameters:

```
MOUNT FILESYSTEM('system.&SYSNAME..DEV')
MOUNT FILESYSTEM('system.&SYSNAME..ETC')
MOUNT FILESYSTEM('system.&SYSNAME..VAR')
MOUNT FILESYSTEM('system.&SYSNAME..U')
```

- *COMMND* - Commands entered at system startup

```
COM='DD NAME=system.SYSDUMP.&SYSNAME..&JOBNAME..D&YYMMDD..S&SEQ'
COM='START product,parm=PARM&SYSCLONE'
```

- *CONSOL* - system console parameters

```
INIT APPLID(SMCS&SYSCLONE.), /* SNA MCS CONSOLE APPLID          *
CONSOLE DEVNUM(900),          symbols can be done for all consoles
        NAME(&SYSNAME.900),
        MSCOPE(&SYSNAME),
```

- *DFHSM* - (hierarchical storage manager) parameters:

```
  SETSYS                                                        -
---
---
        DATAMOVER(DSS)                                          -
            MCDSBACKUPDSN(system.DFHSM.&SYSNAME..MCDS.BACKUP.V0000001) -
            BCDSBACKUPDSN(system.DFHSM.&SYSNAME..BCDS.BACKUP.V0000001) -
            OCDSBACKUPDSN(system.DFHSM.&SYSNAME..OCDS.BACKUP.V0000001) -
            JRNLBACKUPDSN(system.DFHSM.&SYSNAME..JRNL.BACKUP.V0000001))
/*
SETSYS
  MIGRATEPREFIX(DFHSM&SYSCLONE)
```

- **FTPD** - USS daemon that uses TCP to listen to ports - parameter

  ```
  //SYSTCPD DD DISP=SHR,DSN=system.user.TCPIP.DATA(DATA&SYSNAME)
  ```

- **IEFSSN** - subsystem names parameters

  ```
  P&SYSCLONE.1,CSQ3INI,'CSQ3EPX,P&SYSCLONE.1,M'    MQ-SERIES
  P&SYSCLONE.2,CSQ3INI,'CSQ3EPX,P&SYSCLONE.2,M'    MQ-SERIES
  VMCF,MVPXSSI,US&SYSCLONE.xx                       TCPIP
  ```

- **MSTJCL** - parameters

  ```
  //IEFPDSI  DD DISP=SHR,DSN=user.&ZSYS..PROCLIB,VOL=SER=MVIPL1,UNIT=3390
  //         DD DISP=SHR,DSN=system.&ZSYS..PROCLIB,VOL=SER=MVIPL1,UNIT=3390
  ```

- **PORTMAP** - daemon converts RPC program numbers into internet port number - parameters

  ```
  //SYSTCPD  DD DISP=SHR,DSN=system.user.TCPIP.DATA(DATA&SYSNAME)
  ```

- **SMFPRM** - system management facilities parameters

  ```
  LSNAME(IFASMF.&SYSNAME..R30,TYPE(30))
  DEFAULTLSNAME(IFASMF.&SYSNAME..ALL)
  SID(&SYSNAME)
  ```

- **TCPIP** - Internet protocol started task

  ```
  //PROFILE  DD DISP=SHR,DSN=system.user.PROFILE.TCPIP(PROF&SYSNAME)
  //SYSTCPD  DD DISP=SHR,DSN=system.user.TCPIP.DATA(DATA&SYSNAME)
  ```

With these changes, the QA team is now able to change operating systems on a specific virtual system, and has a process in place to update to new versions and service levels as they become available. In addition, when evaluating system records, syslog, and other functions, the naming standards and symbol usage easily identify the system.

■ ■ ■

CHAPTER 10

Updating the Environment

This chapter provides an overview for updating the distributed server environment with more current versions of the operating systems and subsystems.

As discussed in previous chapters, the software versions and levels will be the IBM Recommended Service Upgrade (RSU). Although quarterly RSU maintenance for the operating system and subsystems is sufficient for most development teams, the process in this chapter will be useful regardless of the timing for maintenance. By using logical naming conventions and symbols, shorter software upgrade cycles are more feasible. The naming conventions include standards for DASD volumes, data set names, and parameter library members. The initial setup of standards and symbol usage to match the installation standards of each individual shop takes time, but the resulting ease of implementing new operating systems versions and new operating system levels make the effort worthwhile.

Maintain z/OS Operating Systems with IBM Recommended Service Updates

This section describes the process of moving quarterly maintenance from the mainframe zEnterprise to the DASD repository. The purpose of doing this is to have the latest maintenance running on the zEnterprise machine available to the distributed lab environment as soon as possible. This allows each development team to request the maintenance as needed.

Server Upgrade Process for the Operating Systems

When a new RSU level is available from the IT team, verification on an IT technical support server will maintain a high level of software service. While this server is normally used for testing system utility software and pre-production testing, it makes an excellent staging area for RSU deployment and new server cloning. Cloning of new servers is discussed in detail in Chapter 12.

This procedure upgrades the software of multiple supported operating systems. The steps are as follow:

1. Transfer the new RSU volumes from the mainframe zEnterprise to the DASD repository.

2. Transfer the new RSU volumes from the DASD repository server to the IT technical support server.

3. Make the new RSU volumes available to the first guest system on the dedicated IT server.

4. IPL z/OS system 1 and verify all RSU volumes are available.

5. Run the new catalog jobs.

6. Update the BPXPRM members to reference the OMVS root of the new RSU.

7. Update the device map and z/VM directory to use the new RSU DASD volumes.

8. Verify that the new operating system volumes can IPL, are correct, and the UNIX system services file systems mount properly.

9. Perform a full backup of the IT technical support server.

This process assumes that a shared master catalog and user catalog is in place, thereby eliminating the need to catalog data sets across each z/OS system residing on a server.

Step 1: Transfer the new RSU volumes from the mainframe zEnterprise to the DASD repository

Verify that the volumes are available on the zEnterprise system, and then:

- Submit the job stream on the mainframe zEnterprise system to start the IBM utility used to transfer the DASD volume image to the distributed server.

  - Note: The job could fail if the transfer is not started from the DASD repository within 10 minutes.

- Log on to the DASD repository to transfer the volume.

  - Log on as the Linux userid created for repository logons. For example: dasdrep

  - Use a terminal window to run the IBM utility to load the volumes. This will need to be performed once for each volume transferred. For example:

    ```
    hckd2ckd zoshost /home/dasdrep/Downloads/MVSDxx-RSUxxxx -v MVSDxx
    ```

- Verify that the files transferred successfully by using the IBM utility *alcckd*. It can scan the entire file to verify integrity. For example:

  ```
  alcckd /home/dasdrep/Downloads/MVSDxx-RSUxxxx -rs
  ```

- Move the RSU DASD files from /home/dasdrep/Downloads to the directory where the z/OS operating system volumes reside. For example: /nfs/MFZOS

The volumes are available for transfer to any of the distributed servers to stage for implementation.

Step 2: Transfer the new RSU volumes from the DASD repository server to the dedicated IT technical support deployment server

There are a several options for transferring volumes:

- The network share to NFS (mapped as /z/nfs/MFZOS)

- A graphical FTP application

- Command line FTP

The process shown will utilize FTP. From the IT technical support server:

- Open a terminal window

- Perform this process:

```
cd /z/zos  --> this is the server directory for the volumes

ftp distributedz-nfs --> this is the name of the DASD repository server

dasdrep / password --> DASD repository userid/password

cd /nfs/MFZOS --> this is the directory for the DASD repository

bin       --> set file transfer mode to binary

get MVSBxx-RSUxxxx --> this the name of your linux file for the release 11 RSU
get MVSCxx-RSUxxxx --> this the name of your linux file for the release 12 RSU
get MVSDxx-RSUxxxx --> this the name of your linux file for the release 13 RSU

bye       --> exit FTP
```

Step 3: Make the new RSU volumes available to the first guest system on the IT server

The following process will make the volumes available to the z/OS systems:

- Check the current volumes and corresponding unit addresses in the z/VM User Directory. For example:

  - Enter command: x user direct a

  - Find user ZPRXY

  - The following volumes should exist:

    ```
    MDISK 0AA1 3390 0000 END MVSCR1 R      ALL ALL ALL
    MDISK 0AA4 3390 0000 END MVSBR1 R      ALL ALL ALL
    MDISK 0AA5 3390 0000 END MVSDR1 R      ALL ALL ALL
    ```

  - F3 --> Exit the directory

- Add the new RSUxxxx volumes to the z1090 device map.

  - Note: These definitions will be temporary to make the new volumes available for the RSU catalog jobs.

    ```
    device 0AAD 3390 3390 /z/zos/MVSBR2-RSUxxxx
    device 0AAE 3390 3390 /z/zos/MVSCR2-RSUxxxx
    device 0AAF 3390 3390 /z/zos/MVSDR2-RSUxxxx
    ```

  - AAD, AAE, AAF are the unit addresses for the volumes MVSBR2/CR2/DR2.

- awsckmap devmapname <-- run the check map program to verify no device map errors.

- Shutdown z/VM.
- Restart the IBM z1090 emulator.
- Start the z/VM system.
- Add the volumes to the z/VM directory:
  - Log on to MAINT (IBM z/VM user for maintaining the z/VM user directory).
  - Issue the following command to edit the z/VM user directory:
    - x user direct a
    - Under user ZPRXY

■ **Note 1**   This user is set up so that links can be created to each volume, as opposed to attaching them to each system (as explained in Chapter 5).

■ **Note 2**   These entries are temporary to make the new volumes available for cataloging the data sets jobs. A switch of these volumes for starting the system occurs later in the process.

The following statements are based on the volumes and unit addresses shown earlier in this section:

Existing statements:
```
MDISK OAA1 3390 0000 END MVSCR1 R       ALL ALL ALL
MDISK OAA4 3390 0000 END MVSBR1 R       ALL ALL ALL
MDISK OAA5 3390 0000 END MVSDR1 R       ALL ALL ALL
```

New statements:
```
MDISK OAAD 3390 0000 END MVSBR2 R       ALL ALL ALL
MDISK OAAE 3390 0000 END MVSCR2 R       ALL ALL ALL
MDISK OAAF 3390 0000 END MVSDR2 R       ALL ALL ALL
```

Find the first z/OS system and add these lines:

```
LINK ZPRXY OAAD AAD   R
LINK ZPRXY OAAE AAE   R
LINK ZPRXY OAAF AAF   R
```

- Enter the following commands:
  - save --> save the changes
  - F3 --> exit the directory
  - directxa --> apply the directory changes
  - logoff --> sign off the MAINT user

Step 4: IPL z/OS system 1 and verify all RSU volumes are available

Verify that all volumes are online and available to z/OS. Based on the examples, the operating system volumes and unit addresses are:

```
MVSCR1 unit address is 0AA1
MVSBR1 unit address is 0AA4
MVSDR1 unit address is 0AA5
MVSBR2 unit address is 0AAD    New RSU
MVSCR2 unit address is 0AAE    New RSU
MVSDR2 unit address is 0AAF    New RSU
```

For example, use the following command from an MVS console:

```
D U,,,AA1,1
```

The result of the command should be:

```
0AA1 3390 A          MVSCR1      PRIV/RSDNT
```

This command is for singular verification of each unit address and operating system volume serial.

A variation of the command can sequentially list a specific number of unit addresses. This is convenient if the unit addresses for the operating systems are close within a range. The list will need reviewed to find the operating system volume serials. The following command will work based on the examples in the previous section:

```
D U,,,AA1,15
```

The result of the command could be:

```
0AA1 3390 0          MVSCR1      PRIV/RSDNT
0AA2 3390 A          MVIPL1      PRIV/RSDNT
0AA3 3390 0          F-NRD          /RSDNT
0AA4 3390 S          MVSBR1      PRIV/RSDNT
0AA5 3390 0          MVSDR1      PRIV/RSDNT
0AA6 3390 0          WRK100       PUB/RSDNT
0AA7 3390 0          DMP100      PRIV/RSDNT
0AA8 3390 0          STG100      STRG/RSDNT
0AA9 3390 0          F-NRD          /RSDNT
0AAA 3390 0          F-NRD          /RSDNT
0AAB 3390 0          F-NRD          /RSDNT
0AAC 3390 0          F-NRD          /RSDNT
0AAD 3390 0          MVSBR2      PRIV/RSDNT
0AAE 3390 0          MVSCR2      PRIV/RSDNT
0AAF 3390 0          MVSDR2      PRIV/RSDNT
```

Step 5: Run the new catalog jobs

The next step catalogs the new data sets to the first z/OS system. Perform the cataloging prior to starting the system with the new volumes. If there is an attempt to start the system without the catalog steps, it will have failures because the USS z/FS VSAM data sets are not available.

The catalog jobs should be available from the IT technical support team that applied the maintenance and named the data sets. There should be one job for each new operating system RSU. For example:

- Run z/OS release 11 (B) RSUxxx catalog job

- Run z/OS release 12 (C) RSUxxx catalog job

- Run z/OS release 13 (D) RSUxxx catalog job

Chapter 8 contains detailed instructions for cataloging the operating system data sets.

Step 6: Update the BPXPRM members to reference the OMVS root of the new RSU

Update the BPXPRM members for each operating system.

- Manually edit each of the following members to update the OMVS root to the new RSUxxxx. This assumes a standard parameter library member naming standard. For example:

```
system.SHARED.PARMLIB (BPXPRMZB)
OMVS11.ZFS.ROOT.RSUxxxx

system.SHARED.PARMLIB (BPXPRMZC)
OMVS12.ZFS.ROOT.RSUxxxx

system.SHARED.PARMLIB (BPXPRMZD)
OMVS13.ZFS.ROOT.RSUxxxx
```

Step 7: Update the device map and z/VM directory to switch to using the new RSU DASD volumes

The following steps will start the first z/OS system with the new RSU volumes:

1. Shut down the first z/OS system.

2. Stage z/VM Changes:

```
Update z/VM directory:
Log on to MAINT
Enter command: x user direct a
```

- Change the volser of the normal IPL unit addresses as follows (based on the examples above). These changes are under the ZPRXY user in the user directory. For example:

```
MDISK 0AA1 3390 0000 END MVSCR2 R        ALL ALL ALL    <-- changed to MVSCR2
MDISK 0AA4 3390 0000 END MVSBR2 R        ALL ALL ALL    <-- changed to MVSBR2
MDISK 0AA5 3390 0000 END MVSDR2 R        ALL ALL ALL    <-- changed to MVSDR2

*DISK 0AAD 3390 0000 END MVSBR2 R        ALL ALL ALL    <-- comment out
*DISK 0AAE 3390 0000 END MVSCR2 R        ALL ALL ALL    <-- comment out
*DISK 0AAF 3390 0000 END MVSDR2 R        ALL ALL ALL    <-- comment out
```

- For system 1, comment out the following statements, because the new operating system volumes are now using the unit addresses of the previous operating system volumes. For example:

```
*INK ZPRXY 0AAD AAD R
*INK ZPRXY 0AAE AAE R
*INK ZPRXY 0AAE AAE R
```

  - Note: This process will maintain the same address for each operating system unit address. The advantage is that there are no documentation changes for starting a system. The operating system volumes use the same unit addresses as the previous volumes.

  - Note: The LINK statements that exist under the definition for each z/OS guest system do not need to be changed. They will still work because the unit addresses have not changed—just the volume serials on the MDISK statements under ZPRXY change. For example, the following links under a z/OS guest user for an operating system would still work:

```
LINK ZPRXY 0AA1 AA1 R
LINK ZPRXY 0AA4 AA4 R
LINK ZPRXY 0AA5 AA5 R
```

- Enter the following commands:

  a. save --> save the changes

  b. F3 --> exit the directory

  c. directxa --> apply the directory changes

  d. logoff --> sign off the MAINT user

3. Shut down z/VM.

4. Shut down z1090 emulator.

5. Update device statements in the emulator device map. Change the unit addresses to match the new RSUxxxx files. For example:

```
Change:
device 0AA1 3390 3390 /z/zos/MVSCR1-RSUxxxx - previous RSU
device 0AA4 3390 3390 /z/zos/MVSBR1-RSUxxxx - previous RSU
device 0AA5 3390 3390 /z/zos/MVSDR1-RSUxxxx - previous RSU


To:
device 0AA1 3390 3390 /z/zos/MVSCR2-RSUxxxx - new RSU
device 0AA4 3390 3390 /z/zos/MVSBR2-RSUxxxx - new RSU
device 0AA5 3390 3390 /z/zos/MVSDR2-RSUxxxx - new RSU


Remove (comment):
*device 0AAD 3390 3390 /z/zos/MVSBR2-RSUxxxx
*device 0AAE 3390 3390 /z/zos/MVSCR2-RSUxxxx
*device 0AAF 3390 3390 /z/zos/MVSDR2-RSUxxxx
```

6. awsckmap devmapname; run the check map program to verify no device map errors.

7. Start IBM z1090 emulator and z/VM.

Step 8: Verify that the new operating system volumes can IPL, are correct, and the UNIX System Services file systems mount

Start the first z/OS system using the operating system release 11 DASD volume. There should be no change in the IPL command string to start the system. Once the system starts, enter the following commands on the MVS console:

```
D IPLINFO
      IPL DEVICE: ORIGINAL(0AA4) CURRENT(0AA4) VOLUME(MVSBR2)

D OMVS,MF
      BPX0058I 15.05.47 DISPLAY OMVS        FRAME LAST
      OMVS    000E ACTIVE        OMVS=(ZB,01)
```

The following message will verify that all files mounted properly:

NO MOUNT OR MOVE FAILURES TO DISPLAY

Next, log on to TSO and start an ISPF session. Go to option 6 (Command) and enter *OMVS* to verify that this enters Unix System Services and then exit OMVS by pressing F2 and typing "quit".

While still in option 6, enter *ISH* to verify that this works to enter the ISHELL panel interface for Unix System Services. Once in ISHELL, choose *File_systems* from the menu, then select *1. Mount table...* The following is an example of a mount table:

```
Mount Table:
File system name
OMVSSYS.JAVA31xx.xxxxxx          Available
OMVSSYS.JAVA31xx.xxxxxx          Available
OMVSSYS.JAVA31xx.xxxxxx          Available
OMVSSYS.JAVA31xx.xxxxxx          Available
OMVSSYS.JAVA64xx.xxxxxx          Available
OMVSSYS.JAVA64xx.xxxxxx          Available
OMVSSYS.JAVA64xx.xxxxxx          Available
OMVSSYS.JAVA64xx.xxxxxx          Available
OMVSSYS.MINI.SYS                 Available
OMVS11.ZFS.ROOT.RSUxxxx          Available
```

Start the second z/OS system using the operating system release 12 DASD volume. There should be no change in the IPL command string to start the system from the previous release 12 command string. Once the system has started, enter the following commands on the MVS console:

```
D IPLINFO
      IPL DEVICE: ORIGINAL(0AA1) CURRENT(0AA1) VOLUME(MVSCR2)

D OMVS,MF
      BPX0058I 15.05.47 DISPLAY OMVS        FRAME LAST
      OMVS    000E ACTIVE        OMVS=(ZC,01)
```

The following message will verify that all files mounted properly:

NO MOUNT OR MOVE FAILURES TO DISPLAY

Next, log on to TSO and start an ISPF session. Go to option 6 (Command) and enter *OMVS* to verify that this enters Unix System Services and then exit OMVS by pressing F2 and typing "quit".

While still in option 6, enter *ISH* to verify that this works to enter the ISHELL panel interface for Unix System Services. Once in ISHELL, choose *File_systems* from the menu, then select *1. Mount table...*

The following is an example of a mount table:

```
Mount Table:
File system name
OMVSSYS.JAVA31xx.xxxxxx          Available
OMVSSYS.JAVA31xx.xxxxxx          Available
OMVSSYS.JAVA31xx.xxxxxx          Available
OMVSSYS.JAVA31xx.xxxxxx          Available
OMVSSYS.JAVA64xx.xxxxxx          Available
OMVSSYS.JAVA64xx.xxxxxx          Available
OMVSSYS.JAVA64xx.xxxxxx          Available
OMVSSYS.JAVA64xx.xxxxxx          Available
OMVSSYS.MINI.SYS                 Available
OMVS12.ZFS.ROOT.RSUxxxx          Available
```

Start the third z/OS system using the operating system release 13 DASD volume. There should be no change in the IPL command string to start the system. Once the system starts, enter the following commands on the MVS console:

```
D IPLINFO
    IPL DEVICE: ORIGINAL(0AA5) CURRENT(0AA5) VOLUME(MVSDR2)

D OMVS,MF
    BPX0058I 15.05.47 DISPLAY OMVS          FRAME LAST
    OMVS      000E ACTIVE              OMVS=(ZD,01)
```

The following message will verify that all files mounted properly:

NO MOUNT OR MOVE FAILURES TO DISPLAY

Next, log on to TSO and start an ISPF session. Go to option 6 (Command) and enter *OMVS* to verify that this enters Unix System Services and then exit OMVS by pressing F2 and typing "quit".

While still in option 6, enter *ISH* to verify that this works to enter the ISHELL panel interface for Unix System Services. Once in ISHELL, choose *File_systems* from the menu, then select *1. Mount table...*

The following is an example of a mount table:

```
Mount Table:
File system name
OMVSSYS.JAVA31xx.xxxxxx          Available
OMVSSYS.JAVA31xx.xxxxxx          Available
OMVSSYS.JAVA31xx.xxxxxx          Available
OMVSSYS.JAVA31xx.xxxxxx          Available
OMVSSYS.JAVA64xx.xxxxxx          Available
OMVSSYS.JAVA64xx.xxxxxx          Available
OMVSSYS.JAVA64xx.xxxxxx          Available
OMVSSYS.JAVA64xx.xxxxxx          Available
OMVSSYS.MINI.SYS                 Available
OMVS13.ZFS.ROOT.RSUxxxx          Available
```

Step 9: Perform a full backup of the IT technical support server:

At this point, the only RSU volumes needed on the IT technical support server directory are the volumes that represent the current RSU level for the operating system versions. Delete all operating system volumes for the previous RSU levels before performing the backup.

A full backup of the server at this time will preserve the changes made to facilitate the new operating system software levels.

Operating System Upgrade Is Complete

The operating system upgrade is complete, and a backup of the IT technical support server is complete. The new operating systems RSUs are now ready for deployment to existing development team servers or to a new server.

Maintain Subsystems with IBM Recommended Service Updates

Following a process similar to updating the z/OS operating systems is a useful way of moving a full-volume subsystem DASD to a server from the DASD repository. This section will concentrate on an alternative method for updating and making newer versions of subsystems available.

While moving full volumes would seem an easy solution, the storage required can become enormous. With each RSU, there is a requirement to copy a new volume to the server.

A number of issues can be present with the subsystems:

1. The IT technical team process on the mainframe zEnterprise may maintain each subsystem with SMS managed volumes. This will cause the data sets for the subsystem to move across a pool of volumes with each update. And this means that all volumes associated with each subsystem will require transfer to the server and the data sets recataloged, based on the new location of each data set.

2. With SMS managed volumes, clutter will result on the server if a move is necessary for the pool of SMS managed volumes. This is true for all subsystems.

3. If regular backups are part of the requirements of a server, then the increase in storage usage on the z1090 server will cause longer times for backups. This happens regardless of whether there are many volumes or just one large volume.

4. Server hard drive capacity is an issue with the large amounts of data that are stored. A full accounting of the use case needs to be reconciled to determine space requirements if subsystems are part of the equation for server storage.

An alternative method for copying full volumes is to create a link to the DASD repository and have the required executables for each subsystem transferred to the server. This will allow direct copying from the DASD repository to a z/OS system on the distributed server. It eliminates the effort of creating new files on the server each time a volume with a new service level is available.

This procedure requires an NFS share to the appropriate file system volume on the DASD repository. The next steps are:

1. Update the device map to point to the new files.

2. Start the emulator and z/VM.

If it is possible to keep the volume serials the same, then, once a z/OS system starts, the requisite data sets are available for movement to a DASD volume on the z/OS system.

■ **Note**   The data sets will need to be referenced by volume serial or manually cataloged for access and movement.

Summary

This chapter details methodologies for updating the distributed server with new service levels. The methods presented are for both operating systems and subsystems. They detail the ease of moving full volumes for the operating system upgrades while also offering an alternative method for copying data sets directly to the z/OS system for the subsystem upgrades.

The next chapter presents methods to prepare for recovery of the distributed lab environment. The methodology is valid whether there is only one server or a large distributed lab.

Case Studies
Case 1: Single Laptop System for Mainframe Developer

A developer working remotely has a laptop running multiple versions of z/OS. The environment is set up with a single z/OS running natively (no z/VM). At the outset, the developer did not require any subsystems or other products. However, the need for a current version of an infrastructure product developed by the company has prompted a call to the IT technical support staff.

The need for the product is a one-time request, and there is no expectation on the part of the developer that additional versions or service levels will be needed.

The current infrastructure product volumes are available on the DASD repository. The developer prefers to learn the process for updating and adding DASD volumes to the laptop. Detailed instructions are sent to the developer similar to the "Server Upgrade Process for the Operating Systems" discussed earlier in the chapter. The developer transfers a DASD volume to the laptop and uses it for testing with the product. This requires updates to the laptop environment. The developer:

- Uses FTP to transfer the DASD volume from the repository to the laptop on an existing directory that has the Linux files for the z/OS user volumes.

- Adds a device statement to the z1090 device map to define the new DASD file to the emulator.

- Runs the IBM utility *awsckmap* on the updated device map to verify there are no errors.

- Starts the IBM z1090 emulator.

- When the z/OS system starts, it will have the new volume available.

  - The data sets will need to be referenced by volume serial or manually cataloged for access and movement.

Once the z/OS system starts, the developer can use the new infrastructure product data sets for testing and/or starting a region.

Conclusion

When additional DASD volumes are required for a system, this process will provide additional resources without disrupting the existing system setup. Adding new volumes to an existing laptop or server requires very little effort.

This use case assumes that the I/O configuration definition (IODF) has available DASD unit addresses when adding the volume to z/OS.

Case 2: Server Class Machine Hosting Multiple Mainframe Systems for Software QA Testing

The QA team has been tasked with testing on multiple z/OS operating systems simultaneously. After developing excellent comprehensive testing processes including many automated tests, the QA team now requires regular operating system updates.

The IT technical support team maintains a distributed server with multiple z/OS systems in a shared environment. While this server is for testing internally developed software, it has other uses, such as creating and maintaining base environments. For example:

- Deployment of new distributed servers running mainframe environments

- Deployment of updates to repurpose existing servers

- Testing and verification of each operating system RSU with current system utility and infrastructure products

- Validation of newly developed IT driven code before introduction into the production environment

As such, the operating systems and infrastructure products are at the highest release and service levels available. The technical support staff for the zEnterprise server updates the service levels using IBM RSUs on a quarterly basis.

The QA team requests that the IT staff schedule regular operating system updates. Both parties agree that quarterly updates are sufficient. The technical support staff moves the operating system RSUs to the QA server using the process described in the "Server Upgrade Process for the Operating Systems" section of this chapter.

Conclusion

Maintaining a base server is important when a large distributed environment is used. A base server can serve multiple purposes:

- Deployment of new z1090 environments with the highest level of available software

- Deployment to existing z1090 servers that are being repurposed with the highest level of available software

- Verification of RSUs for each operating system when available from the IT staff

- Verification of each infrastructure product version, release, and service level as it becomes available

The maintenance and testing of each version, release, and service level of software is advantageous when there is a request for an upgrade to software. Knowledge of testing with the latest operating systems and infrastructure products on the base server eases the apprehensions of distributed server system owners when requesting updated software levels.

CHAPTER 11

Preparing for Recovery

The creation of a virtualized mainframe environment requires a significant investment in both capital and time. Once the environment is created, stability is extremely important. The environment must be protected from outages, but if a failure is incurred, there must be a mechanism to recover quickly.

Three techniques for recovering from either system- or user-related failures will be discussed in this chapter. These approaches to recovery provide a wide range of services and can be used individually or combination, based upon the needs of the use case and users.

The first technique is a full backup/restore recovery mechanism. There are several methods that can be employed to provide a full backup/restore process, and they can be used in combination or as solo solutions.

The use of backup volumes that are made available to the users of the virtual systems is a second recovery technique. These volumes are used to provide checkpoints of critical changes in the system between full-environment backups. They are a means of restoring valuable data if there is a general failure to the system.

The third technique is an emergency recovery system that can be started to fix configuration problems on a virtual system that is unable to start. With this method, an emergency system is built that can be started using isolated DASD volumes that will have access to the configuration volumes for a virtual system that will not IPL.

It is increasingly critical that virtualized mainframe environments remain stable. As more teams are added to these environments, every outage, no matter how short or how minor, has a significant impact on productivity. This dependence increases the importance of not only providing stability but also of having a means to recover if there is an outage of any kind.

Backup/Restore Process

One of the most important processes in any data center is the means to restore all or part of a production environment in the event of a failure. IT departments invest heavily in both time and hardware to create processes to protect important data. As the virtualized mainframe environments become more vital to the success of projects, backup and restore processes grow even more critical.

The nature of virtualized environments provides many possibilities for backup and recovery processes. The layered approach provided by the z1090 vendor and the tools available to distributed platforms allow for several variations in how backup and recovery processes can be devised.

One method is to perform a full backup of the Linux host. The backup can be scheduled at regular intervals, and if there is a subsequent system problem, the last backup can be used to restore the system. This is a simple approach and many applications are that can be used to perform this type of backup and restore process.

A second method focuses on the virtual systems. In this method, the emphasis is on the DASD files and the device map that comprise the virtual environment. A systematic backup of the device map and DASD files can be performed on a regular schedule. If there is a problem with one of the DASD files, or the device map, the file can be restored from the last backup.

The last consideration in the backup/restore process is the location of the files created by the backup and used for the restoration of a system. Creating the backup provides no value if it is not available for use when a system needs to be restored. It is important that a process and environment be created to protect and make available the data created during the backup process.

Full Backup of the Linux Host

A simple backup solution to implement is the full backup of the Linux host. Many applications are available to perform this task. The Linux operating system provides utilities that can be used to perform full-system backups. If the tools provided by Linux are inadequate, several independent vendors also provide applications that may provide the functionality required.

If there are other Linux host machines in the corporate data center, there may already be a process in place to perform full backups. In this case, it may be a simple task to add this new host to the list of machines already managed by the IT department.

A major advantage of this backup method is that it provides a full copy of the environment. If anything happens and the system cannot be started, the Linux host, emulator, DASD files, device maps and all the customization that has been completed are available for immediate restore. This may reduce the time needed to get the virtualized environment operational again.

Another advantage to this method is that it captures any customizations to the operating system and virtual environment, and these are available during the recovery process. For example, one of the steps completed during the creation of the virtualized mainframe environment is to apply updates to the Linux host and install any additional software, including updates to the emulator and the Linux host. With a full Linux backup, all of these changes are included if the system requires restoration.

There are, however, several disadvantages to full backups. The first disadvantage is the significant amount of time it takes to complete such a backup because it contains the entire environment. To ensure continuity of the virtual systems, the emulator and the virtual systems it is operating should be shut down during the backup, resulting in users of the virtual environment not having access during the lengthy backup process.

Another disadvantage of a full-system backup is that if the video or other hardware components are different on the system being used for the restore, the Linux recovery may not start because the device drivers will not be compatible. This may require the Linux host to be restored to an identical hardware configuration.

Yet another disadvantage of the full-system backup may be the configuration of the hard drives. If the hard drive configuration of the restoration environment is different, the restore process may not be able to place the Linux file systems to the proper locations. If a hardware failure occurs and there is not a similar machine available, the restoration may fail.

Depending on the organization's requirements, the full backup solution may be sufficient. However, for more complex and user-intensive environments, a virtual system backup/recovery may be more viable.

Virtual System Backup/Recovery

In many instances, system uptime is vital to the success of a project associated with the virtual environment. In such cases, while having a reliable means to recover from a failure is important, it is also important that the environment be available at all times. If system uptime is critical, the backup process adopted must minimize downtime required.

A backup process that focuses on the volatile data of the virtual systems is one method to minimize the system downtime. The virtual system backup/recovery method concentrates on backing up only the virtualized systems, rather than the full Linux host environment. This reduction in data to be managed by the backup process reduces the time that the virtual environment must be stopped.

While the focus of this backup/recovery method is to reduce the time the virtual environment is stopped to perform the backup, the virtual systems and emulator should be shutdown while the backup is being performed to ensure the integrity of the virtual systems. This avoids corruption of data by eliminating the possibility that the virtual systems are updating the DASD files as they are being processed.

There are two variations of the virtual system backup method. The first creates a backup of all the files that comprise the virtual systems. This includes all of the DASD files and the device map. While this method will provide a usable environment when restored, a significant amount of time is spent backing up files that have not changed. For example, if the operating system volumes are attached as read-only, then no updates are possible. There are also volumes that contain volatile data, but that data may not be needed if the system is restored. Some volumes that may fall into this category are the page and spool volumes.

To reduce the time a system is down during the backup process, a second variation is to back up only the files that have useful, volatile data. A process that selectively backs up files can become complex very quickly. Time and careful planning are critical to ensure that all of the important files are included and that any files that are not part of the backup process are available from some other location for restoration if needed.

The best approach for implementing a virtual system backup is to perform the backup and restorations programmatically. Depending on the skill of the programmers involved, there are many ways that this can be accomplished. The approach used in the rest of this section is simple Linux scripting, because this is a straightforward language and easily learned by someone who has little programming experience. Our example of designing a virtual system backup makes the following assumptions:

- All DASD files not backed up are available on a NAS device.
- The following volumes will not be backed up:
    - z/OS operating system volumes (read only packs)
    - z/OS shared product packs (read only packs)
    - z/OS paging volumes
        - An initial backup of these DASD files will be stored on the NAS device with the other read only packs required for a full system restore.
    - z/OS spool volumes
        - An initial backup of these DASD files will be stored on the NAS device with the other read only packs required for a full system restore.
        - All spool files will be lost during a restore.
- A local disk on the server is available to hold the backup files.
    - The file system will be mounted as /backup
- All files will be compressed except for the device map.
- All files will be backed up individually.
- All files will be stored in the same relative directory structure as they are on the Linux host.
    - IE; /zDATA/Common/STG001 ➤ /backup/zDATA/Common/STG000.gz
- After the initial backup is complete, it will be copied to secondary storage.

The first step in the virtual system backup process is to determine what files will be part of the backup and what files will be ignored. As noted, the OS volumes, shared product packs, paging volumes, and spool volumes will be ignored. All other DASD files will be part of the backup process.

The second step is to locate a file system that will hold the backup. In the example that is being used, this will be the /backup file system on the local Linux host.

Once the list of files has been created and the location for the backup has been determined, the third step is to create the scripts. For each file that is part of the backup, there will be two lines of code created. One of the lines is an echo command. This command sends the text enclosed in quotes to the output device—in this case, the monitor.

In this example, the text to be sent to the monitor is the command that is about to be executed. The next line is the actual command to create the backup of the file by compressing the file into a specific location. An example of these two lines of code is the following:

```
echo "gzip -c /zDATA/Common/STG001 > /backup/zDATA/Common/STG001.gz"
gzip -c /zDATA/Common/STG001 > /backup/zDATA/Common/STG001.gz
```

The echo command sends output to the screen illustrating what file is currently being processed, *STG001*. The second command uses the *gzip* utility to compress the file listed first, *STG001*, to the location and file name listed second, *STG001.gz*. To keep this process straightforward, this set of commands can be duplicated for every file that needs to be processed. This allows the programmer to keep the scripting simple.

For a large environment, however, this script could grow very quickly and become difficult to maintain, leading to missing critical files in the backup. One solution to keeping script maintenance simple is to break different components into different scripts. For example, there could be different scripts for:

- z/VM DASD files
- z/OS common DASD files
- z/OS system dependent DASD files
- User DASD files

If the backup is broken out to individual scripts, it would be prudent to create a controlling script to execute each individual script. This script would be executed by the user to start the backup process. It would, in turn, execute all the other scripts needed to complete the backup. This would provide an overview of the entire backup process, but keep the individual components easier to manage. Breaking the scripts out into smaller segments enables the programmer to quickly validate that all of the important data is included in the backup.

Location of Backup Files

A backup is an important step in creating a process to recover an environment in case of catastrophic failure. However, a backup is useless if it is also corrupted or destroyed by the same event that caused the environment to fail. For this reason, it may be desirable to create multiple copies of the backup.

One possible mechanism to provide redundancy is to store the backup images on more than one device that is accessible to a recovery effort. The image may be located on two or more network storage locations. While this protects against a hardware failure on one device, it does not protect against failures caused by a natural disaster, like a flood, or a more localized event, such as a cooling system failure or a fire. To protect against these possibilities, it may be sensible to store copies of the backups in a different physical location. This could be a network storage location in another data center, an external device that is stored in a secure vault, or even storage provided by a cloud vendor. Any of these solutions would protect against localized disasters and provide the ability to quickly recover a system.

Conclusion

Creating backup and restore processes are an important aspect of protecting the integrity of the virtualized environments. However, because of the time required to complete the backups of the systems, it is not practical to execute backups on a frequent basis. To help protect significant system changes, modifications, or progress on an important project, it may be prudent to create a mechanism that allows the system users to protect data between scheduled backups.

Backup Volumes

While the backup and restore process is important to the reliability of a system, there may be times when critical changes are made between backup cycles. Because a full-system outage is required during backups, they may be scheduled for only once a week, or even once a month. Because of the increased usage of these environments and the importance of a quick recovery in case of an error, it is vital to be able to restore critical data if an error occurs between backup cycles. Creating backup volumes that enable users to back up their own data between normal backup cycles should be considered.

The most important aspect of the backup volumes is that they not be located on the same physical hardware as the operational DASD files used by the virtual systems. This way, the data stored on the backup volumes is protected from any hardware or software failure that may occur on the Linux machine hosting the virtualized mainframe environment. For example, if the DASD files used by the virtual systems are located on the local Linux host, then the backup volumes could be located on a NAS or SAN. This provides access to the critical data in case of a hardware failure on the Linux machine hosting the virtual environment.

It is also crucial that the external storage have some type of recoverability, such as using RAID levels to protect against hardware failures. Figure 11-1 shows an example of how this scenario might be configured.

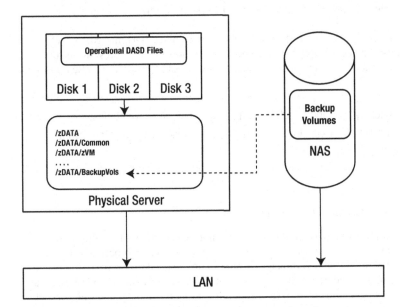

Figure 11-1. *Backup volumes stored on a NAS device*

In Figure 11-1, the operational DASD volumes are located on the local hard drives. To allow the users to back up critical data as needed, several backup volumes are created on a NAS device and mounted on the Linux host at the location */zDATA/BackupVols*. This configuration protects critical user data in the case of a catastrophic failure on the physical server hosting the virtualized mainframe environment. It allows the users to perform restores of critical data if there is a user error that corrupts data. For example, if some changes are made to a database on volumes stored on the physical server and it is corrupted, then the data on the backup volumes could be used to restore the database without requiring a full-system restore.

The backup process used is either configured by the users of the virtual systems or the IT team. There are utilities that can mirror critical volumes, or users can simply copy data over to the volumes as needed. The virtual systems are not impacted by the fact that these volumes are remote.

■ **Note**   An important consideration when determining how backup volumes will be used is the access rates to these volumes. Depending on the device type and how the devices are connected to the system, the access times may be significantly slower than locally attached volumes. Care should be taken in how the backup volumes are used, for improper use may introduce significant latency to the system.

Emergency Recovery System

Another important tool that can be created using the emulator is an emergency recovery (ER) system. When making changes to system parameters, it is possible to create a situation in which the operating system no longer starts. Although the vendor provides a tool that will allow extraction of specific data-set members, this utility may not provide the functionality needed to restore a system to a working state unless the exact cause of the error is known.

A restore of the full environment from a backup is an option, but this takes time and any work that was completed since the last backup would be lost. If the problem is that a few parameters need to be changed to get the virtual systems back into working order, then an easier way to recover the failed virtual system would be through use of an emergency recovery system.

Some virtualized mainframe environments may contain only first-level systems while others may run a z/VM host operating multiple guest systems. The next two sections provide an overview of how to create ER systems to accommodate both of these configurations. For a z/VM with guest systems, both types of ER systems may be required.

■ **Note**   To protect data integrity, the production system and the ER system should never be active at the same time. Because both environments are running in isolated emulator instances, there is no facility in place to prevent simultaneous updates to data, which can cause data corruption.

ER System for a First-Level Operating System

The first step in creating an ER system that can be used to attempt repairs on a first-level system is to create a new Linux userid on the host system. This ID will be used to build and control a virtual system that is separate from the production environment. To reduce confusion, the same Linux userid should not be used to control both the production environment and the ER environment. Since only one environment can be active at a time, it is technically possible to control both environments from a single Linux userid. However, this may lead to invalid and unintended updates to the production systems. For clarity, both environments should be as isolated as possible.

After the userid has been created, the next step is to build the virtual ER system. However, before it can be built, the OS required for the ER system needs to be determined. For example, if the first-level system that is to be repaired is a z/OS system, then the ER system must also be a z/OS system.

Once the correct operating system has been determined, the DASD files to start this operating system must be copied from a vendor-supplied medium. The files are copied to the file system on the Linux host that has been created for the ER DASD files. The device map is then created to start a virtual system using these supplied files.

The last step in creating the ER environment is updating the device map for the ER system. The device map is updated to allow ER system access to the production DASD files that may need data repaired. These updates would add to the *awsckd* stanza any volumes that hold configuration data that, if corrupted, would prevent the production system from starting. It is critical that the device map be properly updated to reflect the correct list of DASD volumes to which the ER system requires access. The ER system will only have access to DASD volumes that are specified in the device map.

Figure 11-2 is an example of a first-level ER system. In this example, the production operating system is z/VM. To access the volumes for the production system, the ER system must also be running a z/VM operating system. In this case, all of the configuration data that may cause the production system to fail is located on a DASD volume labeled *CNFG10*. This DASD volume is shared between both systems so that the production system can use the DASD volume when it is running, but if something is corrupted, the ER system also has access to attempt to resolve the problem.

Linux Host

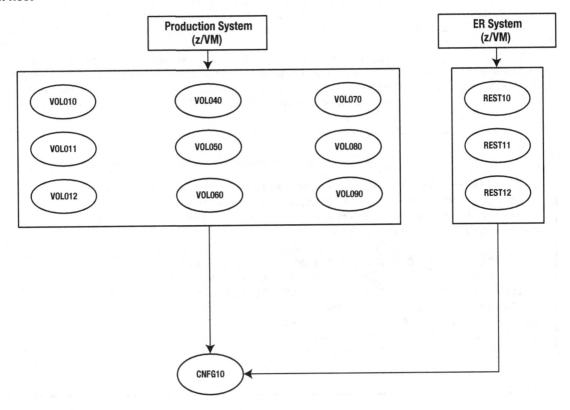

Figure 11-2. *First-level emergency recovery system*

ER System for a z/OS Guest Operating under z/VM

In many virtualized mainframe environments, the first-level system runs a z/VM OS and hosts other operating systems, such as z/OS and z/VSE. This provides users the ability to test with multiple systems and maximize the number of CPUs licensed from the vendor. In an environment like this, it is helpful to have an ER system that is also a guest of the z/VM host.

■ **Note** While this section is focused on building a z/OS ER system for a z/OS guest of a z/VM system, the principles outlined could be used to create an ER system for z/VM and z/VSE guests running as z/VM guest systems.

One reason to create the ER system as a guest is that it does not require a separate Linux userid or an additional device map. This eliminates the need to maintain multiple virtual environments on the same Linux host. A second reason is that it provides more flexibility by using z/VM to dynamically attach corrupted volumes to the ER system for repairs. In first-level environments, access to devices is limited to what is in the device map. That restriction is also in place for the z/VM guest systems. However, since the DASD device is defined to the production system, it is already in the device map. This allows the user to dynamically attach any device to the ER system if the *MDISK* definitions are constructed properly.

The first step in creating the ER guest system is to obtain the DASD files for a base z/OS system from the vendor. These DASD files must be copied to an appropriate location on the Linux host and then added to the production system device map. This will allow the z/VM system to access the files and manage them for the ER z/OS guest system that will be built.

After the device map has been updated, the next step is to start the z/VM host and create a userid for the ER system in the z/VM user directory. Since this system will only be used occasionally to repair damaged configurations for the production systems, the definitions can be kept simple. There should be no need to spend time configuring the system for networking or making any other modifications that are required for the production environment. Logging in with a connection through the z/VM host will allow the user to update and fix problems on the DASD. Figure 11-3 provides statements that might be used in the user directory definitions for the ER system.

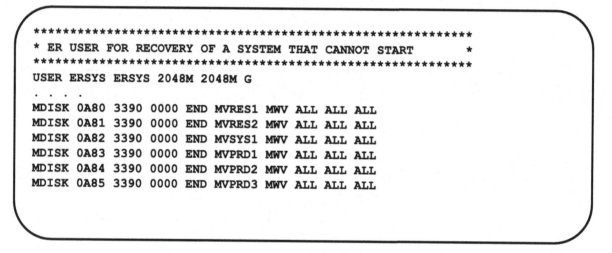

```
******************************************************************
* ER USER FOR RECOVERY OF A SYSTEM THAT CANNOT START            *
******************************************************************
USER ERSYS ERSYS 2048M 2048M G
. . . .
MDISK 0A80 3390 0000 END MVRES1 MWV ALL ALL ALL
MDISK 0A81 3390 0000 END MVRES2 MWV ALL ALL ALL
MDISK 0A82 3390 0000 END MVSYS1 MWV ALL ALL ALL
MDISK 0A83 3390 0000 END MVPRD1 MWV ALL ALL ALL
MDISK 0A84 3390 0000 END MVPRD2 MWV ALL ALL ALL
MDISK 0A85 3390 0000 END MVPRD3 MWV ALL ALL ALL
```

Figure 11-3. Sample user directory definition for the emergency restore system

The user directory statements in Figure 11-3 create the base definition for the ER system, but they do not set up access to the configuration volumes for the production z/OS guest systems. To provide this access, the z/VM LINK statement can be inserted into the user definition for the configuration volumes. Figure 11-4 shows an excerpt from the ZPRXY userid that defines the volumes and the sample *LINK* that could be used to connect the volumes to the ER system.

```
*****************************************************************
* PROXY USER FOR SHARING DATA BETWEEN Z/OS GUEST SYSTEMS     *
*****************************************************************
USER ZPRXY NOLOG 512M 512M G
. . . .
MDISK 0A90 3390 0000 END MVIPL1 MWV ALL ALL ALL
MDISK 0A91 3390 0000 END MVSHR1 MWV ALL ALL ALL
. . . .
*****************************************************************
* ER USER FOR RECOVERY OF A SYSTEM THAT CANNOT START        *
*****************************************************************
USER ERSYS ERSYS 2048M 2048M G
. . . .
LINK ZPRXY 0A90 0AB0 MW
LINK ZPRXY 0A91 0AB1 MW
```

Figure 11-4. *Sample z/VM Link statement to link volumes from the proxy user to the ER system*

The LINK statements will attach the *MVIPL1* volume to the *ERSYS* user at address *AB0* and the *MVSHR1* volume at address *AB1*. When *ERSYS* is started, the volumes will automatically be attached and accessible for read/write access. If the volumes are not attached through statements in the user definition, they can be attached dynamically through use of the LINK command after the ERSYS user is logged onto the z/VM system. Both methods are viable solutions to provide the required access.

Figure 11-5 illustrates how to create a z/OS ER system to fix configuration problems on production z/OS guest systems. In this example, Production Systems 1, 2, and 3 all have several volumes that are only attached to themselves. Each system has its own unique configuration volume—*CNFG10*, *CNFG20*, and *CNFG30*, respectively. Each of these volumes is also attached to the ER system. This provides access to these critical configuration volumes in the event that a production system will not start.

z/VM Host

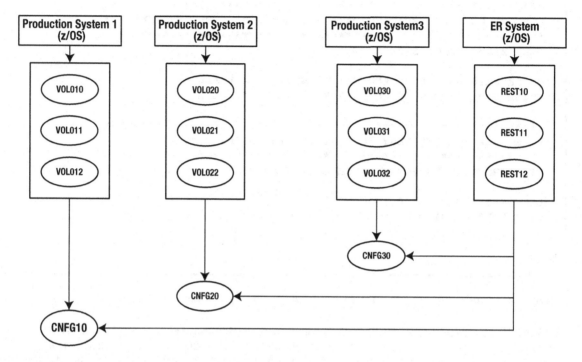

Figure 11-5. *z/OS emergency recovery system running as a z/VM guest*

Conclusion

A virtualized mainframe environment is a significant investment for a company in both capital and time. As such, it is vital that these environments be protected. As discussed in this chapter, there are many ways to recover from unexpected events. The possibilities range from simple backup and restore options to configurations that allow for dynamic recovery from failures. These procedures protect valuable data that is stored in these environments.

As more capabilities are added to these environments by the vendor, additional workloads will be moved to this cost-effective and mobile solution. This will drive the need to provide quick solutions to data and environment recovery requirements.

Case Studies

Case 1: Single Laptop System for Mainframe Developer

The developer now has a couple of months of new code in his environment. He is concerned that if there is a failure, his work will be lost. In order to reduce the downtime in case of a failure, he decides that it would be prudent to start creating backups.

After some analysis and investigation, he determines the best solution is to purchase an external hard drive and perform nightly backups of the entire environment. This includes the Linux operating system, additional utilities that have been installed and developed, the z1090 software, the device map, and the DASD files. When he stops working for the evening, he shuts down the virtual environment and starts the backup. It is completed by the next morning, when he is ready to start work.

To ensure that a minimal amount of work is lost if there is a failure with one backup, he keeps seven backup iterations. After the eighth copy is made, the oldest version is deleted from the external drive. The developer is also concerned about a local disaster destroying his environment. To minimize the loss of data, every Saturday he copies the latest backup to a cloud storage solution. He keeps the four most recent Friday night backups on the cloud storage.

If recovery is needed, a bootable flash drive has been created that will start a small Linux environment on the laptop so that he can connect to the external hard drive and restore the system. Network drivers have also been included so that the operating system started from the flash drive can, if needed, restore the full environment from the cloud storage.

Case 2: Server Class Machine Hosting Multiple Mainframe Systems for Software QA Testing

The QA team has spent a significant amount of time and effort building, maintaining, and updating their virtualized mainframe environment. The team is concerned that if there is a problem, hundreds of hours of effort will be lost. They decide that it is time to create a solution that will allow recovery of data if there is a failure of the environment.

One major constraint is that the virtualized systems are in use almost twenty-four hours a day because of the geographical range of users. Any solution that requires the system to be shut down will affect some members of the team. Another concern is that there are constant updates to the system parameters by various personnel. The changes that are made not only impact the operation of the virtual systems but also may cause startup failures.

To address the concerns, needs, and constraints, a three-step recovery solution is designed. The first step is a streamlined backup process that will be performed on a monthly basis that focuses on the device map and DASD files containing volatile data. The second step is the creation of backup volumes on external storage that will allow the users to store critical changes between scheduled full virtual system backups. These backup volumes are located on storage remote from the physical server hosting the virtual environment. This protects the backup volumes from corruption or loss in the case of a virtual environment failure. The last step is the construction of an emergency recovery (ER) system that can be started to correct any system changes that might cause a failure of a virtual system to start.

The team decides that the monthly backups should be taken on the first Monday of each month. To take the different team members needs into consideration, a rotating schedule of backup times is created so that each team is affected equally by the backup process: the first backup will be taken at midnight GMT; the second monthly backup will start at 8 A.M. GMT; and the third backup will start at 4 P.M. GMT.

The monthly backup will be completed using a set of scripts. Only the device map and volumes that contain volatile data will be included in the backup. The operating system, paging, spool, and checkpoint DASD volumes will not be included. The backup image will be created on an external hard drive. When the backup is completed, the virtual systems can be restarted so that the environment can be used. Once the environment has been restarted, the backup image is copied to a local NAS storage device for redundancy. The additional copy helps ensure that in case of failure there is a viable copy of the latest backup. After the local copy is completed, the backup is also duplicated to another NAS in a secondary data center, to protect against a local environmental disaster.

The monthly backup process minimizes the impact on the team members, but also provides a means to recover data in case of a failure. However, with this procedure taking place only once a month, there is the potential for vital information to be lost between the scheduled backups. To decrease the risk of losing data between scheduled backups, a set of backup volumes located on external storage will be added to the system for the team to use.

A local SAN is determined to be the best solution for the external backup DASD volumes. A file system is created on the SAN and mounted to the Linux host. The SAN array is configured with RAID level 1 to provide protection against a hardware failure. After the file system is mounted, the *alcckd* utility is used to create several 3390 model 9 sized DASD files. These files are added to the production environment device map.

The z/VM user directory is updated to reflect the new volumes and then a z/OS system is started to initialize the new volumes. Once the volumes have been initialized, they are added the ZPROXY z/VM userid with MDISK statements and then added to the z/OS guest systems userids using LINK statements.

After these steps have been completed, the QA team creates a set of z/OS jobs that will copy critical data to these new volumes on a daily basis. Each team member has the ability to run these tasks as needed, but they are also scheduled to run on a weekly basis to ensure that checkpoints are created.

The last step in the recovery process is to build an ER system. The team still has the vendor DASD files and the z/VM userid in place from the original system build. The only change that the team needs to make is to add the *LINK* statements to the ER system z/VM userid to allow quick access to the DASD volumes that hold critical z/OS guest system configuration data sets. Once these changes are made, the ER system is started and access to the required volumes is confirmed.

The QA team documents the new processes and creates a website to store this documentation so that all of the teams can use it. The documentation provides the information needed to perform the monthly backups, use the backup volumes, and start and then use the ER system. Documenting these processes ensures that every member of the team can perform any one of the tasks as needed.

CHAPTER 12

■ ■ ■

Deploying Virtualized Mainframe Environments

If several virtualized mainframe environments are to be created, multiple methods can be employed to complete the task.

- A complete virtualized mainframe environment can be constructed for new use cases, as needed.

- A base image consisting of a Linux host environment, the DASD files, and device map can be constructed and then cloned to identical hardware. The cloned system can then be updated to fit the needs of each individual use case.

- The installation of the Linux host can be tailored to the new hardware. Then a base environment consisting of the DASD files and device map can be deployed to the Linux host.

■ **Note**   For the rest of this chapter, the term *base image* refers to the collection of DASD files and the device map that reside on the medium to be used for deployment. The term *base environment* refers to the collection of DASD files and the device map that compose a basic virtualized mainframe environment that resides on the target Linux host. All discussion of deployment strategies assumes that the hardware, Linux host, and z1090 software have been configured for proper operation.

Constructing each environment individually may be an efficient option if the requirements for each are unique, or if only a few environments will be created. Designing and implementing a process to quickly deploy new environments is not a simple task and the benefits must outweigh the costs. For smaller or unique virtualized mainframe environments, building each configuration individually may be the best approach.

Cloning an entire virtualized mainframe from an existing image is another possible method for deployment. The clone image would include all of the software components of the environment, including the Linux host. This method provides a very quick method to create a new environment and begin the customization required by the use case. The disadvantage to this approach is the lack of flexibility in the design of the environment. Each deployment must be for a hardware configuration very similar to the initial environment.

Individual creation and cloning are simple to implement and can easily be handled by an experienced IT staff. However, neither of these approaches may be viable for a large and diverse collection of virtualized mainframe environments. A third approach is to build the Linux host environment for each server. This allows for hardware and Linux software customizations that may be required by unique use cases. After the Linux host has been created, the emulator is installed, and then a base environment composed of the device map and DASD files is deployed to the new Linux host.

The focus of this chapter is on the third approach. It combines the efficiency of using an existing base environment with the flexibility of using a different Linux host software and hardware configuration.

■ **Note** Once the new environment has been deployed, there are post-deployment activities that must be performed before the virtualized environment will function properly. While the process will vary in the individual environments, many of the most common steps will be highlighted after the deployment discussions.

Creating and Hosting the Deployment Image

The first step in creating a deployment strategy is to create the base image that will be used in the deployment. The base image is simply a copy of the files that will be deployed to any new virtualized mainframe environment that is constructed.

One method is to create one large file consisting of all the DASD files and the device map that compose the virtualized mainframe environment. While this method is simple to implement, it provides little flexibility in creating a deployment strategy. The end user will simply be provided a large file containing the base image. Any customization based upon the use case requirements will need to be performed manually after extracting the DASD files.

A more flexible method is to compress each DASD file and the device map individually. With each file compressed individually, scripts can be crafted to deliver and uncompress only the files that are required by a specific use case. This allows for customization of the base environment according to the needs of each end user. For example, some users may require fewer user volumes or different file system configurations. Controlling individual files during deployment with carefully crafted scripts provides considerable flexibility.

Once the base image has been built, it needs to be moved to a location that can be easily accessed for deploying the virtual mainframe system components. With the advancements in technology, there are several options for hosting the base image: on a NAS device, on a USB flash drive, or in the cloud.

Hosting the Deployment Image on a NAS Device

For a centrally located cluster of virtual mainframe environments, hosting the base image on a network storage device provides a simple and inexpensive solution. Most NAS devices can be configured for either FTP or NFS access, providing multiple methods for deployment. Figure 12-1 illustrates the use of a NAS device for deployment. The base image is hosted on the NAS device and is deployed to Linux host systems through the LAN. In this case, the same base environment is deployed to three separate Linux hosts.

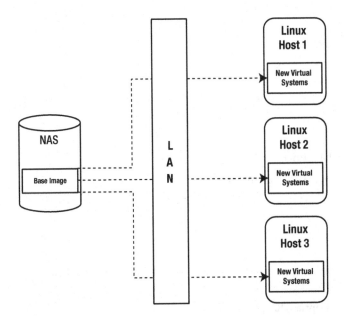

Figure 12-1. *Deployment process using a NAS device*

If a NAS device is the optimal choice for a deployment strategy, the first step in creating the solution is to obtain a suitable NAS device. The recommendation is to purchase a device that has enough capacity for growth and that can be configured for RAID 1. This will deliver a balance of speed and error protection for the critical data that will be stored.

There are many vendors for NAS devices. Each must be evaluated to determine the optimal device for this process. Some of the information to consider is:

- Price
  - What is the total cost of the device?
  - What is the cost per GB?
- Capacity
  - How much capacity is needed to store the base virtual image?
  - Will the base virtual environment grow, thereby increasing the size of the base image?
  - Is there a need to maintain more than one version of the virtual environment?
- Reliability
  - How reliable is the hardware manufactured by the vendor?
  - What is the quality of the support provided by the vendor?
  - What RAID levels are supported?
- User Interface
  - How is the device configured?
    - Web interface?
    - Vendor-supplied application?

- Maintenance
    - How is maintenance performed on the device?
        - Locally through a control panel on the device?
        - Web interface?
        - Vendor-provided application?
- Performance
    - What are the read/write times for the hard drives?
    - What are the network speeds? 10MB? 100MB? 1GB? 10GB?
- Form Factor
    - Is it a desktop model?
    - Is it rack mountable?

Once the appropriate NAS device is obtained, the next step in creating the deployment process is to configure the device. The configuration of the device consists of several steps:

1. The hard drives are configured with the appropriate RAID level.

    - RAID 1 is recommended for error recovery and speed
    - If RAID 1 is not an option, RAID 5 is also a viable solution

2. The security policy is created.

    - May be influenced by the corporate IT policies
    - The administrator password is strengthened
    - Userids are created for accessing the base image
    - The access methods are enabled and secured
        - FTP
        - NFS
        - Samba
    - The location of the base image files is secured and access permissions are granted

3. The base environment files are moved to the correct location on the NAS device to create the base image.

When creating the security polices for the NAS device, several issues require consideration. The first concerns the userids that will be created for access to the base image. Will there be one user defined for access that all new systems will use for deployment? Or will each new virtualized mainframe environment use a unique userid? While using one ID simplifies maintenance of the security policies, it makes auditing device access difficult. Creating unique userids for each Linux host requiring access to the base image provides a better solution when auditing is necessary.

A second consideration is the type of access that will be permitted. Configuring NFS access to the NAS device is the recommended approach, because it can greatly simplify any automation process that may be created. Automation using FTP can be difficult, and both FTP and Samba access may be restricted based upon IT policies.

One last consideration is access to the administrator userid. Use of this ID should be limited to personnel who are critical in the maintenance of the device. This may include only the local IT staff and the administrator of the full, virtualized mainframe environment.

The last step in setting up the NAS device is to copy the compressed files of the base image to the appropriate directory on the NAS share. Once this is completed, these files can be accessed from a new Linux host to create a new virtualized mainframe environment.

Hosting the Deployment Image on a USB Flash Drive

In many environments, the virtualized mainframe environments may not be centrally located. They may be individually positioned across multiple sites, or there may be clusters across a few data centers. Depending on the security and networking requirements for these locations, it may be advantageous to use flash drives for deployment. Figure 12-2 illustrates a deployment using a USB flash drive. In this example, the base image is located on a flash drive. When a new deployment is required, the USB flash drive is attached and the base environment is deployed to the new Linux host.

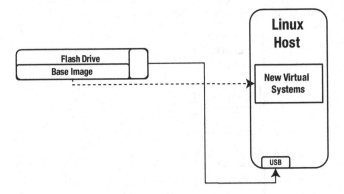

Figure 12-2. *Deployment process using a USB flash drive*

In order to determine if the use of a USB flash drive is part of the optimal deployment, analysis of the following questions is required:

- Does the Linux host have network connectivity?
    - If not, this may be the best solution
    - If so, then using a cloud deployment solution may be advised
- Can a USB flash drive be delivered quickly if needed?
- Does a USB flash drive have the capacity to hold all of the data for all of the DASD files and device map?

If the analysis of the configuration and available technology reveals that a USB flash drive is the optimal delivery solution for the virtual environment, then the USB drive needs to be obtained and formatted for use.

When the flash drive is formatted, there are two critical issues to factor into the process. The first is the type of file system that will be created on the flash drive. The file system must be usable by both the system that is creating the deployment image and the system that is going to be receiving the image. If one of the systems is unable to access the file system, then the flash drive will be unusable. The second factor is that the file system chosen has to be able to store files greater than four gigabytes. Both of these conditions must be met in order to have a usable storage device.

Once the USB device has been formatted, the compressed files of the base image need to be copied to the device. When copying the files to the USB device, there are two options. The first option is to copy all the files that form a base image. This would include all the system DASD files, all the user DASD files, and any other DASD files that have been created to support a base system. It would also include the device map that is used for the base environment. However, depending on the use case, not all files may be needed.

If it is common that each environment requires a different subset of the DASD files, it may make more sense to wait until a new system is deployed before creating the USB flash drive. In this instance, only the DASD files required by the use case are copied to the drive. This enables the creation of an updated device map that reflects any changes to the DASD files included in the image. While this introduces a delay in the deployment, it ensures that no extraneous data is provided during the deployment.

Hosting the Deployment Image in the Cloud

Another option that may be expedient for the deployment of multiple remote images is the use of cloud storage. If storage is obtained from a cloud provider, the base image could be stored in a cloud storage site. This method provides the end user the ability to download the base image from anywhere with a connection to the cloud storage. In Figure 12-3, the base image is located in cloud storage. When a new Linux host has been built, the host is connected to the cloud storage and the base environment is deployed. With this configuration, the Linux host machines can be located anywhere that has access to the Internet and multiple deployments can be executed simultaneously.

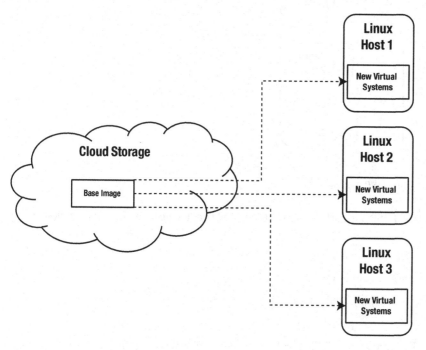

Figure 12-3. *Deployment process using cloud storage*

As with the other deployment models, there are several considerations.

- Do the remote machines have network access?
  - If yes, do they have access to the internet and cloud storage?
- What type of access to information is provided by the cloud storage vendor?
  - Is it available as a NFS mount point?
  - Is it available through a web interface?
  - Is it available via FTP?
  - Is it available via Samba share?

- What is the reliability of the vendor?
    - What are the maintenance cycles?
    - How often do outages occur?
- What are the speeds provided?
    - What is the average download speed?
    - What is the average upload speed?
    - Are there download/upload limits?
    - Are there thresholds that would activate throttling?

To use this method an appropriate vendor would need to be chosen to host the DASD files. The vendor should provide secure, reliable storage that can be accessed by the Linux host. The type of access should also be considered. For most environments, accessing the data through an NFS mount point is preferred, because it provides more flexibility for deployment.

Once the storage vendor has been chosen, the DASD files need to be moved to the cloud storage area. After all of the files have been transferred to the storage provided by the cloud vendor, they can be accessed by any authorized user in order to deploy a base environment.

■ **Note**   One major advantage to using a cloud storage provider to deploy base environments to remote Linux host machines is that it does not require access to the company network.

Pre-Deployment Requirements

In using the deployment strategies outlined above, three steps need to be completed before a new environment can be deployed:

1. Configuration of the hardware
2. Installation and configuration of the Linux operating system
3. Installation and configuration of a compatible version of the z1090 software

Hardware Configuration

Using a base image has the advantage that the only hardware dependency is that it meets the minimum requirements specified by the z1090 documentation. As long as the hardware used meets the requirements of the use case, the configuration can include laptops, desktop PCs, or servers.

The topics discussed in Chapters 2 and 3 apply to a virtualized environment deployment. The memory, hard drive requirements, and RAID configurations (if applicable) all need to be considered when procuring the hardware. Once the hardware has been obtained, it needs to be configured. Depending on the hardware chosen, modifications may be needed to the following:

- RAC or network KVM
- Hard drive configuration
    - RAID
    - Solid-state devices

- SAN configuration
- Network
  - Physical connections
  - DNS entries
  - Static IP address assignments

The use case design should be reviewed as the hardware configuration is created. The final hardware scheme must support the requirements that have been specified.

Linux Installation and Configuration

After the hardware has been configured, the Linux operating system needs to be installed and configured. As described in Chapters 3 and 4, the hardware design and user specifications must be analyzed to determine the correct configuration for the Linux operating system.

The hard drive design must be analyzed to determine where to create the file systems.

- Are there RAID arrays?
  - What file systems should be placed on specific arrays?
  - Where should the file systems be mounted?
- Are there solid-state drives?
  - What file systems should be created?
  - Where should the file systems be mounted?
- Is there a SAN?
  - How many file systems will be available?
  - Where should the file systems be mounted?

Once this information has been determined, the operating system can be installed on the physical box according to the procedures outlined in Chapters 3 and 4. After the Linux operating system has been installed, any additional software can be added to the Linux host. This may range from an x3270 emulator to software development tools. If the Linux host requires network connectivity, the appropriate network information needs to be obtained from the local IT team. The network configuration of the Linux host must be updated to match the use case specifications.

z1090 Installation and Configuration

The last process to be completed before a new virtualized environment can be deployed is the installation of the z1090 software. Before the installation can begin, the version of the software to be installed must be determined. Two common possibilities are:

- Installation of the same version that was used to create the base environment
  - Guarantees compatibility with the base environment
  - May require updating to provide future functionality

- Installation of the most recent version provided by the vendor
  - May require changes to the base system to ensure compatibility
  - May support new functionality requirements without upgrading

The specifications of the use case should be used to determine the optimal version of the z1090 software to install. Once the software has been installed, the Linux host system must be modified according to the requirements detailed for the virtualized environment. These topics are in Chapters 3 and 4 and include:

- Creation of a Linux userid to operate the virtualized environment
- File system permission changes to allow the new Linux userid proper access to files that compose the virtualized environment
- Modifications to the Linux environment as specified in the vendor documentation
- Modifications to the Linux userid used to operate the virtualized environment as specified in the vendor documentation
- Creation of any NFS shares as specified in the environment designs

When these changes have been completed, the system is ready for deployment of the base environment.

Deploy the Base Image

The procedure to deploy the base image depends on the hosting method that has been chosen. Each method provides the ability to create either a full base or a customized environment. Through careful planning, a process can be created that delivers a virtualized environment requiring minimal modifications before it can be started.

NAS

The deployment of a new virtual environment from a NAS device can be accomplished utilizing several different processes:

- The entire base environment may be deployed and then customized
- The base image may be tailored to a specific use case and then deployed
- The DASD files may be compressed on the NAS and uncompressed during deployment
- The DASD files may be uncompressed, reducing steps involved in deployment
- The process may be manual or automated
  - If automated, scripted or high-level programs may be used
- Some combination of the above processes or an entirely different process could be used, depending on the needs of the users

While there may be several processes available to deploy a new environment, most will be based on two common protocols used to connect to the NAS device. These two network protocols are FTP and NFS network services. Most NAS devices are shipped with these capabilities, and each has advantages and disadvantages. The strengths and weaknesses of each protocol need to be analyzed to determine which technology provides the optimal solution.

FTP

FTP is one of the most common mechanisms used to move data between networked devices. Many FTP applications provide both command line and graphical interfaces to transfer the data. Scripting and programming languages can also be used to automate FTP processes.

One of the advantages of using FTP is the speed provided by the protocol. FTP tends to provide faster data-transfer rates. This speed may be beneficial when large amounts of data need to be moved from one network device to another.

Many FTP applications also provide the ability to retry failed transfers. For example, if the transfer of a file fails for any reason, the application may retry the transfer for a specific number of times before failing the transfer. This allows for successful transfer during small network outages or other recoverable error situations.

If FTP is the protocol chosen to deploy the base image, the files can be transferred manually or programmatically. If the transfers are completed manually, the best approach is to use a graphical FTP application. Many graphical FTP solutions provide an automatic method to retry a failed transfer. At minimum, most log a failure so that individual file transfers can be redriven.

Another option to deploy the base image involves creating a programmatic solution. The advantage of creating a program or a suite of programs for deployment is flexibility. Programmatic solutions can be customized to satisfy various design requirements. This enables each deployment to be customized as needed, because each new virtualized mainframe environment may require unique configurations. The flexibility of this solution allows the deployment to deliver either a full base environment or a subset. The device map could also be customized to accommodate any changes to the DASD files deployed.

The disadvantage of using FTP as part of a programmatic solution is the time required to create the program. Depending on the scripting or programming language chosen, the use of FTP as the transport protocol may be very complicated, because the program needs to build the connection and then verify a successful completion of each transfer. The time entailed in creating a programmatic solution must be weighed against the value it provides. However, in a dynamic or growing environment, it is an option worth considering.

NFS

While FTP is a common data movement protocol used across many platforms, NFS is a useful protocol in a Linux environment. It is supported on all Linux operating systems and can be configured in most Linux versions with both graphical and command line tools. This enables users with very basic skills to set up an NFS environment, as well as giving more experienced users the ability to easily share data through NFS shares.

The main advantage NFS provides is that the connected shares appear as if they are a local file system to the Linux host. This allows data to be moved with simple copy commands. As with FTP, this can be accomplished using a graphical application or through automation programs created for the deployment of new base environments.

The advantage of using a graphical application to deploy a base environment is that most applications provide a status bar indicating progress of the copy. However, one major disadvantage when using a large copy operation is that if one file in the group fails to copy properly, the rest of the copy operation is stopped. A new copy operation then has to be initiated to complete the process. Another disadvantage of this method is that it is an all-or-nothing process: there is no filtering; the entire base image is copied to the destination system. This can lead to the migration of data that is not required.

The NFS protocol does afford more opportunities to automate the deployment of a base environment. Because of the nature of the connection, simple scripting tools can be used to copy the base image from the NAS device to the new Linux host. These scripts can be written many different ways and do not require proficiency in high-level languages. Properly constructed scripts can also verify the correct transfer of files, retry failed files, and even log the progress of the deployment. This makes using a NFS connection to a NAS device an attractive option.

USB Flash Drive

Deployment from a USB flash device enables the distribution of base environments to locations that are not possible through other mechanisms. For example, for systems that have no network connections, or very limited network access, it may be the only way to deliver a standard configuration. This method also provides the ability to customize the base image during deployment.

Several questions must be answered before the base image can be loaded onto the USB flash drive:

- Will the files be compressed on the flash drive?

- How will the data files on the flash drive be moved to the Linux host?

    - Will they be copied?

    - Will there be a controlling script?

- How often will the base image be updated?

    - How will the flash drive be updated?

The compression issue is critical because it will influence the deployment design in multiple ways. The size of the base image may be a major factor in this decision. If the uncompressed base image is too large to fit onto a flash drive, compression may be required. If the files are compressed, a smaller drive will be required for the deployment. The resolution to the compression question will also affect how the files will be moved from the flash drive to the Linux host machine.

If the files on the flash drive are uncompressed, two methods can be employed to move the data. The first is to copy the files from the flash drive to the Linux host by using commands issued from a Linux terminal window, or by using a graphical explorer interface. The second method is to use a script to copy the data files to the Linux host and place them in the proper location.

If the files on the flash drive are compressed, they cannot simply be copied to the Linux host. While the files can be manually uncompressed into the proper location on the Linux host, this is not an optimal solution, as it requires a significant investment in time to complete this process for the full base image for every deployment. A better option is to uncompress the files programmatically. This can be accomplished through either simple scripting or a program written in a high-level language, like C or Java.

During development of the process to uncompress and copy the data, methods to customize or modify the deployment need to be considered. As the base environment evolves, simple methods to update the deployment should be considered.

As the z1090 vendor introduces enhancements and support for new technologies, the base environment may be modified to provide support for these updates. Though not as easily updated as a NAS or cloud storage, there are many procedures to update the base image stored on a flash drive. The first is to ship the flash drive back to where it was created and have it updated with the new base image. The second method requires network access on a machine local to where the flash drive is stored. If a local machine with network access is available, then the base image on the flash drive can be updated remotely through the network. Depending on network speeds, this may be time-consuming, but it is more expedient than shipping the physical devices.

One more possibility involves using a flash drive and utilizing scripting and local network access. If network access is available from at least one local machine, scripts can be delivered to create customized deployments for new machines. For example, if a new virtualized mainframe environment requires only a subset of the base environment, a script could be created to deploy only what is needed and then delivered to the flash drive over the network. The customized image can be deployed to the new Linux host. This process affords a little more flexibility to this deployment method.

While deployment using a USB flash drive is not as convenient as other methods, it may be viable where constraints do not allow for use of NAS or cloud methods.

Cloud

The evolution of the Internet and cloud technology has created solutions that would not have been possible previously. In the case of deployment of new virtualized mainframe environments, cloud storage presents a new solution for remote deployment. Through cloud storage technology, remote machines can be given access to a cloud storage area that hosts the base image.

In designing a cloud storage deployment solution, the following factors must be considered:

- What speeds are available?

- Are the files compressed?

- What type of access is provided?

    - File system mapping

    - FTP

    - Browser interface

For any deployment, a critical factor is the speed of the file transfers. Although access from a cloud-based vendor is rarely as responsive as from a local network, varying speeds are available. The download speeds and responsiveness of a cloud storage solution may dictate if automated deployments are required. If it will take hours to download the files, it is not cost-effective to rely on manual efforts for the deployment.

Another important consideration is file compression. Cloud storage pricing is based on capacity, so compression of the data may be required to keep the cost at an acceptable level. Data compression may also lead to the need for automated deployment, as uncompressing each file individually is a time-consuming activity.

If automated deployment is desired, then the type of access to the storage is important. If access to the base image is through a simple web browser interface, and the files can be downloaded only one at a time, automation will be difficult. It will require programming of an application or an applet that can interface with a web browser, dynamically create the list of files to download, determine if the files need to be uncompressed, and copy the files to where they are needed.

If FTP access is required, then the process to deploy the base environment is easier to design, but it still requires more sophisticated programming to accomplish the task. The automation would have to create the FTP connection, copy each file from the cloud, and then uncompress each file into the correct location.

The optimal solution is to access to the files through a share that can be mounted as a file system on the Linux host. This allows for simple scripting to be developed to copy the files and, if needed, uncompress them. Automation for this method does not require the same level of sophistication as using FTP or a web browser to access the files.

Another advantage of using the cloud and programmatically deploying a new base environment is that a customized program or script can be hosted on the cloud storage. With the ability to store scripts or programs on the cloud, automation for the deployment can be customized to the specific requirements of the new deployment. The user can download the program or script and then deploy an image that is tailored to meet the specific needs of the use case for the virtualized mainframe environment.

Post-Deployment Activities

After the base image is deployed, modifications need to be made to adapt the base environment to the requirements of the use case. These updates will include changes to the files that were just delivered, as well as customization of the virtual systems themselves.

Update DASD File Locations and the Device Map

It is important that the new DASD files and device map are in the correct locations and that the device map correctly defines the DASD files that will be used for the new virtual environment. Depending on the level of customization applied during the deployment, there may not be any updates needed. If the deployment scripts/programs or the manual process took into account the required changes, then there may be no updates required to the device map.

Verification that the DASD files are located on the correct file systems is important. Depending on the hardware configuration, some critical files may need to be moved to different file systems. Any changes should be specified in the design of the environment based on the use case.

Once the DASD files have been placed on the proper file systems, the device map may require updates to reflect the changes. This includes any changes to the *awsckd* device manager to identify the location of the new DASD files, as well as any other modifications to support the new use case.

Once these changes have been made, the emulator can be started and the updates to the virtual systems can be made.

Virtual Systems Updates

After the base environment has been deployed and the emulator has been started, there are changes that need to be made to both z/VM and the guest systems. While there may be other operating systems that are guests to z/VM, the focus of this section will be on z/OS guest systems. The changes to the z/VM operating system will be discussed first, followed by the modifications to the z/OS guest systems.

Changes to the z/VM Host

■ **Note**   All of the following changes are described in detail in Chapter 5. They are summarized here to provide continuity in this section.

If access to the network is to be available on the z/VM system, the following updates need to be made:

- Run the *IPWIZARD* utility provided by IBM.
    - Updates the TCP/IP information for z/VM
    - Updates the DNS information for z/VM
- Update the *system config* file.
    - Changes the *SYSTEM_IDENTIFIER_DEFAULT* variable to the new system name
- If a *virtual switch* is required for the guest systems
    - Create a new *MACPREFIX* in the system config file
    - Update the *AUTOLOG profile exec* to allow the guest systems to access the virtual switch for the guest systems

The last updates are to the user directory. These changes will be based upon the guest system names that are defined in the virtual environment design and any updates to the base configuration that were delivered with the customized deployment. The following changes are needed:

- Update or create the z/OS guest users
- Update or add MDISK and LINK statements for any new DASD volumes
- Delete MDISK and LINK statements for any DASD volumes that have been removed

After these modifications have been made, the z/VM host system can be restarted so that the modifications to the guest systems are completed.

Changes to the z/OS Guest Systems

If the system naming conventions and symbols have been created properly, there should be minimal changes to the z/OS guest systems. The guest system changes made to the user directory in z/VM should be properly recognized, and the correct files on the z/OS guest systems should be used for starting and running the systems. The only changes that should be required are for the network access.

Since static IP addresses are required for z/OS operating systems, the data sets for the TCP/IP started task may require changes to reflect the updates involved for local access. These modifications will need to be made for both z/OS network access and USS. The modifications that are required are discussed in Chapter 8. Once these changes have been completed and the TCP/IP started task has been restarted, then the guest system should have full access to the network.

■ **Note**   There may be other changes to the z/OS guest systems depending on requirements specified in the use case. However, these changes are outside the scope of providing a base image that can deploy a base environment with minimal modifications.

Considerations to Simplify Deployment

The topics discussed in Chapters 8 and 9 are based on traditional mainframe operations. While most of these conventions are also useful in the virtualized environment running on a distributed platform, some adjustments to these conventions might prove valuable. The concepts outlined in Chapters 8 and 9 were developed in a more static environment. With the potential for operation with constantly changing objectives and designs, some changes to the base environment may lead to a more simple deployment. The options that will be considered at this point are the naming convention for user DASD volumes and the pre-configuration of network access for future expansion.

User Volume Naming Convention

The naming conventions discussed up to this point have involved including the system name as part of the volume serial number. This is great for large heterogeneous environments where there are many systems and easy identification of DASD volume location is required. However, in a virtualized mainframe environment, there are relatively few systems. In addition, in many instances most of the volumes are shared. This reduces or eliminates the need to have the system name as part of the volume serial number.

To simplify the deployment of new systems, it may be advantageous to eliminate the system name as part of the volume serial number and use generic qualifiers. In Figure 12-4, the volume serial number and DASD file name is *UV0900*. The UV is the generic qualifier that specifies that this is a user volume. The next two digits specify the size of the volume—in this case, 9GB. The last two digits are counters of the number of volumes, starting at 00. If the volume were for a 54GB volume, the first volume would be labeled UV5400.

UV0900

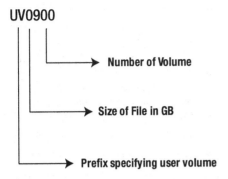

→ Number of Volume

→ Size of File in GB

→ Prefix specifying user volume

Figure 12-4. *Alternative user volume naming convention*

Using a naming convention like this allows for the deployment of DASD volumes to any new complex without the need to change names or reinitialize them.

Networking Pre-Configurations

Depending on the IT infrastructure and requirements, it may not be possible to preconfigure networking components before deployment. However, if it is possible, it saves considerable time, because all the changes can be made at one time.

The first changes are only required if a virtual switch is in use. If so, the *AUTOLOG profile exec* can be updated to grant access to the virtual switch for all the guest systems that may be created. This modification can be made before the base environment is deployed. For instance, if the base image will be used to create z/VM systems *VM01*, *VM02*, and *VM03*, and if each z/VM host will have three z/OS guest systems that will use a virtual switch, then the *AUTOLOG profile exec* can be updated before deployment with the following statements:

- CP SET VSWITCH VMSWITCH GRANT MV11

- CP SET VSWITCH VMSWITCH GRANT MV21

- CP SET VSWITCH VMSWITCH GRANT MV31

- CP SET VSWITCH VMSWITCH GRANT MV12

- CP SET VSWITCH VMSWITCH GRANT MV22

- CP SET VSWITCH VMSWITCH GRANT MV32

- CP SET VSWITCH VMSWITCH GRANT MV13

- CP SET VSWITCH VMSWITCH GRANT MV23

- CP SET VSWITCH VMSWITCH GRANT MV33

Making changes for access to the virtual switch ahead of time will simplify the deployment and allow the new virtual environment to be brought online more quickly.

The z/OS guest systems can also be preconfigured for network access, depending on the policies of the IT department. If the DNS names and the static IP addresses can be obtained for all the virtualized environments, then the networking data sets discussed in Chapter 8 can be created before deployment to simplify the post-deployment process. The primary updates are to the TCPIP.DATA members that are listed in the *TCPIP* proc. These members are the repository for the DNS information, the system hostname and the IP information for the local z/OS system. If the information is known before deployment and the correct naming conventions and symbols are used, the data sets used for TCP/IP access can be created before deployment, allowing the correct TCP/IP information to be available to the system when it is started.

Conclusion

In many companies, the number of virtualized mainframe systems is growing dramatically. This increases the importance of streamlining the creation of these new environments. Building a base image and creating a deployment strategy allow rapid development of new environments and accelerate the availability to the end users.

The topics discussed in this chapter are building blocks that can be adapted and customized to meet the requirements of ever-changing user demands. If time is taken to design a suitable yet flexible deployment strategy, the time needed to create new and increasingly complex configurations can be minimized.

Case Studies

Case 1: Single Laptop System for Mainframe Developer

The initial project has been so successful that the company has purchased more laptops and licenses from the z1090 vendor. The new virtual mainframe environments are being created for several developers and QA personnel around the world. Unlike the developer who was first given a virtual environment to use, these new users do not have extensive mainframe knowledge. In order for this new project to succeed, a mechanism to deploy the new environment must be created so that the end users are not required to build the environments themselves.

Because of the geographic distribution of the users and the availability of Internet access, a cloud solution is deemed the optimal choice for a deployment strategy. The IT team works with several vendors to determine which offerings meet the needs of the team. One is chosen that can provide a virtual share to a Linux host.

In order to keep the deployment simple, an IT vendor is contacted to build the new laptops according to the specifications provided by the developer. The vendor is given details on how to build the Linux host and which Linux components to install. They are also provided information on how to configure the networking for the Linux host. Once the laptops have been configured, they are to be shipped directly to the end users.

While the laptops are being built and configured, the IT team composes detailed instructions for how to install the z1090 software. These instructions and a copy of the z1090 software are copied to the cloud storage solution.

One of the members of the IT team works closely with the initial developer to create a base environment that will meet the needs of the new team. Once the environment has been created, a base image is created on the cloud storage solution. The IT team then creates a set of scripts that will uncompress the files and copy them to the appropriate file systems on the new laptops.

As end users receive the laptops, the IT team helps each user install the z1090 software and deploy the base image. As each virtual environment is brought online, the developer works with the end user to make the modifications required to enable the systems to function properly. These changes include setting a new system name, updates to the networking configuration, and some minor modifications to the system parameter data sets to accommodate the new system name.

Once these changes are completed, the end users are able to begin working on their new project.

Case 2: Server Class Machine Hosting Multiple Mainframe Systems for Software QA Testing

Because of the increase in productivity of the QA team using the current visualized mainframe environment, the company has decided to expand the virtualized lab by four environments every quarter for the next two years. To accommodate this rapid growth, it has been decided to build a base image for rapid deployment of new environments.

After careful analysis of the requirements, it is decided that all of the new virtualized mainframe environments will be hosted in a single lab next to the corporate data center. This will allow the infrastructure to be managed by the IT department.

A decision is made to require the servers that will be used to be the same model and configuration. This will allow a base image to be created and then deployed as needed, saving hours of effort in building the Linux hosts. The Linux host base image will be composed of the Linux OS, an x3270 application, and the z1090 software. In addition, a base image of the virtual mainframe environment will be created. Both images will be stored on a NAS device located in the same lab and will allow rapid deployments.

The first step in creating the deployment solution is to obtain and configure a NAS device. A NAS device is acquired with multiple drives configured in RAID 1 to provide the needed recoverability, speed, and access. This will provide a suitable combination of resiliency in case of a hardware error and speed during deployments. The device is configured with NFS access to provide the ability to mount the file system from the remote Linux hosts. One share is created to contain the image of the Linux host and a second is used to hold the image of the base virtual environment.

The second step is creating the Linux host image that will be used to deploy the operating system to the new servers. This is completed quickly by one of the IT staff that has experience in distributed environments. After the installation of the Linux operating system has been completed, an x3270 application is downloaded to the Linux host and configured. The z1090 software is then installed and configured, with the appropriate updates made to the operating system. Once all of the software has been installed and configured, a full backup image of the Linux host is created and copied to the NAS device.

After the Linux host image has been completed, the third step requires the IT team to work closely with the QA team to create a base image of the virtual systems. They carefully analyze the changes that have been made to build the mainframe zEnterprise-based systems and spend several days recreating a generic version of the environment on a new Linux host. The new environment is composed of a z/VM host system and three z/OS guest systems. They are configured in a basic SYSPLEX communicating through a coupling facility. After the virtual systems have been created, customized, and verified, the files that form the virtual systems are compressed and copied to the NAS device to create the base image for the virtual systems.

The last step is to design the deployment process to be used to create the new virtualized mainframe environments.

The first stage of this process is to build the new Linux host machines. In order to enable a rapid deployment of the host image, a flash drive is created that will be used to start the new servers, connect to the NAS device, and deploy the base Linux host image. This is accomplished by installing a small, bootable Linux operating system on the flash drive and by providing scripts that will connect to the NAS and install the base Linux host image to the new server. After the Linux host operating system has been deployed, the server hostname and networking is reconfigured with information provided by the IT staff.

The second stage is to deploy the virtual systems from the base virtual environment image. This is facilitated by mounting the NFS share to the new Linux hosts and by executing several scripts that will uncompress and copy the files from the base virtual environment image to the new servers. The IT team in charge of the deployments customizes the scripts used for each deployment to meet the needs of the group that will be using the new environment.

APPENDIX A

Software Licensing

A *software license* governs the use and distribution of software. The license grants permission to use the software in certain ways and in certain environments. It is essential and necessary to ensure that all software loaded to the distributed environment is used legally and is not an infringement of its software licensing.

IBM Software Licensing, Approval, and Certification

IBM has a process and procedures in place to provide both approval for use and certification of the software to emulate mainframe zEnterprise software on a non-system z environment. To avoid any infringement of the agreements and before acting upon any assumptions, it is good practice to contact IBM to validate all licensing agreements. This practice will validate your environment and alleviate concerns for the use case that you are committing to establish.

Although many use-case scenario requests may seem prima facie fine to implement, a careful and thoughtful review should nonetheless be conducted to ensure proper licensing in all situations.

IBM documentation provides information for the precise hardware that the emulated software supports. Please refer to current documentation or contact IBM for a list of supported hardware.

Third-Party Software Licensing, Approval, and Certification

Before loading any third-party software (non-IBM) into the distributed environment, discussion with the software vendor is essential for understanding the licensing of the software. Obtaining approval from each software vendor for its software product is important. Do not assume that a software license on the mainframe is a license in the distributed environment. Again, software infringement is very serious; each mainframe software vendor needs to be contacted for verification of licensing on the distributed environment.

Summary

Software licensing infringements carry serious consequences. Careful review and verification is important before implementing any software not provided as part of the IBM software package.

Approach each situation with caution and verify at each stage that the software licensing for each product grants its use on a non-mainframe environment.

APPENDIX B

■ ■ ■

Setting the Standards and Conventions

Naming standards are a major part of managing virtual systems. When properly established, naming standards can enable the implementation of new operating systems and new virtual systems in an easy-to-follow process.

This appendix shows a number of conventions and naming standards that reduce the time to implement and update z/OS operating systems. Another purpose for the standards is to maintain a consistent look and feel for all systems. As operating systems advance or as requirements change, these conventions enable changes in one place to update all systems. This technique creates an environment where less diagnostic research is necessary when a product or testing scenario is successful on one system but fails on another. The understanding that the general system setup is the same allows analysis to begin at a later step. This can be essential when attempting to diagnose and resolve a problem.

The conventions in this appendix assume a large LPAR running z/VM as host to many z/OS guests. The section "Modifications for the Distributed Environment" provides a brief explanation of how these standards change to fit a smaller environment and allow easy deployment when building new servers.

z/OS System Naming Standard

A system-naming standard includes many factors based on the requirements of the installation. These can include items such as location or system type.

The IBM symbol &SYSNAME defines the system name. An effective naming standard can identify the system and where it is located. This facilitates accessing each system and knowing where the system resides. For example, if there are multiple LPARS running z/OS virtual guests, it may be necessary to set a standard based on the LPAR where the system resides. A system name could be ZOSS201 where:

- ZOS is the operating system

- S2 is the LPAR abbreviation for an LPAR named SYS2

- 01 is the system number

Depending on standards, it may be important to ensure that the system number is unique across the different LPARs.

Another example of a naming standard could be ZS201. This also incorporates both the LPAR number and the system number. This standard will work for environments using the same system number across multiple LPARs. For example:

- ZS2*01* is system *01* on LPAR SYS2

- ZS5*01* is system *01* on LPAR SYS5

- ZS7*01* is system *01* on LPAR SYS7

- ZS2*14* is system *14* on LPAR SYS2

- ZS5*14* is system *14* on LPAR SYS5

- ZS5*11* is system *11* on LPAR SYS5

- ZS7*11* is system *11* on LPAR SYS7

DASD Volume Serial Naming Convention

There are a series of naming standards in this section. These represent system standards for utilizing shared parameter library members.

In most data centers, naming standards will separate DASD volume serial numbers by product or function. DASD volume serial naming convention can identify the contents of a volume and where the volume resides. For example, a volume serial that begins with ZOS may represent a z/OS operating system.

Depending on the system and situation, more standards may be necessary than presented here. The prefix of most volume serials presented is a generic xxx. The volume serial naming standard established can support up to 100 systems by starting with system 00 using only numerics. Additional volumes per system can use the sixth position of the volume serial. The prefix setting with three characters is easier to distinguish volume serial usage. For example, TSO02A, TSO02B, and TSO02C represent three TSO volumes for system 02.

However, if the number of systems is greater than 100 or they reside on separate LPARs, then the naming standard needs to be more complex. For example, the following may suffice for some of the examples in this appendix:

- ZOS for operating system volumes

- TSO for TSO/E volumes

- SPL for SPOOL volumes

These are just a few examples that may satisfy the needs of many environments.

Operating System

To set up the systems to switch easily between operating system versions and create new virtualized systems, it is essential to have a standard for naming operating system DASD volumes.

For instance, if the operating system volume has the release as part of the name, then this single number or letter should always be in the same position. See Chapter 9 for a more detailed explanation. As an example, the following volume serials use the fourth position as the release of the operating system.

- xxx*A*xx

- xxx*D*xx

A proper naming standard can work even if the standards change for operating systems. For example:

- xxx*A*xx would work for OS/390 V2 R*10* or z/OS V1 R*10*

- xxx*D*xx would work for z/OS V1 R*13*

- xxx*1*xx would work for z/OS V2 R*1*

Time Sharing Option/Extensions

Time Sharing Option/Extensions (TSO/E) is a place where users can share data, run programs, manage data, and create job control language (JCL) to interact with MVS and other functions.

The purpose is to have DASD volumes available to support all of this and more. These volumes attached to each system are for individual usage for the person or team utilizing the system.

Assume that xxx is the same three characters for each TSO/E volume.

Assuming a system-naming convention, then the following standard will function for different systems. This allows for 99 systems using 01 through 99. However, alphanumeric characters can substitute for numerics or a different naming convention can be established.

- xxx*03*A for system *03*

- xxx*14*A for system *14*

- xxx*23*A for system *23*

- xxx*26*A for system *26*

These volumes each contain the virtual system number and a continuous pattern for labeling each volume (A, B, C, etc.). For example, if you had a system with a significant number of users and need for a large amount of data, the naming standard would work to allow many TSO volumes. The following is an example of such a system:

- xxx*01*A

- xxx*01*B

- xxx*01*C

- .....

- xxx*01*M

In this example, system 01 has thirteen TSO volumes. The standard allows the system number in the same position of the volume serial while allowing multiple volumes for the same type of usage. In the instance here, they are TSO DASD volumes.

The standards depicted are simplistic in nature, but may work for many system environments depending on the number of systems and requirements. It is important to mention that the volumes are not necessarily the same size. Depending on the requirements, the volumes can be very large or very small.

Auxiliary Storage

Another set of volumes that have a standard naming convention are for auxiliary storage. These are commonly called paging volumes. The different types of page data sets should reside on different DASD volumes to improve overall system performance. The types of page data sets are:

- PLPA - The pageable link pack area

- COMMON - Common area paging plus PLPA if it overflows

- LOCAL - Private area and VIO pages

Although there are several different types of paging data sets, a simple naming convention can apply to the DASD volumes associated with each one.

For example, assume that xx is the same two characters for each auxiliary volume. An example of volume serial naming standards would be:

- xx*23P*1 - This is for system *23* and the *P*LPA data set
- xx*23C*1 - This is for system *23* and the *C*ommon data set
- xx*23L*1 - This is for system *23* and the 1st *L*ocal data set
- xx*23L*2 - This is for system *23* and the 2nd *L*ocal data set
- xx*23L*3 - This is for system *23* and the 3rd *L*ocal data set

To illustrate an example for PLPA data sets across multiple systems:

- xx*03P*1 - This is for system *03* and the *P*LPA data set
- xx*17P*1 - This is for system *17* and the *P*LPA data set
- xx*21P*1 - This is for system *21* and the *P*LPA data set

Note that only a two-position prefix is required for the auxiliary storage volumes.

Job Entry Subsystem (JES)

The IBM Job Entry Subsystem JES2 is a component of the operating system that provides job, data, and task management. Essentially, JES2 will receive jobs for the operating system, schedule them, and manage their output.

Two volume types need to be set up for simultaneous peripheral operations online (SPOOL). The following provides a simple characterization for each volume. For more information, please refer to IBM documentation on SPOOL functionality.

- SPOOL - Read/write streams for both input and output on auxiliary storage
- Checkpoint - Backup to the in-storage job and output queues

SPOOL Volume Serial

The SPOOL volume serial naming standard should allow for multiple systems. For example, system 02 may require large amounts of SPOOL owing to the number of users and large job output. The system may require several large SPOOL volumes.

Assume that xxx is the same three characters for each SPOOL volume

- xxx*02*A
- xxx*02*B
- xxx*02*C
- xxx*02*D
- xxx*02*E

By contrast, system 13 may have a small group of users that do not require much SPOOL space and may utilize just one small volume:

- xxx*13*A for system *13*

Checkpoint Volume Serials

The JES2 checkpoint data sets act as a backup to the in-storage job and output queues maintained by JES2. It also performs other functions in a more complex environment.

The volume serials for the checkpoint data set naming standard should be set up for multiple systems. The two checkpoint data sets should reside on separate volumes. A naming standard like the following could suffice depending on the environment.

Assume that xxx is the same three characters for each checkpoint volume

For multiple systems, the checkpoint 1 volume names could be:

- xxx1*02* volume serial for system *02* checkpoint data set 1
- xxx1*13* volume serial for system *13* checkpoint data set 1
- xxx1*24* volume serial for system *24* checkpoint data set 1

For multiple systems, the checkpoint 2 volume names could be:

- xxx2*02* volume serial for system *02* checkpoint data set 2
- xxx2*13* volume serial for system *13* checkpoint data set 2
- xxx2*24* volume serial for system *24* checkpoint data set 2

In this example, there is only one volume for each checkpoint and the possibility for more than one for the SPOOL volume. This is a typical configuration. Important here is the consistency of the system number being included in the volume serial.

Data Set Naming Standards

Data set naming conventions are essential to all mainframe environments and are used to create standards for products and company functional areas such as finance, budgeting, payroll, and other functions. In this section, the references for data set naming will be related to the system and subsystems. Depending on the system and situation, more standards may be necessary than presented here.

Part of each data set name is a generic xxx. The naming standard established can support many conventions. The three-character xxx is not limited to three characters. Similar to volume serial naming, the following may suffice for xxx:

- PAG for page data set names
- SPL for SPOOL data set names
- CKPT for checkpoint data set names

These are just a few examples that may suffice depending on the environment. Most established data centers already have strict standards for data set names. It is essential to have sensible naming standards.

Auxiliary Storage

Having a naming standard for the page data sets is important. There are three types of page data sets:

- PLPA - The pageable link pack area
- COMMON - Common area paging plus PLPA if it overflows
- LOCAL - Private area and VIO pages

In many systems, it is necessary to have more than one LOCAL data set. Each LOCAL data set should reside on its own DASD volume.

Assume that xxx is the same three characters for each page data set name.
A naming standard such as the following example would be for system 23:

- PAGE.xxx*23*.PLPA

- PAGE.xxx*23*.COMMON

- PAGE.xxx*23*.LOCAL

- PAGE.xxx*23*.LOCAL2

- PAGE.xxx*23*.LOCAL3

This convention would work for other systems within the network. For example:

- PAGE.xxx*14*.PLPA would be for system *14*

- PAGE.xxx*18*.PLPA would be for system *18*

- PAGE.xxx*21*.PLPA would be for system *21*

This example shows the PLPA page data set; however, it is valid for the COMMON and LOCAL data sets also. For example:

The COMMON data sets would be:

- PAGE.xxx*14*.COMMON would be for system *14*

- PAGE.xxx*18*.COMMON would be for system *18*

- PAGE.xxx*21*.COMMON would be for system *21*

The LOCAL data sets would be:

- PAGE.xxx*14*.LOCAL1 would be for system *14*

- PAGE.xxx*14*.LOCAL2 would be for system *14*

- PAGE.xxx*14*.LOCAL3 would be for system *14*

- PAGE.xxx*18*.LOCAL1 would be for system *18*

- PAGE.xxx*18*.LOCAL2 would be for system *18*

- PAGE.xxx*18*.LOCAL3 would be for system *18*

- PAGE.xxx*21*.LOCAL1 would be for system *21*

- PAGE.xxx*21*.LOCAL2 would be for system *21*

- PAGE.xxx*21*.LOCAL3 would be for system *21*

Job Entry Subsystem

The IBM Job Entry Subsystem JES2 is a component of the operating system that provides job, data, and task management. Essentially, JES2 will receive jobs for the operating system, schedule them, and manage their output.

Three data set names need to be set up for simultaneous peripheral operations online (SPOOL). The following provides a brief and partial characterization for each data set.

- SPOOL - Read/write streams for both input and output on auxiliary storage

- Checkpoint 1 - Backup to the in-storage job and output queues

- Checkpoint 2 - Backup to the in-storage job and output queues

The following show names for system 01, where "xxx" represent the same three characters for each SPOOL data set name:

- SYS1.*xxx01*.HASPACE for the SPOOL data set

- SYS1.HASPACE.*xxx01*.CKPT1 for checkpoint 1 data set

- SYS1.HASPACE.*xxx01*.CKPT2 for checkpoint 2 data set

For multiple systems, the SPOOL data set names would be:

- SYS1.*xxx02*.HASPACE for system *02*

- SYS1.*xxx13*.HASPACE for system *13*

- SYS1.*xxx22*.HASPACE for system *22*

For multiple systems, the checkpoint 1 data set names would be:

- SYS1.JES2.*xxx02*.CKPT1 for system *02*

- SYS1.JES2.*xxx13*.CKPT1 for system *13*

- SYS1.JES2.*xxx22*.CKPT1 for system *22*

For multiple systems, the checkpoint 2 data set names would be:

- SYS1.JES2.*xxx02*.CKPT2 for system *02*

- SYS1.JES2.*xxx13*.CKPT2 for system *13*

- SYS1.JES2.*xxx22*.CKPT2 for system *22*

Network Naming Standards

In most companies, there are many network naming standards. These standards often include country, office location, lab location, and other potential specifications. In this discussion, the important network convention is domain name server (DNS) host naming. The following could be a standard:

- First two positions for the country—for example:

  - US for the United States

  - CA for Canada

- The next two positions might represent the office—for example:

  - 01 for the corporate office

  - 02 for a satellite office

- The next two positions might represent the system number—for example:

  - 06 for system 06

  - 12 for system 12

- The next position might represent the system type—for example:

  - M for a system that runs natively on a mainframe LPAR

  - V for a system that runs as a virtual guest

If a virtual system is in the United States, is executing at the corporate office, and is the second system, then the DNS is US0102V. Additional examples:

- NAME=US0106M — mainframe system 06 in the US, corporate office

- NAME=CA0312V — virtual system 12 in Canada, Office 03

- NAME=US0417V — virtual system 17, in the US, Office 04

Application Naming Standards

In most data centers, strict application naming standards exist for Virtual Telecommunications Access Method (VTAM). VTAM applications essentially create connections to an application via the network.

A critical VTAM connection is for the JES2 subsystem. In VTAM, the APPLID is the application name. A naming standard should allow for multiple systems. For JES2, the application name could be A01JES2. This would breakdown as follows:

- A   - would be for application name or APPLID

- 01   - would be for the system number

- JES2   - would be for JES2 application connection for VTAM

For multiple systems:

- APPLID=A*01*JES2 for system *01*

- APPLID=A*10*JES2 for system *10*

- APPLID=A*17*JES2 for system *17*

Naming Standards Explained

Whether a site has many virtualized z/OS guests or just a few, good naming standards will help create a sustainable process when new virtual systems are required and built. They enable volume serial numbers or data sets to identify use and location. The naming conventions presented here are building blocks that can be expanded as needed, based upon the needs of the users.

Step 1: System Names are Standardized

The essential first step is to have standardized system names, because standardization enables many virtual systems to run on a single LPAR. A well-conceived naming convention not only enables easy identification of a system but also simplifies the process of creating new systems. The example in this appendix uses a simple naming standard to classify individual virtual systems on a server. However, each installation may choose a different convention to label the system, such as the following:

- ZOS001 - ZOS for a z/OS system, 001 representing system 1

- ZOS022 - ZOS for a z/OS system, 022 representing system 22

Having an easy method to identify the systems is important.

Step 2: DASD Volume Serials Are Standardized

The second step is to ensure standardization of the DASD volume serials. This involves standardizing for these items:

- Operating system release
- TSO/E
- Auxiliary storage (paging volumes)
- JES2 SPOOL and checkpoint volumes

These standards have two essential uses in this book:

- Symbol substitution as described in Chapter 9
- Ease of creating new virtual systems as discussed at the end of this appendix

Step 3: Data Set Names Are Standardized

The third step is to ensure that the data set names are standardized. This involves standardizing for these items:

- Page data sets
- JES2 SPOOL and checkpoint

Step 4: Network Names Are Standardized

The fourth step involves ensuring that the network names are standardized. This involves standardizing for these items:

- DNS host names
- VTAM application naming

Ease of Creating a Virtual System

With sensible, comprehensive standards in place for systems, volumes, data sets, and networks, the creation of new virtual systems is easier. A sequence of events follows for a new system 24 requested by a development team:

1. A new virtual system is defined to z/VM: xx**24**

2. DASD volumes are initialized for the following:

   a. xxx**24**x - This is for the TSO/E volumes

   b. xx**24**P1 - This is for the PLPA data set

   c. xx**24**C1 - This is for the Common data set

   d. xx**24**L1 - This is for the 1st of 3 Local data sets

   e. xx**24**L2 - This is for the 2nd of 3 Local data sets

   f. xx**24**L3 - This is for the 3rd of 3 Local data sets

   g. xxx**24**A - This is for the SPOOL volume

   h. xxx1**24** - This is for the JES2 checkpoint 1 data set

   i. xxx2**24** - This is for the JES2 checkpoint 2 data set

3. These volumes are added to the virtual system

4. The page data sets are created using the following names:

   a. PAGE.xxx*24*.PLPA

   b. PAGE.xxx*24*.COMMON

   c. PAGE.xxx*24*.LOCAL1

   d. PAGE.xxx*24*.LOCAL2

   e. PAGE.xxx*24*.LOCAL3

5. The JES2 data sets are created using the following names:

   a. SYS1.xxx*24*.HASPACE

   b. SYS1.JES2.xxx*24*.CKPT1

   c. SYS1.JES2.xxx*24*.CKPT2

When you are developing a process for building new virtual systems, creating a similar sequence will streamline the building of new systems. The sequence is simple with the proper naming standards.

The conventions covered in this appendix are not a comprehensive analysis and discussion of all the possible naming conventions that simplify mainframe system management. It is a set of building blocks that lay the foundation for good practices. These can then be adapted to the individual needs of the user.

Modifications for the Distributed Environment

The conventions for the distributed environment are subtle, but necessary to provide ease in creating and modifying a new server. Chapter 12 discusses the topic of deploying new servers.

The distributed environment is much smaller, and for the discussion and examples here, the maximum number of systems created for any server is three.

System Names

A naming standard includes many factors depending on the requirements of the installation. These can include items such as location or function. A good naming standard makes it easier to know where a system resides by looking at the name.

The IBM reserved symbol &SYSNAME defines the system name. A naming standard will distinguish the server and the system on each server. This makes for easier access of each system and awareness of the server where the system resides. For example, if a standard is set where the last character of the system name is the server number and the next to the last character is the system number, then xx11 will represent system 1 on server 1.

Here the naming standard is a simple four-character name with the third character being the system number and the fourth character being the server number. For example:

- MV11 is system 1 on server 1

- MV21 is system 2 on server 1

- MV35 is system 3 on server 5

DASD Naming Conventions

This section will cover the differences for volume serial naming. The DASD names are set to one distinguishing position. This allows for up to 36 systems per server. For example:

- SPL*n*00 is for a JES2 SPOOL data set
- CKP*n*00 is for a JES2 checkpoint 1 data set
- PAG*n*00 is for the auxiliary storage data sets

For each of these volume serials:

- The n can be 1 through 3 representing the number of the system
- The 00 represents the first volume of a possible set

Examples follow:

- SPL*1*00 is the SPOOL volume for system *1*
- PAG*2*00 is for page data sets for system *2*
- CKP*3*00 is for JES2 checkpoint data set for system *3*

For deploying systems across servers, the same volume serial is possible for all servers when you consider the system naming presented at the beginning of this appendix:

- xx*1*1 is system *1* on server 1
- xx*2*4 is system *2* on server 4
- xx*3*5 is system *3* on server 5

■ **Note**   Each server does not share any data or resources of any kind with any other server. Therefore, the same volume serials may appear on each server independently. If you are using server 1 to build server 2, then when copying the full server, there is no need to change volume serials.

SPL100 is valid for server xx11, xx12, xx13, and so forth. This is true for all of the other volumes. Once the new server is ready and a need arises for more SPOOL, paging, or other volumes, then additional volumes will raise the 00 suffix to 01, 02, and so forth. For example, if system 2 requires two additional SPOOL volumes, then the following would be the DASD volume serials:

- SPL*2*00
- SPL*2*01
- SPL*2*02

Data Set Naming Standards

The data set names are set to the first three characters of the system name that will relegate the distinction to one position. This allows for up to 36 systems per server.

Using the system-naming convention of xx11, then setting a standard of xx1 in the name will allow each server to use the same data set. This is similar to the volume serial naming convention. For example:

- PAGE.*xx1*.PLPA   for system *1* PLPA
- PAGE.*xx1*.COMMON   for system *1* COMMON
- PAGE.*xx1*.LOCAL1   for system *1* LOCAL - first data set
- PAGE.*xx1*.LOCAL2   for system *1* LOCAL - second data set
- PAGE.*xx1*.LOCAL3   for system *1* LOCAL - third data set
- SYS1.*xx1*.HASPACE   for system *1* SPOOL space
- SYS1.JES2.*xx1*.CKPT   for system *1* JES2 checkpoint 1
- SYS1.JES2.*xx1*.CKPT2   for system *1* JES2 checkpoint 2

Each of these data set names is valid for the first system on any server. The naming standard for systems and servers would be:

- *xx1*1 for system *xx1* on server 1
- *xx1*2 for system *xx1* on server 2
- *xx1*5 for system *xx1* on server 5

The same naming standard will function for systems 2 and 3 on each server. Showing examples for the SPOOL data set:

- SYS1.*xx2*.HASPACE - for system *2* SPOOL space
- SYS1.*xx3*.HASPACE - for system *3* SPOOL space

The naming standard for systems and servers would be:

- *xx2*1 for system *xx2* on server 1
- *xx2*2 for system *xx2* on server 2
- *xx2*5 for system *xx2* on server 5
- *xx3*1 for system *xx3* on server 1
- *xx3*2 for system *xx3* on server 2
- *xx3*5 for system *xx3* on server 5

IEASYS Member Example

This appendix shows a full IEASYS member utilizing symbols and the parameter values after translation.

Note For detailed information on symbol usage, refer to Chapter 9. For detailed information on naming standards and conventions, refer to Appendix B.

IEASYS Member

The following IEASYS example is a singular IEASYS member that, with symbol usage and naming standards, can facilitate multiple releases of the operating system without the need to change any of the parameters.

```
CLOCK=(SS,L),
CLPA,
CMB=(UNITR,COMM,GRAPH,250),
CMD=(DD,O&ZSYS(3:1),SS),
CON=SS,
COUPLE=00,
CSA=(4M,128M),
DUMP=(DASD,03-99),
GRS=STAR,
GRSRNL=00,
ILMMODE=NONE,
IOS=SS,
LNK=(Z&SYSR2(4:1),O&ZSYS(3:1),SS,L),
LNKAUTH=LNKLST,
LOGCLS=L,
LOGLMT=999999,
LPA=(Z&SYSR2(4:1),O&ZSYS(3:1),SS,L),
MAXUSER=255,
MLPA=(Z&SYSR2(4:1),SS),
OMVS=(Z&SYSR2(4:1),O&ZSYS(3:1)),
OPI=YES,
OPT=00,
PAGE=(PAGE.&ZSYS..PLPA,
      PAGE.&ZSYS..COMMON,
      PAGE.&ZSYS..LOCALA,
```

```
        PAGE.&ZSYS..LOCALB,
        PAGE.&ZSYS..LOCALC,L),
PLEXCFG=ANY,
PROD=SS,
PROG=(Z&SYSR2(4:1),O&ZSYS(3:1)),
REAL=0,
RSU=0,
RSVNONR=5,
RSVSTRT=5,
SCH=SS,
SMS=SS,
SQA=(12,24M),
SSN=(SS,O&ZSYS(3:1)),
SVC=SS,
UNI=(1&SYSR2(4:1)),
VRREGN=64,
ZZ=YES
```

The following is the translation of the IEASYS member with the following assumptions:

- &ZSYS = MV2 - This represents system 2

- &ZSYS(3:1)= 2 - This represents system 2

- &SYSR2(4:1)= D - The operating system release is 13 with operating system volume ZOSDR2

```
CLOCK=(SS,L),
CLPA,
CMB=(UNITR,COMM,GRAPH,250),
CMD=(DD,02,SS),
CON=SS,
COUPLE=00,
CSA=(4M,128M),
DUMP=(DASD,03-99),
GRS=STAR,
GRSRNL=00,
ILMMODE=NONE,
IOS=SS,
LNK=(ZD,02,SS,L),
LNKAUTH=LNKLST,
LOGCLS=L,
LOGLMT=999999,
LPA=(ZD,02,SS,L),
MAXUSER=255,
MLPA=(ZD,SS),
OMVS=(ZD,02),
OPI=YES,
OPT=00,
PAGE=(PAGE.MV2.PLPA,
      PAGE.MV2.COMMON,
      PAGE.MV2.LOCALA,
      PAGE.MV2.LOCALB,
      PAGE.MV2.LOCALC,L),
```

```
PLEXCFG=ANY,
PROD=SS,
PROG=(ZD,02),
REAL=0,
RSU=0,
RSVNONR=5,
RSVSTRT=5,
SCH=SS,
SMS=SS,
SQA=(12,24M),
SSN=(SS,02),
SVC=SS,
UNI=(1D),
VRREGN=64,
ZZ=YES
```

Summary

The IEASYS member shown here and the symbol translation are dependent on DASD and data set naming standards and conventions. The singular IEASYS member is practical for setting the standards for a small distributed server environment or a large environment. The primary advantage is that each system will have assimilation with each other, regardless of the operating system version or release level.

LOAD Member Example

■ **Note**   This appendix shows a full LOAD member using naming conventions that support the use of symbols. For detailed information on symbol usage, refer to Chapter 9. For detailed information on naming standards and conventions, refer to Appendix B.

LOAD Member

The following LOAD member example is a singular LOAD member that, with naming standards, can facilitate multiple releases of the operating system without the need to change any of the parameters.

```
IODF      FF SYS1
SYSCAT    MVIPL1113CCATALOG.NEW.MASTER
SYSPARM   SS
IEASYM    SS
NUCLEUS   1
SYSPLEX   PLEXZPDT
*
VMUSERID MV11
PARMLIB   system.SHARED.PARMLIB                    MVSHR1
PARMLIB   system.MV1.PARMLIB                       MVSHR1
PARMLIB   user.SHARED.PARMLIB                      MVSHR1
PARMLIB   user.MV1.PARMLIB                         MVSHR1
PARMLIB   SYS1.IBM.PARMLIB
IODF      FF SYS1
SYSCAT    MVIPL1113CCATALOG.NEW.MASTER
*
VMUSERID MV21
PARMLIB   system.SHARED.PARMLIB                    MVSHR1
PARMLIB   system.MV2.PARMLIB                       MVSHR1
PARMLIB   user.SHARED.PARMLIB                      MVSHR1
PARMLIB   user.MV2.PARMLIB                         MVSHR1
PARMLIB   SYS1.IBM.PARMLIB
IODF      FF SYS1
SYSCAT    MVIPL1113CCATALOG.NEW.MASTER
*
```

```
VMUSERID MV31
PARMLIB   system.SHARED.PARMLIB              MVSHR1
PARMLIB   system.MV3.PARMLIB                 MVSHR1
PARMLIB   user.SHARED.PARMLIB                MVSHR1
PARMLIB   user.MV3.PARMLIB                   MVSHR1
PARMLIB   SYS1.IBM.PARMLIB
IODF      FF SYS1
SYSCAT    MVIPL1113CCATALOG.NEW.MASTER
```

Summary

This member can facilitate any number of virtualized systems. It uses a shared IODF and master catalog. This implies that the systems are similar and probably share data between them.

However, it is possible in this scenario for any of the systems to utilize a different IODF and master catalog. There are reasons why this may occur. Some examples are:

- There is one system with special hardware needs which does not want to share the many devices provided in the IODFFF configuration.

- There is one system with special requirements to update and change the entries within the master catalog.

Glossary

■ **Note**   The definitions in this glossary are designed for the convenience of our readers to dovetail with the use of these terms in this book. They are not intended to be definitive, rigorous, or exhaustive.

1090 dongle. The USB hardware key that determines the number of System z processors to be emulated on the server and that authenticates the environment.

1090 software. The software that provides the processor function and emulation. It also has built-in utilities.

Application Developers Controlled Distributions (ADCD). System z operating systems and subsystems distributed for use with the zPDT (q.v.). Use is restricted in accordance with IBM guidelines and licensing.

BladeCenter Extension (zBX). Blade extensions for Power Blades, Data Power Blades, and x86 Blades; forming part of the zEnterprise (q.v.).

catalog. A system data set for tracking the attributes and location of data sets.

central processing unit (CPU). The module in a computer that executes the instructions of the operating system and the applications that are run on the operating system.

coupling facility (CF). A logical partition that runs coupling facility control code (CFCC) and provides locking functions, high-speed caching, and list processing in a parallel sysplex (q.v.). It ensures data integrity throughout the sysplex.

DASD. See **direct access storage device**.

DASD repository. A storage location that holds DASD (q.v.) files to be used by the virtual environment. The DASD files can be either transferred to a local system for use or mapped by the Linux host for remote access.

data set. A data grouping on a DASD (q.v.). Each data set on a DASD volume must have a unique name. A data set typically contains one or more records. There are many types of data sets and access methods. The differences among types of data sets are in how the records are stored and accessed.

device map. A file created for a z1090 environment that provides device definitions for the z1090 emulator. This file defines specific devices to be emulated by the 1090 software (q.v.) for use by the operating systems that will be run inside the emulated environment. It essentially defines a z series hardware environment for the 1090 software.

direct access storage device (DASD). A mainframe disk device for data storage. DASD volumes come in different architectures and can be different sizes.

Domain Name System (DNS). A hierarchical naming system for servers. This system provides the ability to provide names to specific network-attached components. DNS allows network users to access resources via a recognizable name rather than the numerical address used by the networking hardware to route data.

I/O definition file (IODF). A configuration data structure for mainframe input/output devices. The IODF contains information about the input/output configuration for MVS (q.v.).

Initial Program Load (IPL). The startup procedure for an IBM mainframe operating system. It loads a copy of the operating system from disk into real storage and executes it. This process initializes the system and storage, creates address spaces, and then initializes the master scheduler and subsystems.

IPL. See *Initial Program Load*.

JES2. See *Job Entry Subsystem 2*.

Job Control Language (JCL). Instructions to control and direct work on an IBM mainframe. They identify a job and its requirements to z/OS (q.v.).

Job Entry Subsystem 2 (JES2). A component of the operating system that provides job, data, and task management. Essentially, JES2 receives jobs for the operating system, schedules them, and manages their output.

keyboard/video/mouse (KVM). A device to control the input/output for a computer. This device offers the ability to use a single keyboard, mouse, and monitor to control multiple computers. The device provides a mechanism to allow the user to switch the input/output from one computer to another via a software or hardware switching mechanism.

LAN. See *local area network*.

Linux. An open-source operating system that is based on the Unix operating system. Versions of Linux exist that can run on personal computers, hardware appliances, and mainframe computers.

Linux hypervisor. A Linux operating system that acts as a host to run virtual machines.

local area network (LAN). A network that allows machines to communicate over a limited geographic area. A LAN is normally confined to a single building or floor within a building.

logical partition (LPAR). A subset of resources on an IBM mainframe. Each LPAR on a system z server can run its own mainframe operating system and is IPL'ed (q.v.) independently of the other LPARs. Essentially, each LPAR acts as its own mainframe processor.

mainframe. A computer with extensive capabilities and resources. Recent mainframes are referred to as servers.

master scheduler. An IBM communication subsystem that establishes communication between z/OS (q.v.) and JES2 (q.v.) to control the flow of work.

Multiple Virtual Storage (MVS). An IBM system of services and functions of z/OS (q.v.) other than z/OS UNIX system services.

NAS. See *network-attached storage*.

network-attached storage (NAS). A device connected to a local area network that provides file-level access to storage. While this device could be a computer configured to provide the storage, it is commonly an appliance designed specifically for this purpose.

Network File System (NFS). A distributed architecture file system that enables the sharing of data across a network. This file system is normally used in Linux environments and is a staple of NAS (q.v.) devices for sharing data.

network interface card (NIC). A hardware component of a computer that provides access to the LAN (q.v.). The hardware can be either embedded in the computer motherboard or provided as an add-on component.

Network Job Entry (NJE). A JES2 (q.v.) facility that provides for the passing of jobs, system output, operator commands, and messages between JES2 subsystems.

Network Time Protocol (NTP). A networking protocol that is used to synchronize the clocks on network-attached computers and devices.

Network Time Protocol server. A server that uses the NTP (q.v.) to synchronize the clocks on network-attached computers and devices.

Open Systems Adapter (OSA). A network controller for a zEnterprise (q.v.) server. The adapter supports many networking transport protocols.

paging. The transferring of pages between central storage and external page storage.

processor. Physical hardware with multiple I/O channels and logical partitions. It executes the machine operations that perform the tasks requested by the program instructions.

Queued Direct I/O (QDIO). A data-transfer architecture that improves the data transfer speed for TCP/IP (q.v.) traffic.

Recommended Service Upgrade (RSU). An IBM preventive service philosophy that applies to z/OS (q.v.). Its intent is to reduce the volume of fixes that customers must apply for preventive maintenance.

redundant array of independent disks (RAID). A storage solution using multiple physical disks that constitute one logical container. There are several levels of RAID that can be used to improve performance, increase redundancy, or expand capacity.

Remote Access Controller (RAC). A hardware component of a computer that allows remote control of the machine. This device allows a remote user to control the machine as if that user were using the locally attached keyboard and mouse.

Resource Access Control Facility (RACF). An IBM mainframe security product that provides access control for users accessing the system and authorizing access to protected resources.

Serial Advanced Technology Attachment (SATA). A storage solution interface that utilizes a point-to-point communication method to transfer data to and from a storage device. This is a common hard drive interface in distributed platforms.

Serial Attached SCSI (SAS). A next-generation SCSI architecture that, instead of attaching multiple SCSI devices along a single channel, allows SCSI devices to operate in a serial-connection environment. Each device has a dedicated channel to allow more bandwidth for data transfer.

solid-state drive (SSD). A data storage device that uses integrated circuits to store data instead of spinning platters. Solid-state drives have better performance metrics than older technologies, although they tend to be significantly more expensive.

stanza. A component of a device map (q.v.) that describes a specific piece of hardware or a group of devices that the 1090 software (q.v.) is to emulate or provide a connection with.

storage area network (SAN). A network storage solution that provides access to a block of storage. Unlike a NAS (q.v.) solution, a SAN provides block-level access to the storage so that different file system types can be created. The operating system of the device that is using the SAN storage accesses the block of storage as if it were locally attached.

symbols. Elements that allow different z/OS (q.v.) systems to share parameter members while each system retains unique values for those members.

SYS1.LINKLIB. A data set containing modules for z/OS (q.v.) components and utilities.

SYS1.NUCLEUS. A data set containing the supervisor modules of the system.

SYS1.PARMLIB. A data set containing control parameters for the z/OS (q.v.) system.

SYS1.PROCLIB. A data set containing JCL (q.v.) procedures used to perform system functions.

Sysplex. See ***Systems Complex***.

System z server. Any server component of the zEnterprise (q.v.) environment, such as the zEC12 or z196 enterprise class server or mainframe.

Systems Complex (Sysplex). A group of z/OS (q.v.) systems that communicate using hardware and software to process work.

Systems Network Architecture (SNA). Proprietary IBM data communication architecture that can establish communications among a wide assortment of hardware and software products and platforms.

TCP/IP. The networking protocol suite that drives the primary protocol activity in the networking layer; the most common networking communication method.

Unified Resource Manager (zManager). zEnterprise (q.v.) management interface that allows all systems and hardware resources to be managed from a unified console.

USB key (dongle). The zPDT 1090 (q.v.) hardware key that determines the number of System z processors to be emulated on the server and authenticates the environment. It is the hardware licensing component of the zPDT implementation.

vendor DASD. DASD (q.v.) files provided by the z1090 vendor; distributed via optical media or downloaded from the vendor servers.

vendor-supplied. Provided by the vendor; used in reference to documentation, DASD (q.v.) files, or any other z1090-related information.

vendor system. Any virtualized system based on the DASD (q.v.) files supplied by the z1090 vendor.

virtual switch (vSwitch). A software emulation of a hardware device that allows one network card to route traffic for multiple virtualized environments between network-attached hardware.

Virtual Telecommunications Access Method (VTAM). An IBM communication protocol subsystem that supports Systems Network Architecture (q.v.) and provides an application-programming interface (API) and other features.

Volume Table Of Contents (VTOC). A data structure on a DASD (q.v.) volume that contains information about each data set, including its location on the volume.

z/OS guest. z/OS (q.v.) running as a virtual machine under z/VM.

z/OS. IBM mainframe 64-bit operating system.

zEnterprise. An IBM computing environment comprising both mainframe and distributed technologies in a single integrated system. It has three components: System z server (q.v.), BladeCenter Extension (zBX) (q.v.), and Unified Resource Manager (zManager) (q.v.).

z Personal Development Tool (zPDT). An IBM technology product offering that is a development tool for qualified and IBM-approved Independent Software Vendors (ISVs).

zPDT. See *z Personal Development Tool*.

zPDT 1090. An IBM zSeries emulator. The zPDT 1090 environment is composed of the 1090 software (q.v.) and the 1090 dongle (q.v.).

Index

A

Alcckd commands, 72, 90, 112–114, 123–124
Alcckd utility, 72–73, 110–111, 113, 123, 211

B

Backup volumes
    on NAS device, 205
    RAID levels, 205
Base environment, deployment, 226
    preconfigure networking
        components, 227
    user volume naming conventions, 226
Base image, deployment
    in Cloud, 218, 224
    creation, 214
    DASD files and device map, 225
    on NAS devices, 214
        capacity, 215
        considerations, 216
        form factor, 216
        FTP, 222
        hard drive configuration, 216
        maintenance, 216
        NFS, 222
        performance, 216
        pricing, 215
        reliability, 215
        security policy, 216
        user interface, 215
    on USB flash drive, 217, 223
    virtual systems updates, 225
        z/OS guest systems, 226
        z/VM host system, 225

C

Catalogs
    definition, 6
    master catalog configuration, 7
    shared master catalog, 8
    user catalog, 7
Coupling facility (CF), 81

D

DASD repository. *See also* Direct access storage
        devices (DASD)
    disruption reduction efficiency, 104
    individual product transfer efficiency, 104
    lab environment
        product development teams requirements, 98
        service and support challenges, 99
        service methodology (*see* Service methodology)
        z/OS system contention, 98
    network file system server, 95, 101–102
        DASD volumes, 102
        large data transfer, 101
    product development requirements, 95
    server class machine hosting
        certification chart, 106
        data-sharing environment, 105
        RSU service levels, 106
        server layout, 106
        z/OS layout, systems, 106
    server storage efficiency, 103
    single laptop system, 104
    software levels
        distributed platform, 96
        distributed servers, 97

DASD repository (*cont.*)
  mainframe zEnterprise, 97
  RSUs maintainence, 97
  zPDT servers, 96
  transfer-on-demand efficiency, 103
  zEnterprise availability, 96
  zEnterprise Mainframe Software, 97
  z/OS system, 108
DASD volume. *See also* Direct access storage
    devices (DASD)
  advantages and disadvantages, NFS, 117
  alcckd utility, 110
  couple data sets files, 112
  device map, 114–115, 118
  JES2 checkpoint files, 112
  Linux file system, 116
  MDISK format, 119
  page files, 111
  spool files, 112
  use case, 113
  user files, system MV11, 113
  vendor supplied system migration (*see* Vendor
      supplied system migration)
  virtual system configuration, 110–111, 118
  z/OS guest systems, 112
  z/OS system, 113
Data striping, 20
DEFINE CLUSTER command, 130
Deployment image, 214
  in Cloud, 218
  hardware configuration, 219
  Linux installation and configuration, 220
  on NAS device, 214
    capacity, 215
    considerations, 216
    form factor, 216
    hard drive configuration, 216
    maintenance, 216
    performance, 216
    pricing, 215
    reliability, 215
    security policy, 216
    user interface, 215
  on USB flash drive, 217
  z1090 installation and
      configuration, 220
Device manager stanza
  AWS3274, 60
    channel-attached
        communication, 60
    parameters definition, 60
  AWSCKD
    DASD unit definition, parameters, 61
    example file, 61
    information flow, 60

AWSCTC
  CTC communication network, 63
  device address, 63
  IP address destination, 64
  multiple addresses, 63
AWSOSA
  device line, 62
  network configuration control, 62
  network interfaces, 62
  parameter value, 62
  virtual z/OS system, 61
device manager's, common keyword, 59
vendor documentation, 59
Direct access storage devices (DASD)
  configurations, 6
  data types, 5
  repository (*see* DASD repository)
  volumes, 5 (*see also* DASD volume)
Disaster recovery (DR) process
  considerations, 21
  DR solution, 21
  network-attached storage (NAS), 22
  sample configuaration, 22
Disk mirroring, 20

■ E

Emergency recovery (ER) system, 201, 206
  for first-level system, 206
  for z/OS guest system, 207
    LINK statements, 209
    user directory definition, 208
    as z/VM guest, 209

■ F, G

File system creation
  root file system, 44
  swap file system, 44
  virtual system data
    distinct file system, 45
    multiple raid configurations, 45
FTP, 222
Full backup/restore recovery mechanism, 201
  file location, 202, 204
  Linux host, 201
    advantages, 202
    disadvantages, 202
  virtual systems, 201
    assumptions, 203
    echo command, 203
    gzip utility, 204
    Linux scripting, 203
    variations, 203
    volatile data, 202

■ H

High-level qualifier (HLQ), 129
Hypervisor host, 31
   additional network interfaces, configuration, 32
   hard drive configuration, 40
      file system creation (*see* File System Creation)
      Linux operating system installation, 43
      Network Time Protocol Server, 43
      RAID configuration considerations, 41
      software packages, 45
      storage technologies, 42
   Linux Host Network configuration
      configuration steps, 46
      ping request, 47
   Linux installation, 31
   Mainframe Developer's single laptop system
      base hardware, Linux configuration, 48
      DHCP servers, 47
      graphical FTP tool, 47
      network, file system configuration, 48
   multiple mainframe systems, software QA testing
      ftp utility, 51
      hard-drive configuration attributes, 49
      networking configuration, 49
      virtual system, 49
      /zDATA file system, 50
   networking design considerations
      network connectivity plan (*see* Network
         Connectivity Plan)
      remote access (*see* Remote Access)
   storage configuration, implementation, 31

■ I, J, K

IBM Mainframe Virtualization Technology, 1
Independent Software Vendors (ISVs), 1
Input/output definition file (IODF), 109
Interactive Storage Management Facility (ISMF), 128
Interactive System Productivity Facility (ISPF), 142
Internet protocol (IP), 142
IPWIZARD utility, 76

■ L

Library parameters
   BPXPRM member, 138
   MSTJCL member, 138
   New LOAD and IEASYS Members, 136
   symbol updates, 137
   VATLST member, 138

■ M

Mainframe developer, 199
Multi-server environment. *See* DASD repository

■ N, O, P, Q

Network-attached storage (NAS), 9–10
Network connectivity plan
   environmental connectivity requirements, 35
   IP configuration
      connectivity requirements, 39
      IP addresses requirements, 39
      Static, DHCP address configuration, 40
      virtual machines, network connectivity, 39
   physical network connections, 35
      multiple z/OS configuration, 38
      network configuration, 36
      network ports, 35
      physical host requirements, 36
      virtualized mainframe environment, 38
      virtual machines, 37
Network file system (NFS), 117, 222

■ R

Recommended service upgrade (RSU), 189
   operating systems, 189
      BPXPRRM members, 194
      catalog jobs, 194
      DASD repository, 190
      distributed servers, 190
      FTP, 190
      IPL command string, 196
      system backup, 198
      user directory, 191
      volumes verification, 193
      z/VM directory, 194
   subsystem maintainence, 198
      backups, 198
      DASD repository, 198
      drive capacity, 198
      mainframe zEnterprise, 198
      SMS managed volumes, 198
Recovery, 201
   backup volumes, 201, 205
      NAS device, 205
      RAID levels, 205
   emergency recovery (ER)
      system, 201, 206
      for first-level system, 206
      for z/OS guest system, 207
   full backup/restore recovery
      mechanism, 201
      file location, 202
      Linux host, 201
      virtual systems, 201
   QA testing, 211
   single laptop system, 210
Redundant array of independent
      disks (RAID), 19

Remote access
    card (RAC)
        configuration, 33
        features, 33
        Linux ISO, 35
        mounted ISO, 34
        unique port, 33
    network KVM
        advantages, 32
        solution, 32
Remote network-attached storage, 10
Resource Access Control
        Facility (RACF), 139

■ S, T

Serial ATA (SATA), 17
Serial Attached SCSI (SAS), 17
Service methodology
    distributed servers, 100
    RSUs, 100
Shared parameter libraries, 165
    IEASYS member, 170
        overridden by systems, 167
        sets system standards, 166
    LOADxx members
        IEASYM statement, 169
        IODF statements, 169
        PARMLIB statement, 169
        SYSCAT statements, 169
        SYSPARM statement, 168
        VMUSERID statement, 169
Software testing, 200
Solid-state drives (SSDs), 17
Stanzas
    adjunct-processor stanza, 59
    definition, 58
    device manager stanza (see Device manager stanza)
    system stanza
        controls the memory, 58
        port number, 58
        processor information, 58
Storage area network (SAN), 17
Storage Management Subsystem (SMS), 128
System manipulations
    catalog updates
        clean up the catalog, 131
        master catalog, 129
        multiple user catalogs, 129
        new operating system, 130
    SMS, 128

■ U

UNIX system services (USS), 130
User attributes data set (UADS), 140

User directory
    coupling facility (CF), 81
    proxy users, 81
    service machines, 81
    for z/VM guest systems, 82
        proxy user, 82
        z/OS guest system user (see z/OS guest
            system user)

■ V, W, X, Y

Vendor supplied system migration
    machine hosting mainframe systems, 160
    parameter libraries
        concatenations, 134
        data-set naming convention, 133
        members, 135
    procedure libraries
        concatenations, 132
        data sets, 132
        members, 133
    sharing data sets and volumes, 144
    single laptop system, 146
    system environment, 144
    system manipulations (see System manipulations)
    system migration considerations, 136
        add users, 140
        coupling facility, 144
        dynamic dump data sets, 139
        ISPF, 142
        JES2 migration, 141
        library parameters (see Library parameters)
        page and spool data sets, 136
        RACF, 139
        system data sets, 140
        VTAM (see Virtual Telecommunications
            Access Method (VTAM))
    system verification, 145
    usable backup, 127
    vendor system
        new DASD volume, 128
        shared DASD volume, 128
Virtualized mainframe environment, 13, 53, 213
    base image
        creation, 214
        on NAS device, 214
    base system, 64
    cloning, 213
    DASD files copying
        DASD volumes, 55
        emulator conversions, 56
        virtual environment, 57
        volumes organisation, 56
    device map creation
        locations, 57
        stanzas (see Stanzas)

failsafe system, 25
hardware considerations
    connection types, 19
    CPU specifications, 16
    memory usage, 16
    network connectivity, 18
    network interface cards (NICs), 18
    storage demands, 17
Mainframe Developer's, single laptop system
    case decisions, 67
    device map definition, 66
    Linux kernel modifications, 66
    /zDATA file system, 66
server class machine hosting, 67
sharing data, 23
software update requirements, 23
system failures and outage recoveries
    DR (see Disaster recovery (DR) process)
    hardware fault tolerance, 19
three systems sharing six DASD volumes, 24
use cases
    goals, 14
    mainframe configurations, 15
    network connectivity, 14
    user accesss, 14
    zVM host, 15
user creation, 53
z1090 software installation
    manual updates, 54
    step-by-step procedure, 54
    userid definition, 55
Virtual storage access method (VSAM), 6
Virtual Telecommunications Access
        Method (VTAM), 142

■ Z

zEnterprise mainframe software, 97
z/OS environment, 161
    job entry subsystem, 177
        CKPTDEF, 180
        DNS host names, 182
        INCLUDE additional JES2 members, 183
        LOGON, 182
        NJEDEF, 182
        SPOOLDEF, 179
    master catalog creation, 170
    operating system management
        IEASYMxx, 163
        IEASYSxx, 165
        IODF, 165
        LOADxx, 162
    reserved symbols, 161
    shared parameter libraries (see Shared
        parameter libraries)

symbol substitutions
    IPL string, 174
    LOAD member relationships, 175
    parameter library members, 176
system parameters manipulation, 170
    DASD volume serial number, 171
    page data set parameters, 172
virtual z/VM guest, 173
z/OS guest system user
    CF connection, 86
    CTC definitions, 85
    CTC devices, 85
    DEDICATE statement, 85
    LINK statement, 86
    localhost keyword, 85
    MDISK statement, 87
    memory distribution, 83
    network definition, 84
z/OS Optimization, 109
    DASD volume
        advantages and disadvantages, NFS, 117
        alcckd utility, 110
        couple data sets files, 112
        device map, 114–115, 118
        JES2 checkpoint files, 112
        Linux file system, 116
        MDISK format, 119
        page files, 111
        spool files, 112
        use case, 113
        user files, system MV11, 113
        virtual system configuration, 110–111, 118
        z/OS guest systems, 112
        z/OS system, 113
    machine hosting mainframe systems
        alcckd commands, 123–124
        DASD volumes, 125–126
        device map, 124
        naming convention, 123
        RSUs, 123
    progress, 120
    prospectus, 120
    single laptop system
        commands, 121
        device map, 122
        virtualized mainframe environments, 121
    system volume, 116
zPDT technology
    BladeCenter Extension (zBX), 3
    capabilities, 2
    catalogs
        definition, 6
        master catalog configuration, 7
        shared master catalog, 8
        user catalog, 7

zPDT technology (*cont.*)
 cloud enablement, 12
 cryptographic processor, 3
 DASD (*see* Direct access storage
  devices (DASD))
 data sets types, 6
 IBM Mainframe Virtualization, 1
 mainframe look and feel, 3
 multi-user capability, 2
 Network-Attached Storage (NAS), 9
 network file system server, 11
 remote network-attached storage, 10
 software, 2
 System z Server
  definition, 3
  input/output configuration, 4
  LPAR view, 4
  z/OS systems, 4
 Unified Resource Manager (zManager), 3
 USB key (dongle), 2
 VSAM, 6
 warehoused data, 11
 z/OS parameters, symbols, 9

z/VM Environment, 69
 alcckd utility, 72
 DASD files, 70
 device map, 70
 IPWIZARD utility, 76
 modifications, 71
 multiple virtual systems, 69
 optimization, 70
 paging volumes, 73
 performance monitor, 88
 service machines, 70
 spool volumes, 74
 user directory (*see* User directory)
 verification, 71
 virtual switch, 77
  definition, 77
  DTCVSW1 and DTCVSW2, 77
  for z1090 implementation, 80
  guest system authorization statement, 80
  MACPREFIX keyword, 79
  profile exec file, 79
  start command, 80
  system config file, 78